On Learning

On Learning

A general theory of objects and object-relations

David Scott

First published in 2021 by
UCL Press
University College London
Gower Street
London WC1E 6BT

Available to download free: www.uclpress.co.uk

A CIP catalogue record for this book is available from The British Library.

ISBN: 978-1-80008-000-3 (Hbk)
ISBN: 978-1-80008-001-0 (Pbk)
ISBN: 978-1-80008-002-7 (PDF)
ISBN: 978-1-80008-003-4 (epub)
ISBN: 978-1-80008-004-1 (mobi)
DOI: https://doi.org/10.14324/111.9781800080027

Contents

Preface

This is a general theory of objects and object-relations.[1] There are five object-types in the world: discursive objects, material objects, relational objects, structural-institutional-systemic objects (this type includes discursive and material configurations) and people, including the self, which is always experienced differently from the way other people are experienced. Each of them has different characteristics and, because objects have a dynamic structure, in rare circumstances they may change their status as objects; indeed, what constitutes an object-type is also dynamic. In an object-ontology, objects, including human beings, have acquired dispositions. It is also possible to identify different types of concepts if we understand a concept-type in relation to how it can be used in a way of life. Some of these are: generalisations, abstractions, symbols in the mind, acquired dispositions (this is the use that I will be focusing on in this book), object categorisations, valued configurations, algorithmic formations and semantic conditionals. The reason for doing this is to configure and reconfigure the idea of a concept and, in the process, configure and reconfigure the concept of learning.

I had originally intended the writing of this book to be devoid of references to other philosophers and thinkers. This proved to be too ambitious and I have fully referenced, in both a borrowing and oppositional sense, some key figures in the history of thought: Ludwig Wittgenstein, Aristotle, Martin Heidegger, Robert Brandom, Hans-Georg Gadamer, Charles Taylor, Roy Bhaskar, Michel Foucault and others. There are two reasons for this: first, an inability on my part to develop the full range of ideas required to fill out a general theory of ontological objects and object-relations; and second, an acknowledgement that the theory itself includes a commitment to the way particular ideas, concepts and

---

[1] In contrast to Maynard Keynes' *General Theory of Employment, Interest and Money* (Keynes, 1936), this general theory does not have a representationalist epistemology and clear Humean (Hume, 2000) distinctions between facts and values.

descriptors are embedded in networks of ideas, concepts and descriptors, and have a history.

At the time of writing, the world is infected with the coronavirus, and much of what I have written here seems to pale into insignificance in relation to this threat. However, this general theory is meant to apply to pandemic-ridden as well as pandemic-free societies and worlds, which is another way of saying that it is a general theory. This book, which is a culmination of everything else that I have written (in book, article or report form), is dedicated to my family: Moira, Sarah, Ben, Gail, Lucas, Robin and Jake, with thanks and love.

David Scott
1 November 2020

Acknowledgements

The section on learning in chapter 1 is an extensively amended reprint of Scott (2017a: 57–60), republished here with the permission of the publisher, Palgrave Macmillan. The section on epistemology in chapter 2 is a much-amended and abridged reprint of Scott and Usher (2011, second edition: 27–35), republished here with the permission of the publisher, Continuum Publishing, used by permission of Bloomsbury Publishing Plc. The section on judgements in chapter 3 is a much-amended and abridged version of Scott (2017a: 46–53), republished here with the permission of the publisher, Palgrave Macmillan. The section on theory–practice relationships in chapter 4 is a much-amended and abridged version of Scott (2017a: 112–16), republished here with the permission of the publisher, Palgrave Macmillan. Chapter 5 includes material that was originally published in Scott (2019a). It is republished here with the permission of the publisher, Springer. Chapter 6 includes a small amount of material from chapter 1 of Scott and Scott (2018), republished here with the permission of the publisher, UCL IOE Press. The short section on teacher training at the end of chapter 7 and the short section on comparative education at the beginning of chapter 8 are much-amended and shortened versions of Scott et al. (2018: 1–2; 75–7) and are republished here with the permission of the publisher, UCL Press. Chapter 11 is an amended and extended reprint of Scott (2017a: 60–73), republished here with the permission of the publisher, Palgrave Macmillan. Chapter 12 borrows some ideas and expressions, in minor ways, from Scott (2017a: 74–86), and is published here with the permission of the publisher, Palgrave Macmillan. The short section on formal assessment in chapter 18 and the short section on discourses in chapter 22 are much amended and abridged versions of Scott (2017a: 2–6; 128–32), republished here with the permission of the publisher, Palgrave Macmillan. The first part of chapter 9 and the section on spatiality in chapter 21 are abridged versions of material in Scott (2019b) and are republished here with the permission of the publisher, UCL IOE Press.

Part One
The general theory

The first part of this work fleshes out a general theory of objects and object-relations through an exploration of the important concept of learning. It is important because all human activities supervene on learning practices of one type or another. However, we should be careful not to conflate the concept and the practice, although these are related in both causal and associational ways. Knowledge and learning are homologous concepts, as they both operate in the same way and they share properties and meanings. Knowledge, then, is fundamental to the three types of learning that can be identified: cognitive (relating to propositions), skill-based (relating to processes) and embodied (relating to bodily accomplishments). Prior to each of these three types of knowledge is a set of dispositions, without which cognitive, skill-based and embodied learning would be unsustainable.

However, in order to understand both the concept and the practice of learning, we always and necessarily have to enframe the concept of learning. This notion of 'always and necessarily' has the Wittgensteinian sense of a grammatical notion of inevitability that comes from it being part of a network of other concepts and of a system of convention-governed behaviour. This enframing comprises a semantic understanding of the possibilities of the concept, and these possibilities have political, social, epistemological, functional, ethical and relational meanings. This is the task that I have set myself in the first part of the work, which is an account of the general theory. In the second part, I explore in greater detail the implications of this theory for the concept and practice of learning. I also do what I say needs to be done in the first part of the book: to provide historical, archaeological and genealogical accounts of the concept and practice of learning.

The general theory then has to take account of discursive and material configurations (chapter 1), transcendental knowledge (chapter 2), judgements and criteria (chapter 3), objects and object-relations (chapter 4), ontic and epistemic values (chapter 5), difference (chapter 6), knowledge dualities (chapter 7), institutional and systemic power relations (chapter 8) and identity and consciousness (chapter 9). In order to do this, it borrows ideas, insights and arguments from two seminal books by Ludwig Wittgenstein: the *Philosophical Investigations* (1953) and *On Certainty* (1969). This enigmatic and tormented philosopher provides the inspiration for the general theory that I set out in the first part of the work. His influence continues through the second part. Although the *Investigations* is now over 60 years old, what he had to offer in the way of ideas still seems to me to be of immense significance.

1

Introduction – learning as a concept and as a practice

In his *Tractatus Logico-Philosophicus* (1961), Ludwig Wittgenstein suggested that the world is the totality of facts. A fact, under this conception, is simpliciter a truth bearer. Bertrand Russell (with A. N. Whitehead, 1925–7)[2] had previously developed an argument that there are atomic facts on the one hand and expressions of those atomic facts on the other. Both Russell and Wittgenstein in the end repudiated these atomic unitary philosophies, resulting, in Wittgenstein's case (see his *Philosophical Investigations*, 1953), in the development of a use theory of meaning. Words cannot be understood in relation to the objects they designate, nor can they be understood in terms of the representations of these objects in the mind. Rather, they can be understood by how they are used.

In light of this we need to understand what his use theory might mean, and in particular to relate this to what he actually said in the *Philosophical Investigations* (1953).[3] This may be the wrong place to start, since my purpose in writing this book is to investigate the meaning of concepts and other objects as they are used in everyday life. However, in this case it can serve as a beginning and a methodology; so long as this is understood as a ground-clearing activity and so long as this allows

---

[2] Russell (with A. N. Whitehead, 1925–7) and Frege (1892) before him adopted an essentially Platonic view of logic. For Russell, mathematics is a branch of logic and derives its meaning and credibility from it. In this Platonic sense, he believed in a realm of truth that is separate from everyday life and which is immutable and eternal. The only way that one could gain access to this realm was through reason.

[3] Wittgenstein's *Philosophical Investigations* (1953) is written in a highly elliptical and idiosyncratic style; that is, as a series of units exploring a particular topic or idea in what has been called a hypertextual mode. This form of writing or textuality is deliberate and has implications for the theory of truth he is espousing.

me to elucidate the key concept that I am concerned about in this book: the idea of learning.

Reading a text can be construed in a number of ways, principally either as an action in the world or as a conceptual activity in the mind. In this opening chapter I am more concerned with the latter than the former. A number of approaches to reading texts have been developed. The first of these is monosemic,[4] which means that a definitive reading can be made of a text. However, this type of reading still requires a correct approach to be adopted, which comprises: a bracketing out of values and value-positions (the reader is able to put to one side their preconceptions and prejudgements during the reading);[5] the making of a series of semantic inferences from the text (the reader uses the one correct way of deriving meaning from the assemblage of words and other extra- and para-linguistic forms); and being comprehensive (the reader is not selective in any way). This correct reading is not equivalent to the intentions of the author, as she may not have fully appreciated the meaning of the words that she set down on paper (or on the internet). Furthermore, she may have changed her mind about what her text actually means. However, there is within the text being examined an unequivocal statement of meaning, which can be grasped only through the use of a transcendental method.

A second approach is also monosemic, but here the primary focus is the intentions of the author. The text allows an unequivocal reading because that reading is consistent with these intentions. Again, this type of reading comprises the use of a transcendental method. A number of implications follow from this. It would be wrong to talk about a text being read in a number of different ways, because the author intended it to be read in one particular way. Since the purpose of reading a text is to reconstruct what was in the mind of the author and not to make sense of collections and arrangements of words, the text itself acts only as a piece of evidence, albeit an important piece, from which the intentions of the author can be reconstructed. (It is perhaps appropriate here to point to the real question that should come to mind when we are dealing with a notion of evidence, which is 'what is evidence?' rather than the frequently asked question 'what is the evidence for this or that proposition?'[6] – see chapter 4.)

---

[4] In this case there is a double hermeneutic at work, since a concept of learning will also have to deal (at least in part) with the learning of concepts and the relations between them.
[5] The phenomenological reduction then is this attempt to suspend self and other viewpoints and preconceived perspectives on the world.
[6] The use of a reductionist and detheorised notion of evidence is common in the field of education currently.

There are a number of problems with the idea that, when reading a text, readers should always focus their attention on what the author of the text intended. First, the author may not know her own authorial intention with the required degree of certainty. Second, the author may have deliberately crafted a text that allows a number of different readings. The meaning does not reside in the text, but in the way in which it is read. Furthermore, the form the text takes or the way in which the thought processes of the author are translated into textual form – its textuality – is time-oriented, which complicates the process of inferring authorial intention from the text.

A third approach focuses on reading the text and its enframings. This is a word used by Martin Heidegger (1962), translated from the original German word, *Gestell*, to denote those social, geo-historical, temporal, epistemological, political and discursive frames within which our utterances are ineluctably embedded. The text and the way in which it is read are enframed. Heidegger (1962: 191) pointed to the 'fore-structure' of interpretation; he meant by this that an interpretation is never 'a presuppositionless apprehending of something presented to us', but always involves a 'fore-having', 'fore-sight' and 'fore-conception'. Historical texts are therefore read in terms of their pre-texts: each social and discursive formation has its own way of organising language, discourses and writing, and thus any historical text has a form that is unfamiliar to the reader. Furthermore, each text has a subtext, which operates beneath the text, but which gives it its meaning: those epistemologies and traditions of knowledge that are historical, and which allow a particular reading. Heidegger suggested that if we are to understand the world, what is in the world and how it is constituted, then this understanding has to be seen as a process of *Dasein*'s[7] (being-in-the-world) ability to interpret the world. This ties together interpretation and understanding; and it demonstrates that our interactions with the world are not preconditionless, but involve processes of fore-having, fore-sight and fore-conception.

There are a number of solutions to the problems created by the assertion that textual reading is immersed in history and society. The first of these is to accept that any interpretation made is perspectival, and that is as far as anyone can go. The second possibility is that we can in some way transcend the historicity of our own interpretative stance.

---

[7] *Dasein* is a German word, central to the philosophy of Martin Heidegger, which means 'being there' or 'presence'. (In German, *da* is 'there' and *sein* is 'being'. It is sometimes translated into English as 'existence'.)

Hans-Georg Gadamer (1989) suggested this, although it is not a complete solution. Instead of proposing that an unequivocal reading of a text is possible, he suggested that if we can understand the different contexts and pre-texts of a text, then this in itself constitutes a better way of reading it. For Gadamer, wrestling as he did with the respective claims of authority and tradition, reading a text can be a reasonable activity, provided we understand that this is not an objective endorsement of authority. Heidegger's insistence on the place of the fore-structure in any interpretation we might want to make is in large measure a reassertion of this position.

In making a claim that a conceptual activity such as reading a text may have more than one set of meanings attached to it, I am performing certain actions and these actions are enframed in various ways. Part of this enframing is methodological. I am employing a method that allows me to make a claim – it cannot at the same time provide a justification for the contents of that claim – about the properties of a particular word or word-set. And when I say that an object in the world, in this case a word or word-set, has properties, I am saying that the word-object is characterised by how it is structured or what attributes it has. I am also suggesting that it cannot have an infinite number of properties or attributes – there are limits – and what follows from this is that in the ceaseless repositioning and restructuring of these objects and their properties, those properties, however fleetingly held, constitute the object's potential behaviours and uses in the world. And thus, as Wittgenstein reminded us, there is a particular way of understanding these behaviours: '(w)e feel as if we had to *see right into* phenomena: yet our investigation is directed not towards *phenomena*, but rather as one might say, towards the '*possibilities*' of phenomena. What this means is that we call to mind the *kinds of statement* that we make about phenomena' (Wittgenstein, 1953: §90, his italics). Any methodological statements that I make, and I will be making many of these in the pages of this book, will point in the first instance to the possibilities and, as importantly, limitations, of a word, word-set or linguistically structured concept with the purpose of determining the meaning. The aim, as it was for Wittgenstein, first and foremost, is a semantic one. If the task is semantic then we are necessarily concerned with determining the truth or otherwise of the statements we make about the world, including the one that begins this sentence.

For example, if I assert that true knowledge is language-based, I am suggesting that the truth criterion for this assertion is situated in a language and its structures. I am, as Wittgenstein argued, using criteria, and in using these criteria I am choosing one set of criteria over and against another. The problem with locating truth in language structures is two-fold. First, an assumption has to be made that this language structure has developed as the optimal way of describing and functioning in the world and that the semantic enablements and constraints built into these linguistic structures are not historical corruptions but are responses to changing ontological structures. The second assumption that has to be made is that the development of these language structures does not influence or have an effect on what is there in the world. Making either or both of these assumptions is fraught with difficulty. However, what we can take from this discussion of the semantic implications of reading a text or interpreting a discursive object in the world is that any reading or interpretation is epistemically enframed in some way or another. And this means that ineluctably we have to confront the issue of knowledge creation and its justification.

True knowledge

We are concerned then with the idea of true knowledge. I can think of a number of possibilities as to what this might be, using a Wittgensteinian approach to understanding concepts. For example, true knowledge might refer to hypotheses that work. Here, the burden of proof for whether a statement satisfies a set of criteria is that when this hypothesis, referring to a proposed relationship in the world, is deployed in a practical sense, it works, or at least it leads to effects that the hypothesis predicted. A second example might be that true knowledge is inter-subjectively agreed knowledge. Here the burden of proof is that the truth criterion for this statement about knowledge resides in whether or not the claim being made is agreed with a community of knowers who have an interest in it. A third example might be that true knowledge can be justified empirically; and here the burden of proof for any statement that I might want to make rests with some form of true relationship between what is in the world and my knowledge of it. The most common form that this can take is correspondence or mirroring (cf. Richard Rorty's, 1979, arguments against this position). A fourth possibility is that true knowledge is logically coherent and that it is possible to identify, in a universal sense, certain correct relations and consequently certain incorrect relations between words, word-sets, concepts and forms of knowledge. Another credible position that can be taken asserts that true knowledge is such because we trust it. In effect, we have tried-and-trusted methods, deeply embedded in the social arrangements we have made, for judging whether evidence is reliable, including, as Wittgenstein would have been inclined to say, criteria for making these judgements.

There are five conceptions of truth (there may be more, but they have not yet been invented or codified): truth as correspondence, truth as coherence, truth as what works, truth as consensus and truth as warranted belief.[8] These different theories of truth are framed so that they point to a relationship between a statement and a referent; and thus we can say, if we want to adopt a correspondence theory of truth, that a statement is true if it corresponds to something in the world. Again we can say, if we want to adopt a conception of truth as coherence, that a proposition is true if it is consistent with a further set of propositions, and so on, until we exhaust the possibilities that inhere in this concept.

It is also possible for us to assert, if we ignore those siren voices pushing us towards taking a sceptical position about knowledge, that the referent in each particular case is of a different order. So, for example, a correspondence version of truth refers to a state of affairs, whereas truth as warranted belief refers to whether it satisfies an epistemological test to determine its value. Furthermore, some of these conceptions of truth allow for the possibility of a social element whereas others do not. So, truth as correspondence would suggest that a belief in epistemic relativism is unsound, whereas truth as consensus is predicated on a belief that a universal ahistorical warrant cannot legitimately be developed. These different theories are framed so that belief in one precludes belief in another.

From this list of possibilities, we can perhaps focus on those that could be placed under a pragmatist (in a formal philosophical sense) heading; and this is what Wittgenstein seems to have done. There are a number of knowledge frameworks that can broadly be thought of as pragmatic. C. S. Peirce's (1982) pragmatic maxim was that any theory of meaning assumes that the content of a proposition is the experienced difference between it being true or false. Or, as he put it: 'consider what effects, that might conceivably have practical bearings, we conceive the object of our conception to have. Then our conception of these effects is the whole of our conception of the object' (Peirce, 1982: 402). There has been some debate about what he meant by this, even to the extent that Peirce disowned William James' version of it, leading him to rename his philosophy as *pragmaticism*. However, these different interpretations lead

---

[8] For a fuller explication of these theories of truth, cf. Bridges (1999).

us towards a theory of truth in which truth is understood in terms of the practical effects of what is believed and, particularly, what its use-value is. The concept of use-value is and can be deployed in a number of different ways: making a set of propositions more coherent or consistent; alleviating some need in the world; fulfilling a personal desire; moving from one state of being to another; or, as we have already seen, determining whether a hypothesis actually works in the world.

A further version of pragmatism is that something is true if it enables that person to say that this mechanism or sequence of activities will happen or can be sustained in other situations than those in which it is being applied. It therefore has an externalising dimension. This points to the idea that something is true if it works; and this immediately creates a problem because a further justification needs to be made as to whether what works is ethical – the normative ontological dimension. More importantly, there is a problem with regards to how it works – what is it about its workings that allows us to say that it works? Furthermore, any theory that incorporates an externalising element is realist in principle, although this argument does not specify what type of realism is being advocated.

Another pragmatic justification is that a judgement can be made between two different items of knowledge on the grounds that one is more likely to be useful than the other. It should be noted here that an epistemic judgement (in the traditional sense, and where this refers to a true or false proposition) is being replaced by a pragmatic judgement about efficacy, although in this case a different type of truth theory is being invoked. As a result, it is possible to argue that a theory about an object, a relation between objects or a configuration of two (or more) objects should be preferred to another theory because it is more practically adequate – human practices within which it is subsumed work in a better way as a result of its use. The issue still remains as to what might constitute successful work, or, to put it in a Wittgensteinian way, what criteria could be used to judge whether the practical adequacy of one practice is superior to another. This can be resolved only by arguing that one of these theories contributes to a better way of life than the other, and that this better way of life is determined by the preferences of people in society and manifested through particular networks of power. The problem with this is that those sets of indicators – in a Wittgensteinian sense, these are criteria – that determine whether a theory is practically adequate may not be acceptable to those who hold a different and rival theory. This therefore cannot form a basis for distinguishing between different theories except insofar as this is decided through and as a result of asymmetrical power arrangements within society. Even here it is not possible to say with any certainty that one is more practically adequate than the other as a result of current arrangements in society, because what those arrangements signify might be disputed, and, in addition, they are likely to change over time.

For Roy Bhaskar (2011), judgemental rationality is the key idea and not the natural necessity of objects in the world or the adoption of a use theory of language, although the way that objects become the objects they are, and the relations between these objects as they are and as they will be, still needs to be explained. This requires a unitary theory of knowledge and is a corrective to the many disciplinary or domain-specific forms of knowledge in existence. And what this suggests is that at the extra-disciplinary level, knowledge is capable of being produced that allows us to make a judgement between different theories about the world; in other words, to allow us to say that this knowledge of objects in the world is superior to that knowledge of the same objects. Judgemental rationality consists of four elements or processes. The first of these is epistemic, where one theory is better than another theory because the relationship between knowledge of the world and how the world is structured is better aligned. Bhaskar (2011) identified four possible reasons for the two elements being misaligned: there are social objects in the world and these exist regardless of whether they are known or not; knowledge is fallible because any epistemic claim can be refuted; there are trans-phenomenalist truths that refer to the empirical world and discount deeper levels of social reality – that is, the work of social mechanisms; and more importantly, there are counter-phenomenalist truths in which those deep structures may actually be in conflict with their appearances. The second element or process is where a theory or description of the world is superior to another because within it there are fewer contradictions and logical anomalies. A third approach focuses on the capacity of the theory or model to be more rational than its rivals; and a fourth approach suggests that a theory is to be preferred to another because it is more practically adequate or has stronger links to existing frameworks of meaning (coherentism). These four processes, once they have been reconciled, allow us to make judgements about theories, models and descriptions of the world. In addition, this configurational process can act as criteria of judgement about the object of the investigation – the concept of learning.

There are three problems with this conceptualisation of true knowledge. The first is that since we are dealing here with four processes, we have to address the issue of how they can be subsumed into one set of criteria,[9] which would allow us to determine that this statement or claim is superior to another statement or claim. The second is that these four possible criteria are of a different logical order and this creates difficulties if we want to use them in this way. And, third, each of the processes is valued ontologically, with these valuations being differently arranged in social, geo-historical and discursive environments. What valuations should be given to each of them in the process of reconciliation?

However, for Bhaskar (2011), the power of this explanation (for determining that one account of something in the world is better than another) resides in the disciplines or domains of knowledge, operating as they do as transitory manifestations of temporal and spatial knowledge-development processes. And this implies the use of an immanent critique;[10] that is, critiquing a perspective in its own terms and usually from a specific disciplinary perspective, to establish the possibility of judging that one particular theory is superior to another, which means that this process belongs to a tradition, disciplinary form of knowledge or particular framework. This seems to rule out the possibility of any form of universal or foundational knowledge. However, denying the possibility of universals seems to be a contradiction in itself, since the denial acts in this and other cases as a universal. If this argument is correct, then we are beginning the process of establishing the existence of what P. F. Strawson (1959) called universals of coherent thought,[11] and even some universals relating to ontological relationships such as a mind–world distinction and consequently a connection between them. This is also a denial of true knowledge as being located in the disciplines or domains alone and a reassertion that there are some trans-epistemic elements (understood in a transcendental sense) to knowledge development.

I take up the issue of universals and their possibilities in the next chapter. However, some brief remarks about this important idea are in order at this stage of the argument. Universals can be distinguished from and contrasted with particulars or individual objects. Under this conception, similarity and identity are explained by appealing to general concepts existing only in the mind, although they clearly have some

---

[9] Susan Haack (1993) attempted a reconciliation between these different criteria of judgement, although in her case the criteria were foundationalism and coherentism. She understood foundationalist criteria as being inclusive of experiential, rational and logical elements. She called her reconciliation *foundherentism*.

[10] For a fuller explication and defence of the notion of immanent critique, cf. Isaksen (2017).

[11] This was an attempt by Strawson to reinstate metaphysical entities, although these were somewhat different from traditional metaphysical properties of the world. It was not entirely successful.

connection or relation with particular objects that are mind-independent – both of our minds and other people's. This would suggest that concepts such as learning are not real in themselves; that is, they cannot be located in space and time. In broad terms, universals can be divided into two types. The first comprises meta-statements about matters to do with the relationship between mind and world; for example, our conceptual frameworks, perspectives on the world and descriptive languages interpenetrate what is being called reality to such an extent that it is impossible to conceive of a pre-schematised world (Putnam, 1990). The second type comprises statements about worldly issues; for example, whether smaller class sizes in educational institutions are conducive to improved learning by participants.

My concern in the first instance is to try to defend a meta-notion of universals, the first of our conceptions, and the one that socio-materialists, semiotic-materialists, semioticians and the like[12] embed in their theories, or at least make assumptions about in their theories, without offering any formal justification for doing so. The other important issue that we need to think about at this early stage of the argument is the distinction between these universals and – their antithesis – particulars. Particulars fill regions of space and are located in moments of time. Universals are metaphysical, such as in God or ideal speech situations, or at least outside space and time, as in numbers. The important contrast here is between what is repeatable (universals) and what is not repeatable (particulars). There are difficulties of a philosophical nature with universals, it hardly needs saying, and accounts of these difficulties will feature in the next chapter.

Using criteria, or acknowledging that there are always criteria being used in judgements that are made, points to the purpose or function of these criteria – the use of any criteria signifies a set of enablements and constraints as to how we can use a word or concept. This is a point made repeatedly by Wittgenstein in the *Philosophical Investigations* (1953). What constrains or enables us? Now, this question can be answered in a psychological or socio-material way. If the person answers it in a psychological way, then that person is identifying constraints that relate to the person and not to the object or the conditions for the existence of the object. For example, if the person makes reference or at least points to characteristics that denote personal qualities such as laziness, incompetence, ignorance and so forth, she is implying that it is possible

---

[12] For example, Kress and Bezemer (2015).

for a human being not to be constrained in this way, and in addition she is saying that this particular human being is so constituted at a certain point of time that she is unable or unwilling to perform the activity. If the person answers it in a socio-material way, then she is in effect acknowledging that there are objects, such as linguistic structures, metaphysical framings, conceptual arrangements and more, that are external to human beings and prevent them from doing certain things or allow them to do these things; and these are not just experiences of constraints or of course enablements. We do not have to experience them as constraints or enablements in order for them to effectively constrain or enable us. An example of this process is the formation and reformation of a discursive configuration.

Discursive configurations

There are five types of object in the world, each of which has different characteristics: discursive objects, material objects, relational objects, structural-institutional-systemic objects – this type includes both discursive configurations such as Michel Foucault's (1978b) *dispositif*, and material configurations such as an *educational system* – and people, including the self, which is always experienced differently from the way other people are experienced. Each of them has different characteristics and, because objects have a dynamic structure, in rare circumstances may change their status as objects; indeed, what constitutes an object-type is also dynamic. In an object-ontology – this is the framework within which I am positioning the concept of learning – objects, including human beings, have acquired dispositions (see chapters 14 and 15). Objects may change their form over time. An example of this change process where the object is initially discursive is the invention (insofar as the set of concepts and relations between them is new) of the notion of probability in the late eighteenth and early nineteenth centuries (cf. Hacking, 1990), which changed the way in which other social objects could be conceived and ultimately arranged. The dilemma is that the social world, in contrast perhaps to the physical world, is always in a state of transition, so it is hard to argue that there are invariant laws by which this world works, at all times and in all places, except in a basic logical and rational sense. At the discursive level, then, as this example shows, objects (in general and in particular) change their form over time and act to constrain and enable future configurations. This formulation, which ties together the positive force of an enablement with the negative force of a constraint, is not entirely satisfactory. However, my intention here is to point to the dual role of an object with causal properties and the possibility that it may operate in either way.

If we take one of these object-types, a discursive object-configuration, we can see how discourses are constituted at set moments in time. A discourse is a set of propositions about the world joined together by a series of connectives and relations that offers an account of an object or objects in the world, and it may even act to create objects in the world. It can have a material form – it can be written, orally presented or stored electronically as text – and is usually mediated through a language or languages. Implicit within every discursive formation are: an account of a person, including her dynamic capacities and affordances, and the environments within which she is situated; an account of the relationship between a person and her environments; knowledge about understanding, learning and change, with regards to the person and the environments in which she is located; inferences from these accounts, and conclusions about appropriate representations, media for representations and learning environments. We can say in this context that they are enframed by something or other. Furthermore, what needs to be said time and time again is that a discursive configuration can never be a simple determinant of identity, behaviour or action. Discourses are structured in a variety of ways, and both this meta-structuring and the forms it takes are relative to time and place (see chapters 21 and 22). These meta-forms refer to constructs such as identification, balance of performativity and denotation, relative value, hierarchical binary opposition, truth-value and reference.

The first of these refers to the setting of boundaries between objects in the world – how an object is realised. It is also about the relations between singulars and generalities; and it refers to those items that, when considered together, constitute a general description of a set of objects, such as male/female in a gendered discourse, abled/dis-abled in a disablist discourse, black/white in a racial discourse or heterosexual/homosexual/bisexual/polysexual/transsexual in a sexualised discourse.

A second meta-form concerns the balance in educational and social statements between denotation and performativity,[13] or between offering an account of something with no intention of changing the world and offering an account that is intended to change an object or create a new

---

[13] This distinction is derived from the work of the philosopher J. L. Austin (1962) on denotation and performativity. It has subsequently been taken up by many sociologists, who use the two terms, and the relations between them, in slightly different ways.

one. The person is not intending to merely describe what she thinks is in the world, but in making the statement, she intends to bring something into being. There is of course no guarantee that performative statements will achieve their purpose. Denotative statements have a different function, in that they seek to describe what currently exists, what might exist in the future and what has happened in the past. The intention of the utterer is not to bring anything into being in the world. This distinction between performativity and denotation makes sense only in relation to the intentions of the maker of the utterance and to the perceived relationship between statement and act – it implies that such a relationship exists even if it does not specify what that relationship is. Propositions about learning can be characterised in terms of the balance of performativity and denotation within them.

A third meta-epistemic form concerns the relative value given to an object in comparison with another object. For example, within a race discourse, one of the pair of words is given a greater value than the other, with a fairly obvious example being that white is privileged over black. In a gendered discourse, male is given a more important valuation than female. Dis-ability is understood as being inferior to ability in a disablist discourse and so on.

A fourth meta-structuring device refers to the bipolarity of objects, descriptions and dispositions; that is, an object, description or disposition is defined in terms of another object, description or disposition of which it is the mirror opposite. If the male/female binary is used as an example, it is possible to see that the positioning of the two terms as oppositional in meaning, and the subsequent valuing of one (male) and the devaluing of the other (female) because of their oppositionality, has significant implications for the way the debate about relations between the two concepts can be conducted. Thus, certain words, phrases, descriptors and concepts are understood in bipolar terms, which determines how they can be used as a resource for understanding the world.

A fifth meta-principle refers to the truth-value of a statement. Making an educational or social statement about learning means that a particular type of truth-value is being invoked. So, for example, a correspondence theory represents the truth of whether the statement mirrors the reality that it seeks to describe. As we have already seen, a number of such theories are in existence, some fairly primitive such as naive appeals to facts, others more sophisticated so that they avoid mirror imagery and at least take account of sceptical arguments. On the other hand, coherentist theories are constructed in such a way that they comprise a belief that the truth-value of a statement does not lie in its reference to an external world but rather in whether it fits coherently in a web of knowledge. An educational statement about a category is therefore implicitly or explicitly underpinned by a theory of reference embedded within a theory of truth, and this marks it out as a discursive knowledge form.

A sixth meta-principle refers to the way in which particular ideas, concepts, phrases and descriptors are embedded in networks of ideas, concepts, phrases and descriptors, and have a history. So, for example, learning as a concept is positioned in a complicated network of other concepts, such as innateness (see chapter 15), difference (see chapter 6), valuing (see chapter 5), power (see chapter 8), assessment (see chapter 18), curriculum (see chapter 18), genetics (see chapter 9), pedagogy (see chapter 17), time (see chapter 21), space (see chapter 21), technology (see chapter 13), biology (see chapter 9), intelligence (see chapter 13), progression (see chapter 16), reflection (see chapter 17), evolutionary theory (see chapter 9), identity (see chapter 9), consciousness (see chapter 9), genealogy (see chapter 19) and many more.[14] A web or entanglement is a suitable description here of this set of relations.

I have been focusing on the relations in the discourse between different ideas and notions, and how these can vary depending on the discourse – these meta-relations are those of identification, balance of performativity and denotation, relative value, hierarchical binary opposition, truth-value and reference (cf. Scott and Scott, 2018). These in turn can vary in relation to any of the others. Societies are different because different valuations are given to each of them. (In chapter 5, I will say more about the important role values have in meta-theorising and I will argue that values are both ontologically and epistemologically present all of the time, which means that the judgements we make and the actions we own are subject in every case to a process of normative evaluation. Although this is not an entirely original thought, it is still an important part of the argument I am making in this book.) These are some of the characteristics of discursive objects, although it is important to accept that in the flow of time a discursive object may change its status and consequently its characteristics. It becomes a different object or even in certain circumstances a different type of object. Other types of object, such as material entities, object-relations, structural formations and human beings, have particular characteristics at particular points in time.

---

[14] The emphasis in this sentence should be on the words 'many more', as this is indeed the crux of the matter. In this book I am able to deal with only a small number of all the eligible concepts.

A discursive object then is a form of knowledge and has to be understood as such.

Foundations

However, to use a Heideggerian idea, our being-in-the-world (*Dasein*) is not primarily a question of knowledge. When we talk about being in the world, we are referring in the first instance to entities and relations between entities. When we talk about knowledge, we are referring to ideas, facts, theories and the like. This does not mean that knowledge does not and cannot have a material form or that ideas cannot in principle generate other ideas or influence material objects, object-configurations or relations between objects, because they clearly do. However, knowledge and its contents are not the same as those entities and the relations between them that make up the material world. The mind always focuses on objects that are external to it, although clearly some of these objects have become implanted in the mind and therefore can be reexamined in their mindful form. This is the key to understanding the social world; and consequently, the question needs to be asked: how do we conceptualise and make sense of objects *and* our knowledge of them? These relations can be understood in a number of different ways, ranging from a clear demarcation between the two sets of objects to a weak or integrated one, with each of these conceptualisations referring to how they change internally and in relation to each other, and how they can be justified.

Advocates for classical conceptions of foundationalism (and this is an example of such a relation or connection) argue that any justification for the truth of a proposition rests on identifying those sets of basic principles that underpin the way we describe and use them, and the relevant inferences that allow the researcher to move from premise to conclusion. These basic principles or beliefs must be true propositions, and not in need of any further justification, if they are to qualify as foundational principles.

This strong foundationalist view therefore comprises a process of identifying self-evident truths, which only those human beings with a defective perceptual apparatus cannot recognise. It is worth noting here that these fundamental and self-evident truths are not subject to any forms of argument or development, except insofar as those advocating them might choose to exclude those they consider to have a defective sensibility; they literally present themselves to the normal person – this is, of course, a contested and normative concept – and provide the means by which a foundational structure can be built. And thus, if a foundational belief is to be thought of as credible, it requires no further justification and no further evidence to support it. In effect, it plays the end role in any chain of justification, and there is nowhere else to go if such a justification is sought. This is an epistemic chain of reasoning to a foundational or transcendental notion. In chapter 2, I address the issue of transcendental knowledge in greater detail. A belief in transcendentalism has implications for how we can construe the relationship between knowledge and the world, and this has implications for whether we can and should accept a representational view of the relationship between mind and world.

Representation

Wittgenstein in his early work argued for something that on the surface looks like a representational view of the relationship between mind and world. An influential interpretation of the *Tractatus Logico-Philosophicus* (Wittgenstein, 1961) is that he was advocating a picture theory of meaning, which includes within it the idea of representation. The relationship between what we say and what is in the world under this conception then becomes one of identity or reflecting back the original object. Furthermore, what seems to follow from this is that any proposition that we might want to make about the world is meaningful only insofar as it pictures states of affairs or matters of fact. And again, what this means is that other types of propositions to which we might want to give expression, such as ethical, aesthetic or metaphysical ideas about the world, are literally nonsensical. In the Introduction to the *Tractatus*, Wittgenstein argued that: '(t)he whole sense of the book might be summed up in the following words: what can be said clearly, and what we cannot talk about we must pass over in silence'. This immediately creates a problem, which needs a solution, or at least a tentative solution, before I can continue with my argument. This is because I am searching for the meaning of the concept of learning, and this concept is not designed to picture the world as it is. Picture theories are presupposed by a notion of a state of affairs in the world and this theory of language would seem to deny meaning to the types of statements that I want to make in this book and indeed that Wittgenstein made in the *Philosophical Investigations*.[15]

---

[15] Crude representation theories or picture theories underpin most of the array of tools used by statistical empiricists: basic hypotheses tests such as t-tests, ANOVA, contingency tables and chi-square tests; classic regression modelling including logistic and probit regressions; multilevel regression modelling; and data envelopment analysis, propensity score analysis, stochastic frontier analysis and simulation.

This is all very familiar and in a sense in the *Investigations* Wittgenstein attempted to correct this misunderstanding. However, here we have another of these troubling concepts: the possibility of correction.

In the *Philosophical Investigations*, which in some ways can be interpreted as a reaction against and repudiation of the *Tractatus*, Wittgenstein focused on the truth-value of linguistic propositions and in particular sought to develop an argument or series of arguments against words naming objects, the reduction of language to representation and the adoption of an atomistic unitary philosophy. This is the use theory of language referred to above: 'for a large class of cases of the employment of the word "meaning" – though not for all – this word can be explained in this way: the meaning of a word is its use in the language' (Wittgenstein, 1953: §43). Thus, Wittgenstein placed the emphasis on singulars not generalisations and concrete processes not abstractions.

This leads ineluctably to a notion of a language-game, which is one of the central elements of the *Philosophical Investigations* (1953). What this means is that for certain words and concepts we cannot give a definitive account of meaning and this applies equally to words such as 'language' and 'game', and complex word forms such as 'language-game'. This does not mean that we cannot use these words and many others on the grounds that they are imprecise in definitional terms, but only that the case for establishing the meaning of a word, set of words or word-concept does not lie in the way it is defined. However, what a language-game does is point to the conventional (not necessarily rule-bound) nature of meaning derivation. Wittgenstein's suggestion that 'the meaning is the use' is interpreted by Stanley Cavell (1979: 206–7) as calling 'attention to the fact that what an expression means is a function of what it is used to mean or to say on specific occasions by human beings'. This suggests that the meaning of a word, sentence or proposition resides in and can only be fully understood within the contexts of its utterance (and these in turn need to be explained). This Wittgensteinian assertion, if this interpretation is correct, is a refutation of the notion that meaning is given by the fixed and essential grammar of the word, sentence or proposition, typically addressed by reference to a dictionary or a work of reference.

I also want to suggest that words and word-sets may contain more than one meaning. For example, a notion such as objectivity, a key term in post-truth discursive politics, contains multiple rather than singular meanings, as it is used in the world. It is possible to give six different meanings to the word (Wittgenstein's phenomenal possibilities), namely: that something can exist objectively without it being perceived by human beings; that if something meets a set of truth conditions it is objective;

that something is objective when the relevant knowers' traces such as values and interests are bracketed out; that something is objective if it can be directly accessed through observation; that something is objective if its mode of application to the world is correct; and that something is objective when more than one knower can agree on its truthfulness (cf. Scott and Scott, 2018).

For Wittgenstein, grammar is a semantic idea; in trying to understand the grammar of a collection of words, we are always looking at what is meant by the words and their arrangement. Grammar is not understood in terms of its linguistic reference, but rather in terms of how it can show meaning – what concerned Wittgenstein was the semantic possibilities of the grammar of a word or collection of words. This then is the point of the *Philosophical Investigations* (1953). This viewpoint also provides a reason or reasons for whether we should or should not accept a dispositional view of concepts and a dispositional realist view of the world.

Concepts

A number of concepts are used in the field of education, such as: literacy, numeracy, meta-cognition, emotional intelligence, self-regulation, growth, progression, curriculum, assessment, learning, race, gender, dis-ability, intelligence, behaviourism, constructivism and many more.[16] It is also possible to identify different types of concepts if we understand a concept-type in relation to how it can be used in a way of life. Some of these are: generalisations, abstractions, symbols in the mind, acquired dispositions (this is the use that I will be focusing on in this book), object cate-gorisations, valued configurations, algorithmic formations and semantic conditionals. This class of objects can be understood, as Wittgenstein did, as having family resemblances and not just logical or rationally formed relations or connections. (I discuss this important Wittgensteinian idea in greater detail below.)

I have been focusing on words or complex word-forms in the first instance; however, the same applies to concepts and especially to the concept of learning. How then can we understand the notion of a concept? We can look for the necessary and sufficient conditions by which objects can be said to be parts or exemplars of larger groupings. Or we can reject

---

[16] These are a small sample of all of the available concepts.

what Wittgenstein described as a 'craving for generality' and substitute for it a notion of family resemblance:

> I can think of no better expression to characterise these similarities than 'family resemblances'; for the various resemblances between members of a family – build, features, colour of eyes, gait, temperament, and so on and so forth – overlap and criss-cross in the same way. – and I shall say: 'games' form a family. (Wittgenstein, 1953: §67)

What this means is that the meaning of a word cannot be definitionally, essentially or categorically derived but depends on 'a complicated network of similarities overlapping and criss-crossing: similarities in the large and in the small' (Wittgenstein, 1953: §66). And what follows from this is that how we use a word depends not on a definitional or essential meaning but on how it is used in the way of life that we choose to belong to and this way of life has a history, within which this network is formed and reformed. These overlapping and criss-crossing similarities are events that have happened and are happening – an event precedes another event. In passing, it is worth noting a desire in much political and academic rhetoric to conceal the genealogical element of the meaning of a concept. Even if we decide not to go down this genealogical path, we still have to acknowledge that in any investigation of an idea or an event, there has to be a historical element.

If we assigned a new word to every new manifestation, then we could not and would not have concepts. Rule-following is an example of such a concept, and Wittgenstein addressed this issue in the *Philosophical Investigations* (1953). For Wittgenstein, rule-following is not a question of whether a rule has a definitive abstract form; rather, it is that knowing the rule involves grasping that abstract entity. Therefore, the question Wittgenstein posed is: how do we know that we are following a rule? The claim he made is that there are a number of ways of following the rule and the only way for us to have some faith in it being the correct way to follow a rule is to observe how it is used:

> … no course of action could be determined by a rule, because every course of action can be brought into accord with the rule. The answer was: if every course of action could be brought into accord with the rule, then it can also be brought into conflict with it. And so, there would be neither accord nor conflict here. (Wittgenstein, 1953: §201)

Wittgenstein wanted to reject the common assumption that a rule is so constructed that we are obliged to follow its correct application. This put him at odds with Platonism, where the contents of the rule are understood as integral and abstract (in other words as non-spatial entities), and mentalism, where the contents of the rule are considered to be in the mind. The example he gave of a rule is +2, so a pupil who has developed the rule correctly up to 1,000 continues it after reaching that number in an idiosyncratic way:

> Then we get the pupil to continue one series (say '+2') beyond 1,000 – and he writes 1,000, 1,004, 1,008, 1,012. We say to him, 'Look what you're doing!' – He doesn't understand. We say, 'You should have added *two*: look how you began the series!' – He answers, 'Yes, isn't it right? I thought that was how I *had* to do it.' (Wittgenstein, 1953: §185)

This would seem to suggest that in terms of rule-following anything goes, that there is no absolute or integral meaning that can be given to a rule.

However, Wittgenstein was also concerned to repudiate this scepticism about meaning. In the end he claimed that there is a way of grasping the rule that is not an interpretation – so that it has an unequivocal and unambiguous meaning – and this is to treat each grasping as a case of application and a case in its own right. Here we have an example of Wittgenstein's anti-theoretical stance, although he expressed it – as in a sense he was compelled to do so – in a theoretical or abstract manner. He went on to suggest that rule-following is a practice; that is, how we follow a particular rule is not a universal, ahistorical or atemporal activity – the means for determining how we should follow that rule are embedded in our way of life. And this means exactly and unequivocally what is feared by a great many academics and scholars: that the knowledge process, including the means for determining true knowledge, is located in or relative to the activities of geo-historical social and discursive communities, or so Wittgenstein claimed. He wanted to liberate us from the position of having any metaphysical or foundational authority for rule-following beyond the application of the rule.

Related to this is the notion of Wittgenstein's arguments against the idea of a private language – this is one of his units of meaning. Language both as a means of social expression and as the arena in which semantic games are played out is irredeemably public. Wittgenstein suggested that for a statement to be meaningful (that is, for it to make sense and thus be useable), it must in principle, and in reality, be subjected to public criteria of justification to allow a judgement to be made about its truth-value.

Thus, for Wittgenstein the signs in language can work only where there is the possibility of public (comprising other people in specific time and place locales) affirmation or disaffirmation. Two further notions of some relevance are referred to in the *Philosophical Investigations* (1953): grammar and form of life. Contrary to the position he took about grammar in the *Tractatus* (1961), Wittgenstein chose to develop a semantic notion of grammar. Previously he had understood grammar in a technical sense, as the rules in language for correct usage, rather than the norms for making a meaningful statement. In this new work, the *Investigations*, he wanted to suggest that the norms of grammar describe how we use words to justify our utterances. In doing this, Wittgenstein argued against truth-bearing grammarians: grammatical rules cannot be idealised as an external system of signs. Grammar is not abstract and thus universal (as Noam Chomsky's original work would have it, see chapter 15), but is part of a language-game. It is to here that the principal controversy about Wittgenstein's later work can be traced. He states explicitly in an early part of the *Investigations* (1953: §24) that: '(t)he word "language *game*" [the word-part in the original German, Sprach*spiel*, is also italicised] is used here to emphasise the fact that the *speaking* of language is part of an activity, or of a form of life'. In the *Investigations*, the words 'form of life' are used only five times; however, even this cursory use of the term has provoked a number of contrary interpretations. Two of the most prominent ones are: to understand a *form of life* in relativistic terms[17] – a state of affairs is determined by culture, context and history – and the second is to see a *form of life* as a universal notion common to all human beings.

The key determination of this book, to understand what learning is, also has to come to an understanding of what a concept is. Indeed, there is a need to determine whether learning is a concept at all. The Wittgensteinian approach, as I have suggested above, is to embrace a use theory of meaning and a semantic rendition of the notion of grammar. This is a methodology first and foremost. What this means is that,

---

[17] This can be contrasted with a passage taken from *On Certainty*: 'I believe what people transmit to me in a certain manner. In this way I believe geographical, chemical, historical facts etc. That is how I *learn* the sciences. Of course learning is based on believing. If you have learnt that Mont Blanc is 4,000 metres high, if you have looked it up on the map, you say you *know* it. And can it now be said: we accord credence in this way because it has proved to pay? Again, the argument would seem to be that I cannot *prove* that Mont Blanc is 4,000 metres high, but believing it, on the authority of a map, has "proved to pay". In other words, the social procedures we have for establishing certain types of fact cannot be *justified*, but they are *successful*, they pay, and this is why we employ them' (Wittgenstein, 1969: §170).

if I focus in the first instance on what a concept is, I might come to some conclusions about its possibilities and limitations. So, for example, I can say that concepts are representations in the mind, and consequently that learning as a concept in the mind and doing its actual work represents in a mind-dependent form what is exterior to it, or what is or has been happening in the world. I could of course be wrong, and this in itself constitutes an important part of the general argument that I am making – the possibility of error (see chapter 21).

Advocates for a representational theory of mind believe that these representations are internally structured; that is, a representational theory of mind understands the internal composition of these representations as comprising a system of language-like connections and identity semantics. Or we can say, with Gottlob Frege (1980), that concepts cannot be images in the mind, which represent what is in the world, but should be understood as abstract objects. For Frege, concepts mediate between thought and language and more importantly between thought and the referents of that thought; in short, between mind and world. This means that thoughts are understood as propositions (in the traditional sense). For those who relate these representations in the mind exclusively to the senses (and thus reinstate empiricism as the dominant view of mind), this would seem to raise more problems than it solves. For example, where are there abstract objects in nature to which this form of representational theory refers? Another way of framing this argument is to contrast abstract knowledge with concrete knowledge (knowledge of particulars), an abstraction being understood as a psychological construct in which new ideas are formed if a number of these ideas are analysed together. The object itself is initially conceptualised in its concrete form.

What this also suggests is that a concept – including the concept of corrigibility – can be polysemic and used in a number of different ways. And further to this, concepts in general and concepts in particular such as learning are enframed in a form of life. It is therefore incumbent on us to try to answer a series of questions about concepts in general and then some more questions about the particular concept being investigated – in this case, learning. Some of these general questions are: how do they relate to other concepts?; how do they relate to the world?; how coherent are they?; how relevant are they?; how rational are they?; could one function without concepts?; what functions do they have?; and how are they valued ontologically? In the rest of this book I attempt to find answers to some of these questions, particularly as they relate to the idea of learning.

A theory of learning

In this book I want to focus on learning mechanisms in particular environments and this calls for an engagement with learning theories. Five philosophies of learning are examined in chapter 11: behaviourism, phenomenology, cognitivism, constructivism and materialism.[18] Each of these has particular implications for pedagogic approaches and optimum learning environments, and they are different in their enframings of the concept, and perhaps more importantly in their correctness or corrigibility. Throughout I will be engaging in a modelling exercise. Models are expressions of the real world, without the extraneous detail, and can be understood only as indicative. They are not the real world and it would be a mistake to think that they are. They are designed to help us better understand how the world works (although they might also be understood as activities in the world). However, their use raises a number of questions: for example, what expressive and representational purposes do they have?; what kinds of entity are they?; and what is their learning function? In addition, any model that can be conceived has normative elements; that is, theorists are explicitly suggesting that this model or framework is better than other models or frameworks that have been and could have been devised. This applies, above all, to the activity of learning.

Here is one possible characterisation of the concept of learning. Learning as a process has a set of pedagogic relations – it incorporates a relationship between a learner and a learning object, which could be a person, a text, an object in nature, a particular array of resources, an artefact, an allocation of a role or function to a person, or a sensory object. A change process is required for this, and it is either internal to the learner or external to the community of which this learner is a member. Learning, then, is conditioned by an arrangement of resources, including spatial and temporal elements. Each learning episode has socio-historical roots. What is learnt in the first place is formed in society and outside the individual. It is shaped by the life that the person is leading. It is therefore both externally and internally mediated. Under this conception, learning has an internalisation element where what is formally external to the learner is interiorised by the learner, and a performative element where what is formally internal to the learner is exteriorised by the learner in the world. Within this framework, behaviourists, complexity theorists,

---

[18] There are many more and these five philosophies are only a small sample. They are, however, the most commonly used.

cognitivists, cultural-historical activity theorists, social constructivists, symbol-processing theorists, sociocultural theorists of learning, actor-network theorists and critical realists conceptualise the various elements of learning and the relations between them in different ways.

A theory of learning pivots on the idea that there is an entity called, for the sake of convenience, a human being and this entity has a relationship (both inward and outward) with an environment (for some, this entails a post-humanising and materialising process).[19] As a concept, learning is fundamentally related to knowledge, and therefore if we are thinking about learning and the practices of learning, we also need to make reference to what is to be, and how it is, learnt. Typically what we are aiming at in such considerations is some form of knowledge. Philosophers usually divide knowledge into two categories: knowing-that and knowing-how. (They sometimes add a third category, knowing by acquaintance, but this is not central to the argument that I am making.[20]) These forms of knowledge are understood in modern societies as fundamentally different; in other words, there are strong and impermeable boundaries between them. I want to suggest using a formulation from Robert Brandom (2000) that this is misleading, and that consequently some of the problems that these strong insulations have created can be resolved. In society, these different forms of knowledge are given different statuses or have different levels of importance attached to them, so, for example, vocational knowledge (broadly thought of as being about processes) is considered to be less important than academic knowledge (broadly understood as being about propositions) (see chapter 7). However, these ascriptions of importance do not lie in the intrinsic nature of each knowledge form, but rather in the way in which these knowledge forms are realised in particular societies.[21]

Knowledge, then, is fundamental to the three types of learning that can be identified: cognitive (relating to propositions), skill-based (relating to processes) and embodied (relating to bodily accomplishments).[22]

---

[19] cf. Edwards (2015).

[20] Some philosophers distinguish between knowledge by acquaintance and knowledge by description by suggesting that knowledge by acquaintance is where the subject has direct, unmediated and non-inferential access to what is known, whereas knowledge by description is a type of knowledge that is indirect, mediated and inferential.

[21] In an influential conceptualisation of the curriculum that I discuss later on in this book, strong distinctions between vocational and academic knowledge and between scientific and everyday knowledge are drawn. My position on this matter is that these relations are too strongly framed.

[22] Very little will be said in this book about the notion of embodied knowledge, although this should not indicate its lack of significance. I am using the term in contrast to some philosophers who argue that all knowledge is embodied is some form or another.

Knowledge and learning are homologous concepts; by this I mean that both operate in the same way and that they share properties and meanings. Prior to each of these three types of knowledge is a set of dispositions, without which cognitive, skill-based and embodied learning would be unsustainable. Cognition comprises the manipulation of those symbolic resources (words, numbers, pictures, and so on), which points to (though not necessarily in a mirroring or isomorphic sense) something outside itself. However, the referent might also be construed as internally related or, more specifically, as a part of an already established network of concepts (for example, Brandom, 2000) or as expressive (for example, Taylor, 1985). Skill-based knowledge is different from cognition because it is procedural and not propositional. Examples of embodied conceptual knowledge are sexuality or sexual preference, physicality and motility. Distinguishing between knowledge of how to do something (or process forms of knowledge), knowledge of something (or, in Brandom's, 2000, terms, judging that claim in terms of its relations within and to a network of concepts, and making the subsequent commitments that this entails) and embodied forms of knowledge (assimilating an action and being able to perform in the spaces associated with that action) is important. They are, however, in essence all knowledge-making activities, and furthermore, as we will see, can be formulated generically as acts of learning.

Robert Brandom (2000) suggested that acting in the world requires the use of, and is underpinned by, conceptual frameworks of one type or another. For him, propositional knowledge, or making a claim that this or that is the case, is, in common with the other two forms of knowledge, a process of doing and thus of knowing how to do something or other. And this results in all of these types of knowledge having the same general form, which allows them, in this form, to be understood as learning actions or acts of learning. As a result, propositional knowledge-development activities are construed as individual processes that involve, for example, assertings, claimings, judgings and believings – activity processes.

This means that propositional knowledge cannot be thought of as fundamentally different from procedural and embodied forms of knowledge since assertings, claimings, judgings and believings are of the same order as thinking(s) (about a problem, for example), drawing(s) (a picture, for example), teaching(s) (a class, for example) or analysing(s) (a set of empirical data, for example). Note the way in which these four activities are typically thought of as knowing-how processes, whereas the first four activities are usually thought of as knowing-that processes.

However, what I am suggesting is that in order to make a claim of knowing, we are not, as is commonly thought, providing a description of an experience (that is, constructing propositional knowledge) but making a claim about it in what Sellars (1997) has described as 'a space of reasons' (much more needs to be and will be said about this well-used phrase in the pages of this book). What follows from this is that we can and should understand and use concepts specifically in relation to current and future-oriented networks of meanings. Brandom (1994: 48) has described this as 'playing a role in the inferential game of making claims and giving and asking for reasons', with the notion of giving a reason being understood as the making of an inference, so that if one makes a knowledge claim, the contents of that claim consist of inferential commitments made in applying it in the world and, further to this, these commitments refer to both the circumstances surrounding its content and its consequences.[23] This strong version of inferentialism can be criticised on three counts: the translation of representational contents into inferential contents in every case cannot be satisfactorily made (Fodor and Lepore, 2007); there is an overemphasis on concept development and use and as a consequence an underemphasis on other forms of knowledge development (Standish, 2016); and there is an implied conflation of inferences drawn from knowledge claims and inferences that are a central part of these claims or judgements.

And further to this, the issue of representationalism needs to be addressed. Both Brandom (2000) and Taylor (1985) have rejected crude versions of representationalism that have dominated previous and current theories of learning, such as behaviourism and cognitivism (see chapter 11), and in the process also rejected the idea of non-conceptual sensory representations. Representationalist theories of mind identify an

---

[23] Brandom's (1994; 2000; 2004) support for a notion of inferential semantics is designed to identify the semantic contents of the concepts we use. In rejecting a representationalist viewpoint, where the contents of the concepts that we use are determined by states of affairs in the world, he wants to substitute a notion of inference from concept to concept, from discursive object to discursive object, from concept to what is in the world, and from discursive object to material object. This viewpoint then focuses on the relations between different types of objects. This neo-pragmatist philosophy rests on the superiority (for describing what is in the world) of inferentialism over representationalism in every case. However, this position threatens the idea that some concepts, some discursive objects and some relations between objects have some epistemic content. Further to this, inferentialism cannot describe in a full sense the types of relations that endure between the different elements of language and the world. It does, however, point to the need to enframe our understanding of concepts and discursive objects/configurations in the world (with the implications that this has for pedagogy and learning). The problem still remains that if one rejects in its entirety representationalism, then it is difficult to work out what the semantic contents of concepts such as learning might be (cf. Haack, 1993).

inner realm of representations and an outer realm of objects in the world, which are placed in some form of identity relation. If we reject this approach, the focus of our investigation should be, not so much the existence of these two realms and the possibility of their identification, but the relationship between the two. The question then becomes: how do we understand the relationship between mind and world? Charles Taylor (1985) argued that this relationship is one of action rather than representation (whether this is understood as correspondence, reflection, sameness or manifestation) and this formed the central concern of his expressivist philosophy. Brandom (2004: 2) also sought to heal 'the dualistic wound inflicted by the heedless use of an over-sharp distinction between mind and world'. Both Taylor and Brandom in arguing for an expressivist view of the mind–world relation do so by prioritising expression before representation in the semantic process, that is, in the determination of meaning. (There are some important differences in their solutions to the problem, but they at least agree about the nature of the problem.) Expressing a feeling in action, for example, makes a difference to what that feeling is like. An activity of the mind is not a representation of an action in the world, but, as Taylor (2011: 23) suggested, 'an expression makes something manifest in an embodiment'. Moral judgements bring about something. They do not simply act as reflectors of some preformulated reality. Expression is a form of human activity. If meanings do not come before expression, then it is the expression itself that constitutes the meaning, although there are of course normative constraints on language use, and it is this that allows judgements to be made.[24] This will serve as a brief account of one interpretation of the concept of learning, with the understanding that the concept is potentially polysemic, and can be understood only in relation to how it is used in the world.

Conspectus

A book deserves an introduction. However, there are at least four sets of meanings that can be given to the idea of an introduction. The first is where the reader is presented with a synopsis of the general argument being made in the book without a full account of its elaborations and

---

[24] The central task then of the philosophy that I am advocating in this book is that of determining the relevance, probative force and semantic contents of one reason over another with regards to a claim about something in the world.

justifications. An example is Robert Brandom's text, *Articulating Reasons: An introduction to inferentialism* (2000), which serves as an introduction to his book, *Making It Explicit: Reasoning, representing, and discursive commitment* (1994). This is a separate book; however, it could have been a part of the overall work. It is an overview of the general argument being made, and it is not and cannot be a complete account of the contents of the book. A second type of introduction is where the framing or indeed enframing of the general argument is articulated. The third credible use-function that can be given to the idea of an introduction is that it is reflexive, and this involves a prior reflexive and thus critical account of the argument being made in the text. It is also an account of the book's textuality. I have left, in the main, the discussion of this use-function to the last chapter. A fourth type of introduction is an account of what the reader can expect if they continue with their reading of the book, and this involves a series of signpostings to its various parts and arguments. This chapter, which serves as the introduction to the book, has elements of all four of these.

The framing function, a setting out of the background to the methodology being used in the construction of knowledge in the book, comprises an account of, or reasoned argument to support, a claim about some aspect of the world, whether meta-epistemic or empirical. Such knowledge in this case (see above) refers to the following propositions: i) any claim to knowledge made by a person is enframed; ii) there is a need to articulate and give expression to this enframing as it relates to ontological, epistemological and methodological concerns, and thus any knowledge claim is enframed by a theory of knowledge, what it is and how it can be justified; iii) a relationship exists between a claim to knowledge and its truth-value, and this allows us to talk about 'true-knowledge' as a useful compound word; iv) any divisions or categories that we care to use are in history and could be other than they are, and this includes ontological and epistemological divisions or, more importantly for our purposes here, divisions between our five object-types; v) this requires a theory of mind and thus a theory of the relationship between mind or minds and the world; vi) knowledge and learning are homologous concepts; vii) concepts – including the concept of corrigibility – can be polysemic and used in a number of different ways and are enframed in a form of life; viii) it is possible to determine that any claim to knowledge we might want to make is credible, that there are four ways of establishing the truth or otherwise of any propositional claim we might want to make about knowledge – epistemic, coherentist, rational and logical – and that some form of combination of these is possible and necessary; and ix) this ontology is a form of dispositional realism. All of this and more needs to be established before the central argument of this or any other book can be attended to. I have, I hope, provided in the body of the text convincing arguments in support of these nine propositions. This first chapter has been an attempt at providing a set of convincing reasons for the framing assumptions that I make.

The first part of this book, then, is an account of a general theory of objects and object-relations. There are five object-types in the world: discursive objects, material objects, relational objects, structural-institutional-systemic objects and people. Each of them has different characteristics and, because objects have a dynamic structure, in rare circumstances may change their status as objects; indeed, what constitutes an object-type is also dynamic. In an object-ontology, objects, including human beings, have acquired dispositions.

Two arguments (reason-giving propositions) that are relevant to a notion of transcendental knowledge can be inferred from these brief remarks. The first is that it is possible to identify a type of meta-knowledge, the truth of which does not lie in specific instances of knowledge construction, but in a set of preconditions for the operation of knowledge disciplines and practices. The second is that no sense can be given to a general notion of rationality unless there is also an acknowledgement that all of its generating instances are situated in some form or another. The argument then becomes that our utterances always and necessarily presuppose a set of conditions that are in effect universal. These include context-transcending notions of truth and morality and the rejection of domain-specific notions of correctness. Acts of referring therefore cannot take place without a background of an operating referential system; acts of lying cannot take place outside a system of truth-telling. This argument is set out in chapter 2.

In chapter 3, I suggest that concepts, and this after all is the focal point of my investigation, cannot be fully determined with regards to their meaning in definitional and essentialising ways, but only in terms of how they are used in a way of life. I then suggest that a distinction can be made between knowledge of the world and meta-knowledge, which directly refers to knowledge of this world and not to the world itself. And further to this, all knowledge, including knowledge of learning, uses or is enframed in criteria, whether these criteria are implicit or explicit. I suggest that in addition to the use of criteria, any investigation into the meaning of a concept has a judgemental element: does the object that is being primed for investigation conform to the criteria that are appropriate to the making of a judgement of this type? An answer to this question then needs to incorporate some understanding about reasons (for making these sorts of judgements) and about whether reasons can qualify as evidence for a knowledge claim.

What I am suggesting is that in order to make an ontological claim, we are not, as is commonly thought, providing a description of an experience but making a claim about it in what Wilfred Sellars (1997) described as 'a space of reasons', and that what follows from this is that we can and should understand and use concepts specifically in relation to current and future-oriented networks of meanings. Reasoning within this space involves giving and asking for reasons, where this activity is understood as making a commitment in the world, with that commitment referring to the circumstances surrounding its content and its consequences.

In chapter 4, I focus on the third of the object-types within an object-ontology – an object-relation. If we are able to distinguish between different objects and we want to build into our conception of the world ideas of change, inter- and intra-relationships and continuities (over time), then we need to understand what these are and how they occur. This is predicated on the idea that object-relations inhere in those objects as characteristics of these objects. They are thus interactive, powerful, dynamic and object-specific. This means that in the first case, an object, with a particular set of characteristics, enters into a relation with another (or other) object(s). In the second case, objects in interaction with other objects have the power to change themselves and other objects, object-relations and arrangements of objects. A third characteristic is their dynamism, both in terms of their substance and in relation to how they can be classified as object-relations. And a fourth characteristic of an object-relation is that it is specific to a particular object – its potential power to influence and change other objects in the world in an interactive process is determined by the nature of the characteristics that inhere in that object, and this means that the essential nature of an object is time- and space-bound.

In chapter 5, I make the case (that is, provide sufficient reasons for making a claim of knowledge) for values as being centrally implicated in both our descriptions of the world and in our life choices. There are two dimensions to this claim. The first is ontological, and this amounts to a claim that objects in the world and human beings are valued in relation to each other and to other object-types. A second dimension is that values are epistemological. If we accept that value-free knowledge is an impossibility, that we inevitably make prejudgements about the world in our investigations, then being in the world is understood as a practice, primed for investigation, but resistant to the algorithmic and value-free methods for describing it used in the natural sciences.

In chapter 6, I examine the issue of divisions and boundaries between objects. I make the argument that processes of classifying and reclassifying change the nature of objects, object-relations and object-configurations. All references to the world involve the identification, manipulation, transformation and reconstruction of the categories, and we cannot avoid this. The scientific method – with its claims for the possibility of positional objectivity, that concepts can be reduced to measurable constructs, and that we should adopt a representational ontology – is negligent of these.

In chapter 7, I examine two important binary categories (scientific/practical and educative/training) – they are important because they act as cultural conditioning agencies for many of the institutions and systems that exist in the field of education and learning. The strength of the boundary between two contrasting manifestations of a concept influences how learning institutions (buildings, pedagogies, curricula, environments and the like) are constructed; for example, if a strong boundary between vocational and academic education is in place, this can mean that children are assigned to different types of schools, are taught in different ways, follow different curricula and learn in different environments.

In the first part of the book, I focus on some important ideas in the history of thought: what concepts are, the relationship between knowledge and learning, the possibility of universal knowledge, excellence in a practice, what evidence is, the distinction between epistemology and ontology, the role and place of values in our descriptions of the world and in the world itself, the notion of difference, different epistemic categories and powerful practices (see chapter 8). I also relate these to a notion of human identity in chapter 9, referring as it does to our fifth object-type: human beings and human consciousness. The problem with a physicalist notion of consciousness is that not everything can be explained by this view of the mind–body relationship – every action of the mind cannot be explained fully by an identical movement in the brain. It is this missing knowledge that constitutes the core of consciousness. Consciousness under this conceptualisation is more than what we already know about the mind and the brain, and more than we can literally ever know. Consciousness is thus too complicated to explain through the methods of physicalism or neurophysiology. In chapter 10, I discuss the concept and disposition of theorising.

In the second part of the book I focus exclusively on learning in its two guises: as a concept and as a practice. They need to be analysed separately because they are different types of object, and what this also requires, then, is an explanation of how they are or how they can be connected at both ontological and epistemological levels. This key relation in the lifeworld is between the world itself and our knowledge of it. I start off by examining five important philosophies of learning: behaviourism, phenomenology, cognitivism, socioculturalism and socio-materialism (chapter 11). Theoretical and contextual considerations impact on how elements of teaching and learning are realised. Acknowledging this allows the construction of a number of learning models: observation, coaching, goal-clarification, peer-learning, trial and error, hypothesis-testing, reflection, meta-cognition and repetition. And each of these in turn is underpinned by a particular theory of learning. What this means is that any model of learning used in the world is constructed in relation to a particular view of how we can know the world and what it is. These models or learning sets give different emphases to the various elements of a learning process (chapter 12). In chapters 13 and 14, I examine four important concepts that relate to learning – technology, artificial intelligence, literacy and numeracy – treating each in socially semiotic ways in terms of their meanings and their possibilities.

This relates to an important element of the claim or series of claims that I am making about learning in this book, which is that any coherent theory of learning needs to embrace a dispositional essentialism, and consequently an object – whether discursive, material, relational, configurational or person-oriented – has causal properties and thus dispositional powers. In accepting this, I am committing myself to an approach that suggests objects have real powers by virtue of what they are, although those powers are not always realised. Conceptual learning or, as I have transposed it, dispositional learning, then, has a place in the language of learning. What this means is that concepts are understood as the properties of a person, as elements of knowledge and as having dispositional powers. Knowledge is transformed at the pedagogic site, through processes such as: simulation, representation, amplification, pedagogic control, progression, textual construction, temporality and feedback. This means that in the learning process, the learning object takes a new form as a result of changes to its properties.

In chapters 15 and 16, I show how arguments for nativism or innateness can be refuted and suggest that learning has to incorporate a notion of progression; that is, movement from one state of being to another, with the latter being understood as better in some form or another. This introduces an ethical dimension to the concept of progression, and thus ineluctably an epistemological dimension. We can rise to or reach higher kinds of knowledge only through a supersession of what we perceive to be a lower kind. As I argue in chapter 17, a concept, such as pedagogy, is both a material and discursive object and consequently has all of the characteristics that we have come to associate with these types of object. In the real world, boundaries are drawn between objects. As a discursive object, the concept of pedagogy has certain properties, such as being polysemic, semantically contested, networked, interactive, powerful and dynamic. In addition, as an object it has causal powers, both as a conceptual object and also because it is in the world, or at least in a world.

In chapters 18 and 19, I focus on learning as curriculum knowledge and its historical, archaeological and genealogical connections and relations. With regards to the second of these, I consider how these three types of event-methodologies, which refer to events in the past and in the present-past, can be distinguished from each other. Historical, archaeological and genealogical methodologies are framed by time, although this core category is construed differently in each of them. A further shared element is that they produce configurations of discursive objects, such as learning discourses relating to, for example, disengaged reasoning, curricularisation, scientism, atomisation, innatism, bureaucratisation, naturalism and representationalism. These discursive object-configurations are understood in different ways historically, archaeologically and genealogically. The key, then, to understanding what they are lies with the types of relations that exist between objects in their formation and reformation.

An important dimension of learning is time and temporal relations (chapter 20). This works through activities such as: progressions and trajectories of the learner; knowledge formations; progression and emergence of learning objects and relations between them; logical prerequisites of learning objects and relations; institutional temporal relations such as timetables, lesson durations, school days or learning holidays; examination and test progressions; age-related competences and more. Indeed, it could be said that time and temporal flows are essential to understanding the concept, process, institutionalising and practice of learning. In chapter 21, I discuss its companionate concept, that of space. In the last chapter (22), I return to two important episte-mological issues: what knowledge is and how we can know anything at all. In this concluding chapter I focus on the reflexive importance of understanding the textuality of the work that I have written. I have used a variety of textual devices in this book and I point to some of them here: referentiality, linearity, fragility, corrigibility, enframing and coherentism. A key determination of the meaning of the concept of learning is whether and in what way it relates to a meta-theory, which invokes a relationship between mind and world, and which has transcendental elements. In the next chapter I address these concerns.

2
Transcendental knowledge

In this chapter I examine interrogatively three dimensions of the knowledge-construction process. The first is the possibility of some universal or transcendental elements. The second refers to those epistemic properties that result in forms of knowledge in a community, such as: the means for determining what is true knowledge; the arbitration of good practice; the semantic formulation being used; the types of values that are attached to concepts; and the types of power mechanisms that are in place. And the third refers to the development of a credible account of epistemology and ontology and the relationship between them. The first of these is an examination of whether and in what way there are transcendental elements at work in the development of knowledge.

Here are a number of statements that can be thought of as universal or transcendental: i) a distinction can be drawn between the way the world works and how these workings can be expressed; ii) social reality has ontological depth; iii) the social dimension of reality can be understood as an open system; iv) our conceptual frameworks, perspectives on the world and descriptive languages interpenetrate what we are calling reality to such an extent that it is impossible to conceive of a pre-schematised world (Putnam, 1990); v) there are such entities as universals of coherent thought, and even some universals relating to ontological relationships such as a mind–world distinction and consequently a connection between them; vi) disciplinary and inter-disciplinary forms of knowledge supervene on universal or transcendental types of knowledge; vii) curriculum knowledge is derived from our understandings about knowledge in general; viii) true knowledge refers to hypotheses that work; ix) any form of knowledge, and its justification and grounds for legitimacy, has constructed elements, and this means that knowledge is relative to particular human environments, structured differently in place and time; and x) statements about the world and about knowledge of the world are potentially and ineluctably corrigible. These are all meta-knowledge statements; that is, they refer to a material world, can be construed as discursive objects in the world and are expressed as true statements about this and other worlds. They do not seem to be relative to particular manifestations of human existence but are universal in intent and scope. They are deemed to be rational, or at least they are seen as parts of a system of thought, where the criteria for determining whether something is rational or not includes some notion of what could constitute intelligibility.

A minimum set of conditions for a belief to be thought of as intelligible is as follows (this set is not necessarily correct): there are reasons that can potentially be made available for supporting a belief and these reasons can be construed in evidential form; these reasons are relevant to this belief insofar as they are necessary and sufficient for holding it and using it in the world; there are no contrary reasons publicly available or imagined for not holding that belief; this set of reasons is internally coherent, which means that the four conditions for intelligibility are met (the rule of non-contradiction, the rule of conformity to a truth criterion, the need for logical connectives, and the need for conditionals/inferential methods); and there are a series of logical connectives, conditionals and inferential methods available for use, so that there is a reliable method that can be used for connecting evidence, reasons and beliefs (adapted from O'Grady, 2002: 145). Each of these five requirements or conditions is designed to be universal or transcendental in substance.[25] But even then, we need to understand what a universal might be.

Transcendence

Basarab Nicolescu (2002), in his *Manifesto of Transdisciplinarity*, suggested that transdisciplinarity is holistic, stratified, semantically and practically unified, multi-referential and multidimensional, non-metaphysical and progressive. It should be noted here that although Nicolescu presented this menu of specifications as not aspiring to be a new metaphysic, it certainly seems to be just that. And the fact that this is a manifesto would take it out of the realm of a philosophy or

---

[25] Intelligibility is of course another of these contested concepts. It could be understood as a precondition of saying anything at all that is not nonsense, gibberish or false.

philosophical argument and place it within the bounds of a political treatise. Nicolescu (2002) explicitly characterised transdisciplinarity as complementing those approaches that have been called disciplinary or domain-specific (see Young, 2005, for an example in the field of education and see chapter 18 for a critical evaluation of this approach). Since complexity is, for Nicolescu (2014), an important feature of reality, and reality is stratified (and contains the logic of the included middle),[26] then consequently there is a need, as he saw it, to rethink and reconceptualise the traditional relationship between subject and object.

The etymological root of transdisciplinarity is that the object under consideration is transcendent (from the Latin word *transcendentem*, meaning surmounting or rising above – see *Online Etymology Dictionary*), rather than the corruption that has taken place, which positions it within those forms of knowledge, which we might want to call, generically, interdisciplinary. The word-forming element, 'trans-', embraces a number of disparate meanings: across, beyond, through, on the other side of, going beyond. This can be traced back to the Latin word, *trans*, which in turn has been translated as across, over or beyond, and perhaps to its verb form, *trare*, meaning to cross. This in turn may have its roots in the Proto-Indo-European suffix *tra-*, or a variant, *tere*, both of which mean to cross over, to pass through or to overcome. Since we are talking here about a corruption and an evolution, and indeed about a word with multiple meanings, we can perhaps distinguish three meanings from its likely etymology. The first of these is a going beyond with the implication that it is more basic (foundational) and operates at a higher level of reality. An example of this is Mylonakou-Keke's (2015) notion of an ongoing dialectical synergy between different methodologies, different disciplines and different types of researchers at different levels of reality, which generates a 'syn-epistemic wholeness'. It is this wholeness that qualifies it as being beyond disciplinarity and the various forms of interdisciplinarity on offer. The second of these is that transdisciplinarity is understood as the equivalence of interdisciplinarity, with the emphasis now on a bricolage or synthesis across the disciplines. The third notion is that of movement between the two, so that transdisciplinarity consists of a process of passing through or crossing over, with the implication that the knowledge developer needs to go through a process of inter-disciplinarity before reaching a state of transdisciplinarity.

---

[26] Another negative obstacle for Nicolescu is the 'either/or' law, or 'law of the excluded middle' (*tertium non datur*), which states that if a state A and a state not-A exist, a state T that is simultaneously A and not-A cannot exist.

The first of these notions then is that transdisciplinarity signifies a unity of knowledge beyond the disciplines. This unity might be expressed in the form of Platonic universals (Plato, 1997),[27] a Christian Godhead[28] (cf. Van der Meer et al., 1961), the European Enlightenment notion of reason[29] (cf. Israel, 2001), a Hegelian notion of teleology[30] (cf. Taylor, 1985), Martin Heidegger's (1962) phenomenological perspective,[31] Umberto Eco's (1997) conception of a perfect language,[32] Jurgen Habermas' (1981) idea of an ideal speech situation or E. O. Wilson's (1998) theory of consilience.[33] This unity implies movement from segmentation of knowledge to boundary crossing, from fragmentation to wholeness, from working alone to collaboration and cooperation, from simplicity to complexity and from detheorisation to full theorisation. In a Wittgensteinian sense we have to be careful not to essentialise the meaning of these terms and consequently we should understand them as being both corrigible and semantically oriented to how they are used in the way of life we choose to belong to or to some or other way of life in another possible world.

We can take one of these, Jurgen Habermas' (1981) ideal speech situation, and examine its transcendental qualities. For Habermas, communication is a basic social need. He argued that all human communication implicitly involves the making of validity claims. A communicative transaction involves four such claims: that what is said and done is intelligible, truthful, justified and sincere. Given this, Habermas suggested that undistorted communication allows all four

---

[27] Plato's solution to the problem of universals is to say that they do exist, but not in an ordinary common-sense understanding of this term. They are outside space and time, and human beings cannot have direct sensory contact with them. Nevertheless, they have an existence and can be conceived of.

[28] Christianity has been the dominant cultural tradition in certain parts of the world for 2,000 years. Its central belief is a transcendent creator.

[29] This is the European Enlightenment notion of reason, in French *siècle des Lumières* (century of the Enlightened) and in German *Aufklärung*, in which God, reason, nature and humanity were redefined.

[30] A Hegelian notion of teleology is where there is a finality or complete explanation for something, human history perhaps, in terms of its endpoint, purpose or goal. It comes from two Greek words: *telos* (end) and *logos* (reason).

[31] Martin Heidegger's phenomenological perspective is extensively referred to in the pages of this book. This perspective was a reaction to and disputation of Husserl's original phenomenological perspective, and in particular his notion of *epoché* (bracketing out the natural world around us).

[32] Umberto Eco's search for the perfect language was conducted through a belief in an Ur-language, a universal medium of unambiguous expression. As with Habermas' notion of an ideal speech situation, it does not and cannot solve the many philosophical problems with universals.

[33] E. O. Wilson's theory of consilience describes the ultimate synthesis of all knowledge types, and especially those from specialised fields of the life course.

validity claims to be met – a situation that he referred to as the ideal speech situation.

Habermas saw the ideal speech situation as involving rational agreement reached through critical discussion, an agreement or consensus that can be distinguished from one arising from custom, faith or coercion – a critical dialogue conducted through known public criteria. Here, justifications become explicit as people talk about their reasons for what they do and do not do just in terms of their desires. In an ideal speech situation, all participants have an understanding of the technical issues involved, in addition to having a procedural understanding of how to act appropriately and a competence to participate fully and equally. An ideal speech situation, with its absence of external and internal constraints, is characterised by openness and a commitment to deep explanation, where each participant has an equal chance of participating and therefore where all of its validity claims can be successfully redeemed. In this way, any consensus achieved through dialogue will be based on the force of the better argument rather than the force of ideology, where this contentious idea is understood as being against an idea of a true (and thus rational) account of the world.

Indeed, the very notion of a language makes no sense without some idea of an ideal speech situation. To engage in dialogue while repudiating it is to contradict oneself. It follows, therefore, that the values and criteria of the ideal speech situation are universal; they are present in any language and any dialogue and are in effect context-free. However, this is not the end of the matter, for the ideal speech situation can function as a norm or regulative ideal, an idealisation of rational practice, even though most actual conditions of social interaction and communication are nothing like this. In this sense, it provides a critical measure of the inadequacies of existing forms of interaction. Thus, actual situations can be examined (an important task for researching and ultimately knowing the world – see chapter 4) to ascertain the degree to which they deviate from an ideal speech situation and appropriate action can be taken to bring them closer to the ideal. But more significantly, an ideal speech situation seems to provide the ideology-free position from which ideology can itself be rationally critiqued: it is universal and transcendent; it provides public and shareable criteria for justifying and choosing; and it cannot be denied without falling into substantive contradiction.

However, the fact that an ideal speech situation is rarely if ever present poses other difficulties. Should we endeavour to bring it about? If research, or even our daily interactions with and in the world, is not to be either an instrument for the further dominance of technical-rationality (see chapter 4) or for the furtherance of human understanding and communication, then something else is needed. The ideal speech situation is the condition of possibility of language as a communicative tool. But this now suggests a further question, which is to do with what makes the ideal speech situation possible. The most plausible answer is undistorted language, because if language is distorted then the rationality that constitutes the ideal speech situation becomes distorted and in effect it becomes yet another ideology.

What is required for language to be undistorted? Such a language would have to be pure and transparent – a language free of the distorting effects of particular practices, readings and interpretations. What is being asked for here is a totally decontextualised language that can fulfil its referential function without vagueness, variation or ambiguity. It is not difficult to realise that such a view of language is highly problematic. Apart from the impossibility of finding such a language, it cannot even be posited as a norm or regulative ideal, since even if it were achievable, it would actually end all communication rather than undistort it. It is precisely because language is distorted that we can communicate through it, so any realisation of an ideal speech situation, far from making for undistorted communication, would actually stop all communication in its tracks. And thus it can be said that the ideal speech situation as a transcendental concept is flawed. In addition, this does not and cannot solve some of the problems I have alluded to already, and will do so below, with transcendentalism or a monistic epistemology.

Monism

The initial task, then, is to understand what monism or transdisciplinarity might be. Transdisciplinarity, monodisciplinarity, interdisciplinarity and disciplinarity constitute different forms of knowledge. A form of knowledge is constituted by its fidelity to certain types of norms, practices and protocols. Examples of these include the accepted means for determining what is true knowledge in a community; the arbitration of good practice within the community, over, for example, what constitutes *excellence* (see chapter 3); the semantic formulation currently in use; the type of values that are attached to concepts within the community; and the types of power mechanisms that are in place to regulate these practices and protocols. Transdisciplinarity is sometimes treated as equivalent to interdisciplinarity and this is a mistake, because transdisciplinarity, or its equivalence, monodisciplinarity, is monistic in a fundamental sense: knowledge of everything can be justified only in one fundamental transcendental way. Medieval conceptions of the transcendentals by scholars such as Thomas Aquinas[34] (cf. Fester, 2009), Henry of Ghent[35] (cf. Porro, 1990) and John Duns Scotus[36] (cf. Spade, 1994) in the end are monistic,[37] leading to a notion of God.

Immanuel Kant (2007) developed a different type of transcendental argument, which he described as transcendentally idealistic. There are conditions for how human beings can know objects in the world, such as space, time and human intuition,[38] and these conditions in part contribute to the formation of the object. We cannot know these objects in themselves, but only as they appear to us: they have been filtered through the mind's functions and categories. These epistemically inaccessible real objects are transcendentally real and fundamentally mind-independent. In Kant's terms, these are noumena.[39] Phenomena, on the other hand, are objects as they appear to us: empirically real, and in part dependent on the means of knowing them.[40] Science can study only the empirically real and not objects in themselves. Roy Bhaskar (2008a) argued that the objects of science are not just objects as they are for us, or objects that are meaningful to us in relation to how we can access them; they are mechanisms or objects regardless of how we access them. He suggested that the existence of these objects as independent of human judgement is a transcendental precondition of doing any form of science.

Two arguments (reason-giving propositions) that are relevant to a notion of transcendentalism can be inferred from these brief remarks. The first is that there is a type of meta-knowledge, the truth of which does not lie in specific instances of knowledge construction, but in a set of preconditions for the operation of knowledge disciplines and practices. The second is that no sense can be given to a general notion of rationality unless there is also an acknowledgement that all of its generating instances are *situated* in some form or another. The argument then

---

[34] Thomas Aquinas argued that in addition to it having ontological properties, a first known is credible propositionally.

[35] For Henry of Ghent, although the idea of God is still thought of as the first known, being is redefined as that which is known first. In contrast to Aquinas, Henry's interpretation of key concepts such as being and thing was essentialist.

[36] Duns Scotus began his theology with the idea that all things naturally knowable of God have to be a transcendental, and this includes a notion of the divine. Scotus argued that there is nothing above it except being and that a transcendental is not common.

[37] Monism is characterised as being operative of one single principle, being or force, and can be applied to knowledge as such.

[38] *Anschauung* in the original German.

[39] *Dinge an Sich* in the original German.

[40] *Erscheinungen* in the original German.

becomes that our utterances always and necessarily presuppose a set of conditions that are in effect universal. These include context-transcending notions of truth and morality and the rejection of domain-specific notions of correctness. Acts of referring therefore cannot take place without a background of an operating referential system; acts of lying cannot occur outside a system of truth-telling. An example of a monist philosophy is critical realism.

Critical realism – a unitary philosophy

Roy Bhaskar (2011), a philosopher whose primary concern was to reinstate ontology as the singular most important dimension of humankind (this is a unitary or transcendental philosophy), made three claims about the world: there are important differences between knowledge of the world and the world itself, that is, between the transitive realm of knowing and the intransitive realm of being; reality has ontological depth; and the social world is an open system. The first of these establishes a clear distinction or demarcation between the ontological and the epistemological spheres of influence, although this does not and cannot rule out a dynamic relationship between the two. Thus, in certain circumstances but not in every circumstance, knowledge of an object, a network of other objects and the relations between them can act to change those objects, networks and relations. In a similar fashion, objects, networks and relations in the world are the referents for knowledge. These networks, confluences and conjunctions are constantly changing; with the consequence that the point of reference for the knowledge gatherer is always the dynamic object, the dynamic network and the dynamic system of relations within and between objects.

The second of Bhaskar's requirements for a unitary theory is that social reality has ontological depth. This means that these objects, networks and relations are structured and because of this they possess powers. He described these objects as mechanisms to indicate that they are dynamic. The powers held by these mechanisms have three forms: they can be possessed, exercised or actualised. Powers that are possessed belong to objects regardless of whether they have been triggered by circumstances or by contact and interaction with other objects. Powers that have been exercised are now operating within an open system and interacting with the powers of other objects in different types of ways. However, these powers may not result in any new phenomena (objects, networks and relations) because other powers may be acting as constraints on their actualisation. A third manifestation of these powers is that they are generating effects in the open system of which they are a part. These effects have not been suppressed or counteracted by other objects, networks or relations. What this means is that embodied, institutional, systemic or discursive powers can be possessed by an object but are not actualised, or they can be actualised but not have any real effects in the open system they are operating in, or they can be influencing present and future arrangements of objects, networks and relations dynamically. As a result, causation cannot be understood in terms of processes of spatiotemporal contiguity, succession and constant conjunction (as David Hume [2000] would have wanted us to believe), but rather generatively.

The third of Bhaskar's requirements is that reality and especially the social dimension of reality should be understood as an open system. In closed systems there are always two conditioning factors: objects, networks and relations operate consistently and do not deviate from their essence or essential nature. In open systems neither of these conditions is present. It is characteristic of the social world that objects, networks and relations between objects within networks operate in these open systems, and one implication of this is that it then becomes difficult to make predictions and develop law-like propositions about the social world. For Bhaskar, these three dimensions of reality are central to what the world is like and to how we can conceptualise it, and these fundamentals have transcendental qualities.

Interdisciplinarity

The issue then of what knowledge is, its justification, constitution and rationale, is a concern. If knowledge is understood as disciplinary-based or domain-specific, then the mode of production and justification is located within a discipline or domain of knowledge. If knowledge is understood as interdisciplinary or transdisciplinary, then its mode of production and justifying rationale is located in the spaces between different academic disciplines or knowledge domains or outside of those different academic disciplines or domains altogether. What this also means is that disciplinary knowledge, discipline-derived rationales for knowledge and discipline-based epistemic practices are in some important ways insufficient and inadequate.

The real question we need to answer (and this is one that is frequently ignored by philosophers, sociologists and knowledge developers alike) is: what is there in and about the world that makes interdisciplinarity and consequently transdisciplinarity possible? Answering this question requires the identification of limits to inter-disciplinarity as a feature of the knowledge theory, as well as the development of transdisciplinary constructs as features of it. And this in turn is to understand knowledge, its development, and its derivative capacity as having ontological and objectifying dimensions, and as being more than what is produced by and in the disciplines. Disciplinary knowledge then is always a pale reflection of deeper-lying knowledge constructs. Any form of knowledge, and its justification and grounds for legitimacy, has constructed elements; and this means that knowledge is relative to particular human environments, structured differently in place and time. For example, logical positivists such as A. J. Ayer (1936) understood the limits of true knowledge – what constitutes true knowledge and what cannot be considered as true knowledge – in a different way from Aristotle (2018a; 2018b; writing as he did in the fourth century BCE in Athens). However, underlying this and much more besides is some universal notion of what knowledge is, what constitutes true knowledge and what relations there are between the development of knowledge and what it refers to. Consequently, it is possible to suggest that almost all knowledge development requires interdisciplinary and transdisciplinary processes of one type or another. The conditions for this depend on complexity and object-dynamism, and since dynamism is an important feature of human life, all knowledge development that is concerned with human beings and their activities in the world is both interdisciplinary and transdisciplinary.

Interdisciplinarity and transdisciplinarity overlie and encompass disciplinary knowledge because they comprise a truthfulness and comprehensiveness that is denied to the various forms of disciplinary knowledge. If truth can be conceived in unitary terms (through the development of a unitary philosophy), then there can be only one version of truth; and thus, there cannot be multiple truths generated from different disciplines.[41] A solution to this problem might be to posit a hierarchy of truths, so that there are partial and whole versions of the truth. Disciplinary knowledge is frequently understood as partial, but

---

[41] For example, the title of a book, written by the philosopher of education Chris Winch, *The Philosophy of Human Learning* (2002), seems to imply that philosophers, sociologists, historians, psychologists and other groups of people have produced accounts of human learning that are of equal standing. The position I take in this book is that philosophy is not just another way of looking at a concept, but as a concept it has transcultural and transcendental attributes. This puts me at odds with Winch's view of the world, which is still essentially disciplinary or at best interdisciplinary.

partiality implies wholeness: it is not possible to make any sense of partiality unless it is also understood as partial to something else that is not in itself partial. What this also shows is that there is a relationship between disciplinarity and interdisciplinarity, as there must be between interdisciplinarity and transdisciplinarity.

These relationships are important. As a result of the interaction of these three knowledge forms, variously described and formulated, a tradition of knowledge is developed, and it is either morphogenetic or (usually) morphostatic. In the field of education, a number of disciplinary, interdisciplinary and transdisciplinary traditions of knowledge have been developed. In most of these cases, as we shall see, the trajectory of the tradition is static, resulting in undeveloped or immature configurations. (Young and Muller, 2010, and the Research Excellence Framework [REF], 2014, are examples.) The reason for this immaturity is that in each case transdisciplinary elements are neglected in its formation and reformation, with these referring in the main to four processes of validation: whether the framing of the object is empirically or practically adequate, coherent, rational and referenced to networks of meaning. The first task is to identify these traditions of knowledge in the field of education, and to remind ourselves that our quest is for an in-depth understanding of the notion of learning.

Traditions of knowledge

Traditions of knowledge in the education discipline can be broadly divided into three types: academic knowledge traditions, practical knowledge traditions and integrated knowledge traditions (cf. Whitty and Furlong, 2017). However, their designations as particular traditions of knowledge cannot guarantee that they are empirically or practically adequate, coherent, rational or referenced to/part of actual frameworks of meaning. Academic knowledge traditions position themselves as in some way detached from the object being studied and can be distinguished from everyday forms of knowledge (see chapter 8, for an unpicking of this sharp Durkheimian distinction between sacred and profane knowledge forms; Durkheim, 1995). Basil Bernstein (2002) characterised this distinction as being between vertical and horizontal discourses. Vertical discourses are specialised symbolic structures, which attempt to be context-independent, conserved by enclosed social institutions, such as disciplines, though not exclusively so, taught in specialised institutions that seek to develop nomothetic, abstract and generalised knowledge of objects in the world, and most importantly take the knower beyond his everyday and immediate experience. Horizontal discourses are context-dependent, used in everyday life, involve commonsense knowledge and are exchanged through unsystematic processes and procedures.

In addition, Bernstein (2002) distinguished between singulars and regions of knowledge. Singulars are bodies of specialised knowledge that exist within their own intellectual field, have distinctive practices and established boundaries between themselves and other practices, and rules of procedure within them. There are two types of singulars: those with a strong grammar, hierarchical arrangement, unitary means for testing knowledge, and a strong community of practice with a common language of expression by participants; and, in contrast, those with weak grammars, more eclectic knowledge structures, and that are composed of subgroups within the overall specialised knowledge tradition, members of which speak a plethora of languages and adopt different methodo-logical and epistemological frameworks.

Regions of knowledge, on the other hand, are traditions of knowledge that borrow from a number of singulars, do not claim to be underpinned by distinctive logical and discursive framings and operate both in the field of practice and the intellectual field. However, the distinction that Bernstein made between singulars and regions of knowledge neglects epistemological issues and subsumes in its generality a number of important distinctions as they play out in possible conceptions of relations between theory and practice.

A particular regional tradition of knowledge that was influential in Anglophone education systems comprised an amalgam of singular forms of knowledge, that is, sociology, psychology, philosophy and history of education, although it became increasingly obvious that this hybrid tradition was beset with some significant difficulties in relation to notions of objectivity, relations between theory and practice, the designation of scientific knowledge, the means for determining quality in the practice and so forth. As with many of these hybrid forms of knowledge, this regional form of knowledge became increasingly unstable, while at the same time evolving into something approaching a singular. In France, it became known as the *Sciences de l'éducation*. The German tradition of educational knowledge (*Erziehung*) at a more foundational level is a singular form of knowledge in Bernstein's terms, although it should perhaps be suggested at this point that Bernstein's categories of horizontal and vertical knowledge are insufficient for a complete understanding of the complex relations between scientific knowledge and everyday knowledge (see chapter 7).

Another form that an academic knowledge tradition can take is applied educational research and scholarship, which manifests itself in the study of particular educational domains. In reality, these are ideological epistemic constructions that offer particular views on particular aspects of education. Examples are leadership and management, comparative and international education, and higher education (a subdiscipline that at the moment is dominated by statistical empiricists). They achieve their influence by providing the means of an intellectual identity for their members. In Bernstein's terms they are not singulars in their own right because they lack a sense of epistemological coherence.

A manifestation of a practical knowledge tradition is what Bernstein called a generic modality. These are forms of knowledge produced outside of and thus external to the disciplines. An example is the Research Excellence Framework (REF) in the UK, involving as it does educational judgements, sorting processes and extra-disciplinary epistemic judgemental frameworks. The problem with categorising practical knowledge traditions as generic is that it ignores the genuine argument that in the social sciences, disciplinary knowledge – whether of a singular or regional type – is by virtue of what it is insufficient or incomplete. Another example of a practical knowledge tradition is the use of generic standards in course design in universities and colleges of further education in the United Kingdom.

Whitty and Furlong (2017) identified a third tradition, which they called integrated (although hybrid would be a more appropriate term), insofar as there are some traditions that are neither academic (usually though not exclusively disciplinary) nor practical: they are a mixture of the two. The problem with designating Latvian *Pedagogija*, practitioner enquiry and clinical practice, as Whitty and Furlong (2017) do, as particular forms of knowledge and knowledge development is that practice enters into the discourse in different ways and at different points in the sequences of activities that constitute them. So, for example, although this may be disputed, practitioner enquiry using action research approaches draws on existing literature (specifically, literature that describes research completed outside the specifics of the practice being primed for investigation) to design interventions, which are a direct response to practical problems in situ. The Latvian *Pedagogija* tradition describes itself as a multidisciplinary science that takes a particular approach to teaching and learning. However, it engages directly with practice as the source of its theorising and as the experimental setting for re-forming that practice.

The problem with adopting a Bernsteinian framework for knowledge production is that epistemological concerns are consequently neglected.[42] What this means is that classifications about and relations between different knowledge types are undeveloped because they are not able to adequately describe mind–world relations. I therefore need to address the issue of epistemology here, since learning as a concept is epistemologically enframed, or so I am claiming.

Epistemology

Epistemology has traditionally been concerned with what distinguishes different knowledge claims, specifically between legitimate knowledge *and* opinion and belief. When in the nineteenth century the social sciences were beginning to be developed, they did so under the shadow of the physical sciences. Therefore, as immature sciences they sought to mirror the procedures and approaches adopted by the natural sciences (or at least by an etiolated version of scientific methodology that rarely equated with how scientists actually behaved).[43]

Such approaches can be characterised in the following way. There is a real world out there and a correct way of describing it. This allows us to think that theorising is simply a matter of following the right methods or procedures. What follows from this is that the knowledge produced from this algorithmic process is always considered to be superior to common sense understandings of the world, because it is systematic and rigorous. Science works by accumulating knowledge – that is, it builds incrementally on previous knowledge. Even given this, it is hard to argue that the social sciences have developed a body of knowledge that presents unequivocal truths about its subject matter. (There are many reasons for this, not least that objects, relations and object-configurations are dynamic.) Furthermore, twentieth- and twenty-first-century philosophy has generally accepted that any observations that we make about the world, including those that are integral to the research process and can be construed as 'facts', are always conditioned by prior understandings we have of the world. There are no theory-free facts,[44] and this puts

---

[42] This is the view of Maton (2014), although his solution is not satisfactory.

[43] cf. Comte, 2009.

[44] cf. Quine (1951) – in this article he suggested that the distinction between synthetic and analytical truths is unsustainable. Sellars' (1997) rejection of the sensorily given if we are to have any perceptual knowledge at all gives support to Quine in his attack on the foundations of representationalist and empiricist traditions.

at risk the distinction made by logical positivists such as A. J. Ayer (1936) between observation and theory. Fact-based semantic theories, including Wittgenstein's early representationalist theory of the *Tractatus* (1961) and Searle's (1995) status object theory,[45] are equally guilty of not addressing this foundational and fundamental problem, which is that they ignore or misconstrue the real relations in social life – those between knowledge of the world or knowledge construction and the world itself.

The positivist/empiricist method (cf. Durkheim, 1995) incorporates an idealised view of scientific activity and is characterised as a set of general methodological rules. A clear distinction is made between knowers and objects in the world. Facts can be identified, free of the values and personal concerns of the observer. Any assertions or statements made about this world refer to observable measurable phenomena, and this implies that two theorists if they apply the correct method would come to the same conclusions. It is the correct application of the method that guarantees certainty and trust in the theories that are produced. Although all of these assumptions are significant in their own right, they give the impression that positivism and empiricism are simply highly idealised abstruse doctrines; however, such theories have important social consequences and speak as authorities in the world about social and physical matters.

This conception of theory development is and has been disputed by interpretivists, critical theorists and postmodernists, who, in their turn, have been criticised for not providing a way of developing their theories that fulfils the Enlightenment desire for universal knowledge – knowledge that is shorn of superstition, personal preference and special pleading. Interpretivists, critical theorists and postmodernists therefore sought to provide an alternative to a view of theory building that prioritised reduction to a set of variables, a separation between the knower and what they sought to know, a means of predicting and controlling the future, and a set of perfectly integrated descriptions of the world with a view of the social actor as mechanistic and determined. Interpretivists provide one possible alternative. They generally focus on the meanings that social actors construct about their lives and in relation to the world and argue

---

[45] In *Making the Social World*, John Searle (2011) writes as follows: 'Humans have the capacity to impose functions on objects and people where the objects and the people cannot perform the functions solely in virtue of their physical structure. [For instance, a five-dollar bill can't be physically transformed into a grande latte.] The performance of the function requires that there be a collectively recognized status that the person or object has, and it is only in virtue of that status that the person or object can perform the function in question.' (Kindle location 194)

that human beings negotiate these meanings in their social practices. Human action, then, cannot be separated from meaning-making, with our experiences organised through preformulated interpretive frames. Interpretivists believe that we belong to traditions of thought, and the task of the theorist is to make sense of these interpretations, even though such interpretive activity is mediated through the theorist's own frame of reference. This is a practical matter for each individual, although of course they cannot develop meanings on their own, since all meaning-making is located within cultural, linguistic and historical communities of practice (see Wittgenstein's, 1953, arguments against the idea of a private language and thus against private meaning-making practices). The field of study is therefore the meaningful actions of social actors and social institutions; and one of the consequences is that the social sciences are now thought of as distinct from the natural sciences. Being in the world is therefore understood as a practice, primed for investigation, but resistant to the algorithmic and mechanistic methods for describing it used in the natural sciences.

All of these frameworks cannot be equally correct (an assumption is being made here that all knowledge is essentially and potentially amendable), and this explains why theorists produce conflicting and contradictory accounts of important educational matters, such as the concept of learning. However, the situation is more serious than this, as, even though two theorists may subscribe to the same epistemology, they may still disagree with one another, even if they are focusing on the same set of social problems. The dispute might be about the correct and incorrect uses of the method, different views and interpretations of the epistemological tradition to which they claim to belong, or the use of different interpretive frameworks. This has precipitated what has been called a crisis of representation; however, the resolution is already given in the way the problem is conceptualised. There is no crisis of representation because representation is not an intelligible way of understanding or conceptualising the relationship between knowledge and the world. There are better ways of doing this (see Brandom, 2000;[46] and Taylor, 1985).

---

[46] Brandom's anti-representationalist inferential philosophy amounts to a claim that meaning cannot reside simpliciter in a relationship between a unit of language and something that it represents in the world. In contrast, and not in addition, an inferential relationship logically implies other relationships with other linguistic units (from word to word-complex, for example), with other semantic units (from discursive object to discursive configuration, for instance), and with relations between objects in the mind and material objects. The problem with this is two-fold: saying that the meaning of a discursive unit resides in a network of other semantic units cannot show how in any absolute sense the relationship between the particular and the general can be configured; and

Theorising is too important to simply ignore the supposed problems of representation alluded to above. Indeed, we need to understand how our theories are constructed and how power is ever present in their construction (see chapter 8). This is because theory development is conducted with and through other people (some of them more powerful than others), and the theorist is always in the business of collecting, collating and synthesising accounts by social actors of their lifeworlds and activities in the world. One of the key concepts implicated in these epistemological debates is criticality and I now want to address the issue of its use (and thus for Wittgenstein, 1953, its semantic possibilities) in discursive and methodological frameworks.

Criticality

Adopting a critical approach ineluctably implies that a state of affairs is flawed or incomplete and therefore needs to be replaced by an alternative that is not flawed or incomplete in the same way. Here I want to focus in the first instance on the argument used by Bhaskar (2008b) in his *Dialectic: The pulse of freedom*. That is, from the premise that people have needs and that these needs are unfulfilled, we are logically enjoined to meet those needs. Thus, we have moved from two factual statements without recourse to the addition of a value statement or even a practically prescriptive statement to a value conclusion. Identifying a need implies that it must be met. We can conclude only that inherent in an explanatory critique there is a statement of value and a means for deciding between correct and incorrect actions; in other words, the argument is practically adequate. Social researchers make truth claims about objects in the world. However, in the social world the objects of knowledge include the ideas that people have about those objects and, further to this, those ideas do not just operate as descriptions or explanations but may causally effect and thus transform the original objects. Many of these ideas seek to explain the characteristics of that same society. If social scientists seek to explain society, and their explanations differ from those held by people in society, then both cannot be right. All this shows is the possibility

---

it does not take account of how the meaning of particularities and generalities relates to changing discursive and material objects. Brandom wanted to make the link between meaning and reference explicit, so that language or linguistic expression is located in the rules that pertain to 'the game of giving and asking for reasons', and thus meaning resides in the role an expression might acquire vis-à-vis inferential rules.

of critique. This is different from the natural sciences because physical objects have no conception of themselves and no means of providing an explanation for what they do; in short, they cannot be reflexive (see chapter 17).

Social researchers can go further than identifying inaccuracies in the accounts that people in society hold about their lives – they may also want to explain why these false beliefs are held. What is the false belief-causing mechanism? Once this is identified, logically and ineluctably, the next step is a negative evaluation of it. If we say that some institution or structure causes us to misdescribe objects in the world, then necessarily we are criticising it and seeking to ameliorate its harmful effects, and thus change it. Furthermore, even just reporting the results of an evaluation not only subverts the false belief-causing mechanism, but in addition has the potential to undermine its false meaning-making powers. Explanation thus has the three-fold purpose of describing, explaining and subverting.[47]

Criticality, however, is a polysemic concept. Indeed, this is part of the problem, for the term itself has a complex range of connotations and applications. This means that there is disagreement as to what actually constitutes a critical approach. It tends to be the case that when critical theory is used in its capitalised form (Critical Theory), the reference is to the Frankfurt School of social theory founded in the 1930s.[48] Indeed, it could be argued that all critical theory contains elements of Critical Theory. This is hardly surprising, given the powerful model of the critical forged by the Frankfurt School and its successors, and the continuing relevance of the attempt to both critique and redefine modernity. However, this is not to say that all critical theory is simply a gloss on Critical Theory, or that all critical approaches simply comprise the modelling and enactment of the tenets of Critical Theory. The *critical* can therefore be said to be marked by a disengagement from the scientific as conventionally conceived, with an accompanying critique of its

---

[47] Hammersley (2002) criticised Bhaskar's emancipatory realism with regards to research and in particular to this argument.

[48] Some of the most prominent scholars of the first generation of critical theorists were: Max Horkheimer, Theodor Adorno, Herbert Marcuse (see chapter 13), Walter Benjamin, Friedrich Pollock, Leo Lowenthal and Erich Fromm. The concern of the social theorists associated with this school was to rethink the meaning of the European Enlightenment at a time when the ravages of totalitarianism seemed to be making a mockery of Enlightenment ideals. The spiritual successor of the Frankfurt School was Jurgen Habermas, whose work foregrounded the need to reformulate the project of modernity. A third generation of critical theorists included Andrew Feenberg, Albrecht Wellmer and Claus Offe. All of them owed much to the pioneering work of Habermas, and all of them took as the central theme of their writings the inescapable relation between knowledge and criticality.

distinguishing features such as objectivity, value neutrality and the strict separation between knowing subjects and objects to be known, or, to put it another way, the self and the world.

In interpretivism, research takes everyday experience and ordinary life as its subject matter and asks how meaning is constructed and social interaction negotiated in social practices. Human action is inseparable from meaning, and experiences are classified and ordered through interpretive frames; that is, through pre-understandings mediated by tradition. The task of research then becomes to work with, and make sense of, the world, through the frames and pre-understandings of the researched rather than the categories of the social sciences. The process of meaning-making and negotiation over meaning is always a practical matter for individuals in the sense that it is located in their social practices. Situations are interpreted and, while these interpretations may be faulty or misleading, they reveal for researchers, and indeed everyone in the world, the shared and constructed nature of social reality; and this would have been missed had they been objective in a positivist sense. Positivism, or positive science as Auguste Comte (2009) called it, can therefore be critiqued on the grounds that its proponents fail to understand the complexity of the lifeworld of individuals. This lifeworld is instead reduced to an oppressive uniformity through the imposition of scientific categories and through the reductive processes that are integral to the common scientific method. Given, then, that the field of study is the meaningful actions of individuals and the social construction of reality, the social sciences must be distinct from the natural sciences, with different methods, different ways of explaining things and different criteria about what constitutes valid knowledge. This means that explaining the social world involves understanding or making sense of it, and it involves understanding the meanings that both construct and are constructed by interactive human behaviour. The goal of research becomes that of providing interpretations of human actions and social practices within the context of meaningful, culturally specific, arrangements.[49]

---

[49] Some elements of knowledge, which we may want to describe as transcendental, could be an exception to this. Richard Rorty (1998: 57) wanted to deny even this and settle for a version of knowledge that employs a strategy 'for escaping the self-referential difficulties into which "the relativist" keeps getting himself [and this] is to move everything over from epistemology and metaphysics into cultural politics, from claims to knowledge and appeals to self-evidence to suggestions about what we should try'. This move does not allow a real escape from relativism or from the possibility of some form of transcendental knowledge; indeed, it is a thoroughgoing sceptical argument.

If all sense-seeking and sense-making is through culturally and historically located interpretive frames, then knowledge of objects is perspective-bound and partial – it is relative to these frameworks. Gadamer (1989) argued that it is impossible to separate oneself as a researcher or person from the historical and cultural context that defines one's interpretive frame since both the subject and the object of research are located in pre-understood worlds. Frames (or pre-understandings) constitute 'the initial directedness of our whole ability to experience ... the conditions whereby we experience something – whereby what we encounter says something to us' (Gadamer, 1989: 173). Underlying Gadamer's argument is the notion of a universal hermeneutics where understanding always involves interpretation and where this interpretation is universal. Interpretation is not, however, arbitrary, but, as we have just noted, takes place through interpretive frames, which are themselves located within the background of all of our beliefs and practices. Even apparently simple actions, such as arm-raising, can be understood only in terms of an immersion in and inseparability from a background and are therefore never fully specifiable. They are enframed.

At the same time, this background should not be seen as a reified object, since it can be manifested only through partial interpretations. For example, the meaning of this book is manifested through each of its chapters (the parts), yet each chapter's meaning depends on the meaning of the whole book.[50] At the same time, there is also a background that comes into play: of practices, of reading, of culture and history, for example, about what constitutes a book. This background is meaningfully present, but also absent from the awareness of the reader. This determination of meaning in the interaction of part and whole against an unconscious background is the hermeneutic circle. But it is important to note that the circular and perspectival qualities of interpretation, which make it always partial and incomplete, are not extraneous, but they make interpretation possible; in other words, they act as conditions of possibility.

As a social practice, research is itself a meaningful human action constructed through interpretive frames. Researchers are also in the sense-making business, so unlike the situation in the natural sciences, in social research both the researchers and those being researched are sense-makers and knowers. Research into learning therefore involves

---

[50] An example of a knowledge mechanism in which this is ignored is the Research Excellence Framework, in which a book is given an assessment evaluation rather than a proper reading because the latter is considered to be time-consuming and too expensive.

interpreting the actions of those who are themselves interpreters. It is an interpretation of interpretations. Any inquiry, including the one that I am conducting here – and we should remind ourselves that this is a conceptual inquiry and an inquiry about what concepts are – has as its starting point the pre-understandings that researchers have of what they are researching simply through sharing a world with them. Thus, the purpose that motivates and animates inquiry, the carving out of a field of study and the emergence of criteria and standards by which that study can be evaluated, are all dependent on the historical situatedness of scientific activity and therefore on the pre-understandings of researchers. But this immediately brings us back to the problem of objectivity touched on in chapter 1. How can researchers, as interpreters or meaning producers, be objective about the meanings produced by those they are researching? Furthermore, how can they themselves be objective in the sense of not falling into an arbitrary subjectivism? One answer to this problem has been that, although researchers must recognise their situatedness, they must also bracket out, that is, temporarily suspend, their subjectivity and explanatory frames (see chapter 11).

Yet this position is not altogether satisfactory, and an alternative suggested by Gadamer (1989) shows why. He argued that it is impossible to escape from our pre-understandings even temporarily. But at the same time, it is precisely through the interplay between our interpretive frames or pre-understandings and the elements of the actions we are trying to understand that knowledge is developed. In other words, our pre-understandings, far from being closed prejudices or biases, actually make us more open-minded because in the process of interpretation and understanding they are put at risk, tested and modified through the encounter with what they are trying to understand, and this includes the dispositional exercise of doubting, as Wittgenstein (1969; and chapter 22) was so keen to affirm. So rather than bracketing out or suspending them, we should use them as the essential starting point for acquiring knowledge. In order to know, we must be aware of our pre-understandings even though we cannot transcend them. At the same time, however, while they are an essential starting point, they need to be left open to modification in the lifeworld.

Since knowledge always involves interpretation within historical and cultural contexts, it is grasped not by eliminating subjectivity but through the inter-subjective relationship between the knowing subject and the object to be known. Knowledge is not a matter of subject and object becoming identical, but of them entering into a necessary dialectical relationship. What is involved, then, is a dialogue, or what

Gadamer (1989) called a 'fusion of horizons', where knowledge is an unpredictable emergent rather than a controlled outcome. Here, an analogy between literary texts and social phenomena becomes useful, since both are complex systems of meaningful elements that are in need of interpretation. Interpretivism is the view that human life is essentially historical, and that human societies and behaviours need to be read like a complex text. Thus, what is involved in understanding is translation, empathy, dialogue, participant observation and thick description. As a hermeneutic inquiry, the task for research becomes one of working out as many meanings as possible of a complex social life (and in relation to concepts of trying to understand their possibilities in a Wittgensteinian sense). So, if social phenomena can be read as and like texts, Gadamer argued that understanding a text is only partly a function of the historical situation of the interpreter, as there is also the subject matter itself that must be given due weight. In the fusion of horizons, the term 'horizon' refers to our standpoint or situatedness (in time, place, culture, gender, ethnicity, and so on) and the standpoint or situatedness of that which we are trying to understand. The fusion results from an understanding that is grounded in both standpoints, neither of which can be bracketed out. We could say that a fusion of horizons occurs when authors and readers, both of whom are historically situated, create shared meanings. Because it is situated, every horizon is inevitably limited, but it is also open to connecting with other horizons (perspectives or standpoints). The resulting fusion is an enlargement or broadening of our own horizon through a process of learning that leaves open the possibility for continual reinterpretation and different meanings as horizons move and change. It is the outcome of inter-subjective agreement where different and conflicting interpretations are played out and possibly harmonised. Through the comparing and contrasting of various interpretations, a consensus can be achieved despite differences – indeed, because of differences.

The fact that both researchers and researched (or people acting in, and on, the world) engage in interpretive practices means that the social sciences and social research cannot help but be engaged in a dialogue with their subject matter. In other words, they cannot help but be reflexive, although this is not to say that it is always seen in this way. Theoretical knowledge is floated off into a context-free vacuum, the matter of research is detached from its locating background, and researchers are cast as ideal knowing machines who can know the world only by being outside it, even though they still seek to grasp it. Interpretivism is a popular approach to research, because in emphasising the social it offers a more fruitful and human-centric way of doing research. Through the foregrounding of interaction, meaning and social construction, it avoids both the scientism and objectivism of traditional positivist approaches and the remote theoretism of critical theory's more structural emphasis.

What I have not yet succeeded in doing is providing some certainty, in a Wittgensteinian sense, about the meta-knowledge that I have discussed in this chapter. This discussion of criticality and meta-knowledge ends up with an implicit nod in the direction of scepticism, pointing to the need for more work to counteract this. This will be one of my tasks in the rest of the book. Before that, I need to address the issue of quality or excellence in research and, in particular, to take us back to Wittgenstein's notion of criteria for making judgements about knowledge.[51] The fundamental question, then, in relation to any propositions that we might want to make about learning is not what evidence there is for this or that proposition, but what would constitute evidence for making a proposition about learning in the first place. All too frequently, it is the former rather than the latter that is used as a criterion for the truth or otherwise of the knowledge statements we might want to make about learning in particular and concepts in general.

---

[51] Wittgenstein's notion of criteria is complicated. In, for example, *The Blue and Brown Books* (1958: 24), he suggested the following: 'When we learnt the use of the phrase "so-and-so has toothache" we were pointed out certain kinds of behaviours of those who were said to have toothache. As an instance of these kinds of behaviour let us take holding your cheek. Suppose that by observation I found that in certain cases whenever these first criteria told me a person had toothache, a red patch appeared on a person's cheek.' He went on to say that the way he knew that red patches meant someone had toothache was because of the coincidence between the appearance of the red patch and the person holding her cheek. He further suggested that ultimately such knowledge is conventional. The argument was then taken by Wittgenstein into the realm of defining what a criterion for making a judgement might be and he distinguished between criteria and symptoms. Criteria for him were those signs that allow a judgement about a state of affairs to be made; symptoms were those observational states that allow us to conclude that the feature is actually present. Finally, he suggested that in actual cases of language use we cannot distinguish between criteria and symptoms. This anticipates the idea of a form of life in the *Investigations*.

3
Judgements and criteria

It is at this point in the argument that I need to retrace the steps I have taken so far. In line with Wittgenstein, I have suggested that concepts, and this after all is the focal point of my investigation, cannot be fully determined as to their meaning in definitional and essentialising ways, but only in terms of how they are used in a way of life. I then suggested that a distinction could be made between knowledge of the world and meta-knowledge, which directly refers to knowledge of this world and not to the world itself. And further to this, that all knowledge, including knowledge of learning, uses or is enframed in criteria, whether these criteria are implicit or explicit. I want to suggest that in addition to the use of criteria, any investigation into the meaning of a concept has a judgemental element: does this object that is being primed for investigation conform to the criteria that are appropriate to the making of a judgement of this type? An answer to this question then needs to incorporate some understanding about the reasons (for making these sorts of judgements) and about whether those reasons can qualify as evidence for this or that. From this very brief summary of where I have got to so far, it is obvious that I have made only a small amount of progress and indeed that I have barely touched on learning as such. However, the issue of evidence/reasons is an important next step. If we are to include reasons in evidential justifications, then we also have to value or evaluate those reasons when we make a claim about knowledge.

Within the community of practice that I belong to, I make judgements all the time: judgements about the quality of a piece of work, about what excellence in the practice might be, about the reasonableness of accepting an application for promotion, about the effectiveness of a teaching programme and so forth. All of these are inferential judgements about evidence and the conclusions that can be drawn from this process. In making a judgement about a learning event, evidence and its use are central. There are two types of evidence: primary evidence, which is not and cannot be atheoretical, and comes in the form of testimony or direct observations of worldly events or happenings; and a codified chain of reasoning that comprises the collection and analysis of primary evidence and its positioning in an inferential sequence to allow a judgement to be made on whether and to what extent a proposition about learning is reliable and valid – with the proviso that these two terms also need to be interrogated. Evidence can be more or less authentic, reliable and accurate, and, more importantly, more or less salient, where this is understood as a chain of reasoning involving evidence and inference leading to a conclusion about a set of activities and involving judgements at every level. So, a piece of evidence may have a weak indirect relationship to the chain of reasoning, or a strong direct relationship to the chain of reasoning because it refers to the chain itself and not to evidential elements of it.

Furthermore, salience as a criterion for determining the suitability of a piece of evidence for supporting a judgement is practice-specific.[52] This refers to the kinds of information that serve as supporting facts in making a claim, and these, I am suggesting, are practice-dependent: what is a relevant fact is determined within a practice. Therefore, evidence may not be salient because it does not fit with the evidence base within which the claim is embedded, and which gives it some measure of credibility. And further to this, each and every evidence set also has within it a threshold for determining the required probative force of any claim that is made.

Evidence in relation to a judgement about the quality of learning may therefore be invalid for a number of reasons: domain incommensurability; non-conformity to the implicit and explicit rules of the domain; a lack of probative force to achieve credibility within the domain; a lack of fit with the way the domain is formed; the degree and type of fallibility accepted in the domain;[53] and the degree to which

---

[52] The notion of a practice is contested. MacIntyre (1981) argues that practices are cooperative, integral and have boundaries between them and other practices. They also have internal standards of excellence that make them what they are.

[53] There are a number of different types of fallibilism: i) the individual believes that because she is positioned in relation to the external world, then her perspective is limited and thus the knowledge she produces is compromised and incorrigible; ii) it is possible to make mistakes that in theory could be corrected; iii) the individual holds that no true knowledge is possible because there are no convincing arguments to refute the possibility of being radically deceived; and iv) knowledge is produced through processes of conjecture and refutation, but this can never attain to a perfect form of knowledge, since the changing and emergent nature of reality means that knowledge always lags behind its referent.

the evidence set provides a complete account of the activities being investigated. The content of that evidence and the form it takes differs between domains. And this in turn means that domain-specific judgements are illegitimate if and when they are applied in other domains and in particular to domain-specific sets of evidence and inference, and this refers above all else to any claims that are intended to be generic or universal.

There are a number of ways in which such judgements can be made. The first is deontological, where the judgement is made in terms of a set of absolutely right actions or a set of universal precepts. A second way is consequentialism. This suggests that a normative judgement can be made in relation to the consequences of the actions of people, and not to intentions, circumstances or processes. A third way in which such judgements can be made is by examining intentions, and then comparing what has actually happened with what was intended to happen. There are a number of problems with this. Intentions are always future-directed and, fundamentally, they reflect what people think can be achieved in relation to what currently exists and how what currently exists may change in the future; that is, they are predictive. Furthermore, they may be wrong, misguided, poorly formulated or incorrectly predictive.

The discussion so far has focused on how we can and do make judgements about learning. I have already suggested here that these judgements and the way in which they are made are underpinned by particular epistemological and ontological positions. The issue of whether it is possible, within the limits of language,[54] to develop lists of evaluative criteria or even whether it is possible to judge between different views of knowledge is therefore of immediate concern.

A wide range of criteria and criterial systems are in use. And when I say in use, I am referring to systems such as the Research Excellence Framework (REF),[55] or systems for promotion in universities, or review processes undertaken by editors of journals in the field. For example, Furlong and Oancea (2005) suggest that in relation to applied research about learning, where the focus is on texts of various types, there are four interrelated and interdependent dimensions of quality: epistemic, technological, capacity development and economic. Within each of these

---

[54] This phrase, 'limits of language', is derived from Wittgenstein's *Tractatus* (1961: §5.6): 'The limits of my language mean the limits of my world.' It is intended to show that words, word-sets and language in general can never give us a full and perfect account of the world. There is always a gap between knowledge of the world and the world itself; and to believe otherwise is to adopt a mistaken view of what language is and can do.

[55] For a fuller discussion of this regressive mechanism, see chapter 16.

dimensions, they suggest a number of subdimensions. So the epistemic dimension comprises trustworthiness, capacity for making a contribution to knowledge, explicitness, propriety and paradigm dependence. The technological dimension comprises purposivity, salience or timeliness, specificity and accessibility, a concern for enabling impact, and flexibility and operationalisability. The capacity development dimension requires the piece of work being judged to be plausible, collaborative, reflexive or deliberative, receptive and/or transformational. And the economic dimension comprises marketability, cost-effectiveness, auditability, feasibility and originality. The implication of their argument is that for a piece of work which describes a learning activity to be judged to have reached a threshold of excellence, it should meet the requirements of these dimensions and subdimensions, or at least that when a judgement is being made, these criteria should be central to the way the judgement is made. There are three types of criteria.

Internal, external and parasitic criteria

A fundamental distinction can be drawn between all of the different criteria that have been suggested, and this relates to their internality or externality. Internality refers to the quality of the piece, with the focus on validity, sufficiency of evidence, sufficiency of process of evidence-gathering or systematicity, which in turn is validated by inter-subjective judgements within a particular discourse community, or by judgements made by individuals who subscribe to the values of a discourse community. However, whether subjectively or inter-subjectively validated, the focus is not on the impact it makes on that community or any other community, but on the quality of the piece – internal criteria are epistemically focused. External criteria, on the other hand, refer to the impact of the piece, so the piece is judged to be sound if it can be shown to have had an effect on an agent or agency in the world. A single external criterion may be deemed to be necessary, though not sufficient, for making a judgement about the quality of the piece, especially if a multi-criterial approach is adopted. The reason for distinguishing between these two types of criteria is that a piece of work can be internally sound but have made no impact; and conversely, a piece of work can be internally flawed but may still have made an impact, either positively or negatively, on a discourse community.

A piece of work can be internally sound, that is, it represents the world adequately; however, it still may not be adequate at the level of external satisfaction. For example, it may not be useful, it may not have had any impact and it may not have contributed to the development of the research community or to any capacity within it. It is internally sound in the sense that it is epistemically valid. The assessor, in using external criteria in judgement, is switching her attention from the original account and focusing on a different problem – that of the impact of that account on different discourse communities – and this requires a different range and type of evidence to be collected to determine whether or not it is adequate. As I have suggested above, this still requires the use of epistemic criteria, although these are now being invoked to determine the adequacy of a different activity.

There are a number of criteria that cannot be treated as criteria in their own right, but which are parasitic; that is, their value relates to the values given to first-order criteria, such as epistemic validity or the impact on a discourse community or communities. For example, a piece of work can be valued only for its transparency if what is being made transparent is epistemically valid. If this is not epistemically valid, then the attribute of transparency has no value.

An example of a second-order criterion is intentionality. It has been suggested that the stated intention of the author or authors should be a necessary, but not sufficient, element in any judgement about worth that is made. A piece of work should in part be judged on whether it conforms to its stated purposes. In this case, no overall judgement should be made as to its impact or its internal validity, or even the soundness or otherwise of those intentions, without at least some reference to the stated intentions of the author or authors, if they can be safely understood. Thus, if the intention of the author is that it should have no impact, it may still meet the requirements for soundness in relation to this intentional criterion because there is an intention behind the piece, which acts as a satisfier for quality.

However, if we have good grounds for believing that the stated or implicit intention of the researcher is flawed, or even that, in all of the possible cases that have come to our attention and all of the possible cases that could come to our attention, there is the possibility that a researcher could have a misguided intention, then the inclusion of intentionality as one of our criteria is suspect. A criterion such as intentionality can be used in this way only if it has a close relationship with other epistemic criteria, such as truthfulness, validity or reliability. It is therefore a second-order concept. The assessor is being asked to make her judgement not in relation to whether the researcher has an intention but in relation to whether the intention or purpose of the piece being assessed is sound. Furthermore, this means that no value can be given to intentionality in a criterial set unless a further judgement is made that this intention is sound or reasonable, and this involves a further judgement about the background to the research being made. It also requires a judgement to be made about whether the implicit recommendations of a piece of research are binding on participants in the setting under consideration or not.

Probative force

Another issue then that needs to be addressed is the probative force of the conclusions made in a piece of research.[56] If a researcher makes a theoretical claim about learning, she is also claiming that this theory is a better theory for explaining all of the available evidence than every other possible theory, and the truth claim embedded here would compel the practitioner to modify her practice if it was relevant to that practice. To do otherwise would be to base her practice on custom and experience rather than on the prescriptive force of research findings. However, much research does not make the claim that it has an absolute view of truth, but rather hedges its findings as helpful guidance or lacking in contextual detail or as tentative, and therefore deliberately does not make the claim that it should be accepted as the complete truth about the matter in hand. In this case, an acknowledgement is being made that the exercise of practical wisdom comprises a selection from all of the available evidence. This does not mean that the practitioner ignores the evidence and does what she feels was right all along, but it does mean that evidence and hypothesising are treated here as being strictly non-determinative.

A criterial judgement is considered to be sound if it satisfies the requirements for that judgement to be made.[57] For a piece to be judged to have met the requirements of being significant, for example, it must have conformed to a model of what significance means to the person making the judgement, and this comprises two processes: first, that the criterion

---

[56] Most research currently has attached to it an inadequate notion of truth, whether the author explicitly states this or not. This amounts to an assertion that because that author has collected, collated and analysed data (of whatever type) and drawn the appropriate conclusions, then what she is presenting to the reader must be truthful. It is a mistaken assertion.

[57] Wittgenstein (1953: §354) distinguished between criteria and symptoms, while at the same time making it clear that all knowledge claims were determined by criteria: 'The fluctuation in grammar between criteria and symptoms makes it look as if there were nothing but symptoms. We say, for example, "Experience teaches that there is rain when the barometer falls, but it also teaches that there is rain when we have certain feelings of wet and cold, or such-and-such visual impressions." As an argument in support of this, one says that these sense impressions can deceive us. But here one overlooks the fact that their deceiving us precisely *about rain* rests on a definition.'

is adequately defined; and second, that this general definition is applied to the particularity of the piece in a satisfactory way, so that this piece in part or in its entirety is an adequate example of the criterion. A criterion, then, is a statement about the quality of a piece or any future piece, and implicit within it is a model of what constitutes sufficient evidence for a judgement to be made that it conforms to the criterion, and evidence in the particular example being considered here (its significance) refers to the structure of the piece, whether it shows to the reader that the argument made is significant and so forth. The reader, who is making the judgement that it is significant, needs to have found good reasons or evidence as to why it meets those requirements. The reader may also have looked for evidence that the piece has not met the criterial requirements; in other words, she is looking for evidence or examples of places within the text that would indicate that the satisfiers for the criterion have not been met. If she finds a sufficient number of examples in which the author has not adopted a significant approach, then she is likely to judge that it has failed to meet these satisfiers. Thus, moments of positive affirmation and negative disconfirmation are implicit within the process.

Furthermore, two conditions have to be met. First, the relationships between these criteria have to be clarified. Are they for instance in a hierarchical relationship with each other? Do they have different values attached to them? If they do, are these implicit or explicit? And second, the application of criteria still requires an interpretive process to be undertaken by an assessor or assessors, and this involves the surfacing of background knowledge and the reaching of agreement between those assessors. This reaching of agreement is fraught with difficulties, especially if the discourse community is fractured or consists, to use Bernstein's (2000: 67) phrase, of 'a variety of specialised languages'.

However, it is not a question of abandoning one set (such as internal criteria) at the expense of another (such as external criteria), but of deciding on the relative value of each. This is inherently problematic; first, because different types of research may have different purposes and thus to give a low value to a piece, which is designed to have no practical or instrumental purpose, would be to discriminate against it. The second reason is that a further justification, which is an addition to the individual justification for each criterion, has to be provided, and this refers to why one criterion should be given a higher or lower value than another, and this applies even if all of the designated criteria are given equal values. In the process of identifying these criteria, an implicit value is given to each, and this value is relative to values that could be given to other criteria within the set, and in turn, these relative valuations need to be justified.

Those making these judgements then need a meta-theory that provides a rationale for the values given to the different criteria.

Assessors make judgements about quality, although the background to their judgements may be implicit. What is the origin of their judgement? They may have had experience of performing the same action before, and although their understanding of what is involved has changed over time, it has been influenced by previous encounters with the same type of problem. They may in the past have had their view moderated by examples of other people performing similar actions to their own, and they have assimilated these experiences into their repertoire of beliefs, leading to certain well-rehearsed practices/actions. Knowledge in judgement is still tacit, even if at various points in time that tacit knowledge is surfaced for reflection and contemplation and amended accordingly. They have a model of what good research looks like when they make a judgement and, in part, they match up the piece under scrutiny with this model. There may, however, be a further process at work, which is that because they are aware of a number of different and conflicting ways to make a judgement about a piece of research, they suspend their own set of beliefs and judge the work to be sound if it conforms to the collective judgement of the discourse community in which they work, as they understand it. However, what we can say is that evidence-providing or reason-giving activity has a judgemental element.

Evidence in judgement

All judgements about educational matters are inferential; that is, evidence is collected, and a conclusion is drawn from that piece of evidence or evidential set. In making a judgement about a piece of research in relation to a set of criteria, evidence is investigated. However, the relationship between evidence and judgement is complicated. The evidence or evidential set has either a strong or a weak warrant and is domain specific – the kind of information that will serve as supporting facts in making a claim is dependent on the practice within which it is embedded. Claims that are made in the world, then, are domain specific, so one set of practices or a domain requires a different type of evidence base from another.

In making a judgement about a piece of research using a set of criteria, the issue of fallibilism is salient, both as it relates to the judgement made by the assessor and as it relates to the use of evidence by the researchers to support their hypotheses. This is because in making a judgement, true knowledge (that x is better than y, where x and y refer to different pieces of work) may consist of an acceptance that a weak form of evidence to support the hypothesis that is being made and/or a weak relationship between evidence and hypothesis is all that is required. In this case, knowledge is fallible; however, it may still be acceptable either to the reader or user of research or to the discourse community in which she works. Thus, when a judgement is made that a piece of research is relevant, plausible, transparent or whatever, no assumption is being made that it is perfectly plausible, transparent or relevant. It is accepted that it meets some but not all the requirements of these criteria.

There is a further dimension that needs to be considered, and this is the nature of the evidence itself and, in particular, the way in which it has been gathered; in other words, its implicit (usually) warrant. If evidence is contaminated by vested interests, then it may be considered to be unsound. However, at a foundational level, there may be disagreement about the possibility or otherwise of any evidence being produced that is not imbued with interest values of one type or another. If, for example, a Gadamerian perspective is adopted (see chapter 2), then the soundness of the evidence is judged by whether a sufficient acknowledgement of the background to the collection and presentation of the data is made (Gadamer, 1989), and this is underpinned by the idea that no value-free evidence can be collected. This, however, is treated not as sufficient for designating a piece of evidence as sound or unsound, but only as a necessary element of such a process.

A piece of evidence on its own may not be enough to confirm or falsify a belief that is held, since it may be that a collection of evidence is required to confirm or falsify a belief. Thus, the problem arises with regards to the relationships between these different items of evidence. Again, more evidence of the same type merely gives the researcher greater confidence that she is correct in holding this belief. However, the belief that she has may not require more of the same type of evidence, because even if she collects many instances of the same type, this can never prove conclusively that she is correct to hold that belief. It may be that different types of evidence are required to confirm or disconfirm that belief. Furthermore, the strength of the evidence, which leads the researcher to hold a belief, is always undermined – it becomes weaker – if alternative hypotheses generated from those data can be identified.

Perhaps the most fundamental sense in which we can understand the social processes involved in knowledge formation, even more than with the making of judgements about texts, is the activity of learning itself. Before that we need to address the issues of reasons and causes, whether reasons are causes, and whether human beings *and* material or discursive objects can be distinguished by their capacity or otherwise to operate in the realm of reasons.

Reasons and causes

In chapter 1, I suggested that there are five generic types of objects: discursive objects, material entities, object-relations, structural formations and human beings. What is missing then is a set of reasons for or a justification of an object-ontology.[58] This will have to wait. For the time being I want to address one element of this argument: the reason-giving disposition of human beings. Objects, such as material entities, structural formations and human beings, have particular characteristics at particular points in time. Here I want to concentrate on the most important of these object-types, human beings, and suggest that the principal characteristic of human beings is their capacity to work with and through reasons.

What I suggest is that in order to make an ontological claim – that is, a claim about being – we are not, as is commonly thought, providing a description of an experience but making a claim about it in what Wilfred Sellars (1997) described as 'a space of reasons', and that what follows from this is that we can and should understand and use concepts specifically in relation to current and future-oriented networks of meanings. In his *Empiricism and the Philosophy of Mind*, Sellars suggested that 'in characterising an episode or a state as that of knowing, we are not giving an empirical description of that episode or state; we are placing it in the logical space of reasons, of justifying and being able to justify what one says' (Sellars, 1997: §36). This is a spatial metaphor and a marker that can distinguish human beings from other types of objects, insofar as trees, rocks and buildings do not seem to reason, employ reasoning strategies or attempt to provide a justification for a course of action. Reasoning within this space involves giving and asking for reasons, where this activity is understood as making a commitment in the world,

---

[58] By calling it an object-ontology I am affirming that anything I say here has a realist element to it, and that it is possible to differentiate between things in the world. What I am also suggesting is that the type of realism I am espousing is far from the type of realism argued for by positivists/empiricists or the type of realism that postmodernists set themselves against. Realism does not necessarily entail representationalism.

with that commitment referring to the circumstances surrounding its content and its consequences.

Such an argument makes sense only within a particular enframing of the object-world; for example, if one adopts a physicalist view of the world, with no distinction being made between mind and matter, then reasons and separately rationalisations for those reasons are literally irrelevant to true explanations of these phenomena. They can play no part in the causal sequence that we might want to explain, which includes learning activities. This would suggest that if a non-physicalist approach to volition and constraint is adopted, then a notion of giving and asking for reasons as the essential characteristic of the human being is needed. Although this is an argument that on the surface seems to suggest that human beings can will certain things, this would be to claim too much. There are two obstacles to us believing this. The first is that I have to provide an argument or set of arguments for the giving of reasons in the first place, and any subsequent rationalisations of those reasons (all of this may be below the level of consciousness) and this reason-giving activity have to be different from the way in which a physicalist causal sequence might operate. Otherwise reasons are simply epiphenomenal and are irrelevant to how we explain this or that – especially when we are dealing with learning as a concept or even an episode of learning. And second, I still have to provide an argument within a space of reasons for a non-physicalist approach. (I do this in chapter 9.)

There may be a way out of this dilemma: to construe a reason and the giving and asking for a reason in physicalist terms. This would involve stripping away all of the elements of the process of giving and asking for reasons – the activity of giving, the activity of asking, the notion of a reason and more – and understand them purely as physical unwilled objects that conform to certain laws of nature, as a neuropsychologist would argue. (See chapter 9 for a fuller explication of this argument.) This would, I think, render them as meaningless and the space of reasons would become an empty concept.

I have suggested here that a temporal distinction needs to be made between reasons and rationalisations of those reasons, and this would be in accord with the view that human beings have intentions and that these intentions are not irrelevant to any explanation we might want to make of an event or causal sequence. So, in the first instance, the rationalisation of the action might not be a part of the explanation of the original causal sequence at the first time point. However, this rationalisation might in turn be an important part of a new and different causal sequence, with a different object as its endpoint. A rationalisation of an explanation is a post-hoc explanatory mechanism and may have nothing to do with the original reason-causing activity, except insofar as it may constitute evidence for the identification of the original reason for the action.

The key is answering the question as to whether reasons can be causes. This is of some importance because it impacts directly on the choice of methods for collecting evidence to confirm or disconfirm the theories we might have about human activities. Is it possible to determine ex post facto that the reasoning activity of an individual can provide an adequate explanation for a particular event in which this individual played a prominent part? Texts produced through interactive processes such as interviewing and involving interpretative activity can provide truthful accounts of them. This argument hinges on the idea that the reasoning process undertaken by an individual can lead directly to actions; in other words, intentionality is a genuine idea. This does not mean that rationalisations of the reasons for their actions by individuals do not take place and, indeed, interviews as a methodological tool generally focus on these post-hoc rationalisations. However, the post-hoc rationalisation is emergent from the actual reason for the activity and thus retains elements of it, although it is not reducible to it.

The difficulty then becomes that these reasons (which by necessity have a directive quality about them) are embedded in networks of reasons for doing things, which exist independently from the consciousness of the individual, although clearly the individual has the capacity to access them. A person can have a reason for her action, be convinced that the reason she gives is the actual reason for why the action took place, and believe that the action would not have taken place without the reason being developed prior to the action. And yet, the reason given is not the real reason for that action. Furthermore, the rationalisation of the original reason is not necessarily a distortion of that original reason; it may comprise a re-forming of that reason, which now entails the placing of the action in wider social, political, economic and discursive contexts (some of which are developed during the research process by the researcher, trusted-other or teacher). The purpose is to grasp the reasoning action in its setting of rules, practices, conventions and, fundamentally, people's expectations. What this implies is that there is always an intentional relationship in any particular action or event. And this in turn implies that in most circumstances the person is a skilled knower, especially with regards to her own reasons for her actions, even if the original and motivating reason is subsequently rationalised over time.

In pursuing a causal explanation of learning via a constant conjunction model, with its stress on that which can be observed and controlled, researchers, and human beings in the lifeworld, have tended to overlook the liabilities, powers and potentialities of the programmes and people whose behaviours they are trying to explain. If this is correct, then the data-collection methods and the research design are going to be different. The reason for this is that researchers are now committed to understanding mechanisms that may not actually operate in practice (that is, produce effects) because the external conditions for the release of the generative mechanism may not be present. Researchers therefore have to adopt a two-fold strategy: identifying the appropriate generative mechanism and examining the actual conditions that have produced the effects they have observed. Since the reality, which they wish to describe, is social in nature and comprises social actors interacting with each other, they cannot simply assume that those actors are compelled to behave in particular and specific ways by causal mechanisms that they cannot observe and which they do not understand. These types of causal relations need to be understood as configurations of social actors making decisions, whether appropriate or not, within certain determinate conditions and, further, that the making of those decisions and the subsequent retroductions that are made change both the contexts in which future decisions are made and the identity of those social actors. I have focused here on the reason-giving capacity of human beings and the implications of this for how we can research into and consequently understand learning, both our own and that of other people. In the next chapter, I address these issues in more detail and, in particular, the third of our object-types, object-relations.

4
Object-relations – research into learning

The third of the object-types within an object-ontology is an object-relation. If we are able to distinguish between different objects (and the justification for doing this is complicated, but nevertheless essential to the argument being made in this book – see chapter 13 for a fuller explication) and we want to build into our conception of the world ideas of change, inter- and intra-relationships and continuities (over time), then we need to understand what these are and how they occur. This revolves around the idea that object-relations inhere in those objects as characteristics of these objects. They are thus interactive, powerful, dynamic and object-specific. This means that in the first case an object, with a particular set of characteristics, enters into a relation with another (or other) object(s). A person opens a door and walks through it, closing the door behind him. In the second case, objects in interaction with other objects have the power to change themselves and other objects, object-relations and arrangements of objects. A third characteristic is their dynamism both in terms of their substance and in relation to how they can be classified as object-relations. And a fourth characteristic of an object-relation is that it is specific to a particular object – its potential power to influence and change other objects in the world in an interactive process is determined by the nature of the characteristics that inhere in that object, which means that the essential nature of an object is time- and space-bound. These object-relations act as hinges in the interaction between objects, object-configurations and people.

I have already suggested that one requirement for a coherent theory of knowledge and being is that social reality has ontological depth. This notion of ontological depth has two elements: that the world is stratified or can be characterised as having different levels of being; and that it is possible to identify (but not necessarily through the senses or experientially) concrete manifestations of phenomena operating at these different levels. One such stratificational hierarchy is Roy Bhaskar's (2011) three levels of reality:[59] the empirical level (the level of experiences), the actual level (the level of events and states of affairs) and the real level (the level of underlying structures and generative mechanisms). For Bhaskar, the real level constitutes a more fundamental level of explanation – this has implications for how we can know reality, since the real level is not immediately available to consciousness. In order to access this level of reality, we have to operate in a backwards or retroductive fashion to determine what the real relations in any causal sequence that has already taken place might be; and in turn this means that we cannot safely predict at any time point what is going to happen in the future. Objects, relations, networks and people are dynamic and do not change in relation to some predetermined pattern or plan. In addition, objects, networks, relations and people possess powers. The powers held by these objects have three forms: they can be possessed, exercised or actualised. What this means is that material, relational, personal, institutional-systemic or discursive powers can be possessed by an object but are not actualised, or they can be actualised but not have any real effects in the open system they are operating within, or they can be influencing present and future arrangements of objects, networks and relations dynamically.

---

[59] Bhaskar (Scott with Bhaskar, 2015: 35) in one of his last writing projects suggested that: 'There are two basic features of the new ontology that was established by the same sorts of arguments that established the necessity of ontology itself. There were two ontological characteristics of the greatest importance. Well, let's say two concepts. The first concept is that of an open system, and this is an index of the differentiation of the world, and the second concept is that of ontological stratification, or a distinction between, what I call, the real and actual, bearing in mind that the actual is also real, the real level then signifies the non-actual real, and of course this was part of a triple distinction between the real, the actual and empirical. And so, the key feature of this is stratification, and if I could just go into stratification a little bit. There are two senses that can be given to stratification, which I think it is important to differentiate, all of which are in critical realism. So, the first is the idea of the distinction between structure or mechanisms and the events they generate, or the distinction between the real and the actual, or the distinction between powers and their exercise or between powers and their realisation in actuality. And the second is the idea of the multi-tiered stratification of reality, and this is opposed to the idea that there is just one level or stratum, where there isn't even one level of difference. The distinction between structures and events is in principle infinitely repeatable in reality. So, for example, here we have a table, and the table is constituted by molecules in motion, and the molecules in motion are constituted by atoms, which in turn are constituted by electrons, which are to be explained in turn by quantum fields of singularity. In the history of modern physics, we have identified these five levels of structure, and critical realism has a very nice schema to show how science gets from one level to another. This I call the D-R-E-I-C schema and it basically tells you what happens in any round of scientific discovery and development.'

Examples of these object-relations expressed dualistically are: one-to-one or one-to-many relations (where the relation between objects is manifested as an object-to-object relation or as an object-to-objects relation); strong or weak relations (where this refers to the probative force of the object-relation); vertical or horizontal relations (where this refers to whether hierarchies or flat structures of objects are being created); corrosive or developmental relations (where this refers to the consequences of the activation of the powers of an object on another object or objects – what type of change results); endogenous or exogenous relations (where this refers to the direction of change in the original object – internal or external); enabling or constraining functionality (where the direction and impulsion of the object-relation is towards one or the other); feed-back or feed-forward relations (where this refers to the temporality of the change process); convergence or divergence (where the end point is towards a monistic or pluralistic categorisation of knowledge); framing or reframing relations (where this refers to the epistemology of the change process); categorising or recategorising relations (where the concern here is with the essence or non-essence of objects in the world); and subsumptive or contiguous relations (where this refers to the impact of the interaction on both objects, whether the impact is integral or peripheral). Each of these examples of object-relations is expressed in terms of its potentiality to influence object-arrangements at a particular point in time.[60] So, for example, some objects can be characterised as having one-to-one, feed-back, weak and contiguous powers, and it is these powers or orientations that in conjunction with many other powers and orientations enable us to distinguish between objects. As a result, causation can only be understood as being generative, productive and retrospectively understood. These three knowledge claims need in the first instance to be distinguished from claims about causation that are false or insufficient.

Causation

Aristotle's causal explanatory framework comprises the following: i) material causation – an object such as a statue is generated from something else, such as a basic metal; ii) formal causation – an object

---

[60] This is the crucial point. It is not just that objects have tendencies to influence other objects, it is that they have tendencies to influence them in particular and specific ways. These tendencies are relational.

such as a statue represents something else and thus this something else can be said to have caused the object; iii) efficient causation – an object can be said to have been intended, so we can say that it has been caused by the intention of the person and the work of that person in fulfilling his or her intention as in a sculptor making a statue; and then there are iv) final causes where we are dealing with ends or purposes – the statue has some purpose such as satisfying an aesthetic need or honouring an important public figure (cf. Aristotle, 2018a: Book II, chapter 3).[61] In order to provide a satisfactory account of causality, the philosopher must also develop a satisfactory account of epistemology – the former supervenes on the latter.

Those subscribing to empiricist and positivist philosophies claim that it is possible to predict events, and this is founded on the idea that both the original account (at the first time point – T_1) and the predicted account (at the second time point – T_2) are sufficient in all essential respects. On the other hand, as I have argued above, it may not be possible to make law-like predictions about social and educational matters. What this means is that laws should not be thought of as constant conjunctions, or even as determinate causal sequences, but as tendencies of powerful objects, and these tendencies are understood as the properties of those objects, and not as predictive behaviours that have not yet been performed.

Scientific realists and statistical positivists generally subscribe to a Humean theory of causality as spatiotemporal contiguity, succession and constant conjunction, and this is founded on the idea that although it is not possible to observe a relation between cause and effect, it is possible to identify a persistent association between two or more events, and then infer a causal relation.[62] A repudiation of this view of causality is an essential building block for a notion of dispositional realism, or at least a view that objects have causal properties and thus dispositions of one type or another – an argument that I will take up in chapter 15.

Objections to Hume's theory of causality have frequently been made. It cannot account for spurious associations or order cause and

---

[61] In this exposition, Aristotle was giving an account of the different ways in which causation can be understood semantically. He was not in this particular passage showing how causation actually works in the world.

[62] This is one interpretation of David Hume's notion or idea of causality and the most common one, and he makes this point repeatedly in his writings. Here is one instance of it (Hume, 2000: 161): 'All ideas are deriv'd from, and represent impressions. We never have any impression, that contains any power or efficacy. We never therefore have any idea of power.' There are many other instances in his *A Treatise of Human Nature*.

effect, and there is no guarantee that all of the possible interacting variables have been identified. Furthermore, it is reductive because it treats these variables as real, and therefore elides epistemology with ontology. The meaning of a concept is always embedded in a framework of other concept-meanings, and in pointing to the detheorisation of much contemporary research I am suggesting that traditional and reductionist forms of research separate out the concept from the framework, in order for it to have the properties of a variable. Having detheorised the concept, relations are then identified between these different variables, even if the variable itself does not have a meaningful relationship with the world. (Such relational exercises include descriptive statistics; basic hypotheses tests such as t-tests, ANOVA, contingency tables and chi-square tests; classic regression models, including logistic and probit regressions; multilevel regression models; factorial analysis and structural equation models; and data envelopment analysis, propensity score analysis, stochastic frontier analysis and simulation.[63]) Most research in the field of learning is predicated on a detheorisation and a semantic reduction of the concept(s) being examined. The frequently cited injunction that in order to make a comparison between institutions or systems of learning, the first move one has to make is to reduce the various elements of the setting being examined to sets of numbers is to adopt a restricted view of the concept and how it is used in the world – with the consequence that this detheorisation process means that the researcher understands objects, relations between objects, arrangements of objects, people and causality in a particular way, which cannot relate to how these objects actually behave and have their being in the world. It is the enumeration of the object that acts to delimit the way the object (material or discursive), the object-relation, the object-configuration or the person can be understood, and what follows from this is that it can produce a distorted view of what is being investigated.[64] Some objects (both conceptual and material) are already framed enumeratively, for example, money[65] or

---

[63] The use of some of these techniques has been described by a leading quantitative researcher in the field of education as getting us closer to the real world. He was wrong then and is still wrong now.

[64] There are three possible alternatives for how we can understand the use of mathematics to illuminate concepts: i) mathematics as a useful formal linguistic system; ii) mathematics as a system to enable us to discover causally inert and non-normative objects in the world; iii) foregoing a representationalist meta-semantics and a causal theory of knowledge implicit in i) and ii) *and* adopting a use theory of meaning and accepting that mathematical statements have normative as well as descriptive elements, as Wittgenstein argued.

[65] It should be said here that if we are dealing with monetary relations, such as exchange, distribution, storage and the like, then enumerative distortions are likely to detheorise these objects.

runs in the game of cricket, and thus are not detheorised or semantically distorted if the mode of investigation or appreciation is broadly quantitative; however, most objects, especially those that operate in the space of learning, are not framed enumeratively or at least not framed exclusively in enumerated ways.

Another view of causality is that people cannot observe these causal relations, and in addition, those relations do not exist in nature since events are not caused. There are only apparent regularities, and therefore what is understood as a causal relationship – that is, a first event has led to a second event on every occasion in which they have interacted – is a product of chance. There is nothing in nature that causes anything to happen. This is an extreme version of causality, effectively a denial of causality as real. An alternative view is to suggest that there are different types of causes, which are different in kind because they operate in different ways; a person having a reason for doing something that also causes him to do it, such as keeping an appointment, is different from that person not being able to leave a room because the door is locked. If asked what caused him to do it, he might provide a different reason for his action from the one that motivated him in the first place or conditioned his action. This however, is not a refutation of the belief that reasons can in certain circumstances be causes, but only an observation that a person may be misled about the actual reasons that caused another person's actions, or even that the person himself may have been confused about what actually caused him to do something.

Let us now imagine that the world is not random, and thus it does have causal elements. Again, there are a number of possible models. The first of these is that everything is caused: the universe is a closed system of objects, including individual human beings; these objects have causal powers that may or may not be activated; and if they are activated, they behave mechanically. And what this means is that if an object comes into contact with another object, then a new object is formed, which is what constitutes a causal sequence. All events are caused whether observers are fully able to understand them or not. Incomplete or deficient understandings occur because a person does not know enough about the world, or because he does not know how he could investigate the event in a reliable way, or even because he could never be in a position to conduct a reliable investigation. Indeed, he might think that he knows the cause of something, especially if the cause–effect–cause sequence involves an intentional act; however, he could be mistaken even if he is the intentional being. This process takes place regardless of whether it can be or is described or theorised about; thus, notions of probability do not come into the equation at this level of explanation. The important point to note about this model is that intentionality is treated in the same way as any other material or ideational causal substance. Thus, one substance in conjunction with another substance necessarily causes a new substance to be formed. This ineluctably implies determinism and necessity.

A second model is different and is predicated on the idea that reasons can be and are causes. However, this needs to be qualified by the adoption of a further premise, which is that reasons are not causes in the same way that events have antecedent conditions which necessarily have to be present for that event to take place. We need to distinguish here between actual reasons for an action and rationalisations of those reasons after the event or activity. However, even if we distinguish between the two, we are not identifying a new justification, because we are not ruling out the possibility that a reason has caused something to happen, even if, subsequently, that causal mechanism of which the action is the central component has been incorrectly described.

A reason has to relate to the action it seeks to explain; it has to, in other words, be relevant. It takes the form of a justification for an action yet to be performed, and this therefore implies that there are competing actions between which a human being has to choose. (This would include all of the possible ways of behaving that are relevant to the proposed course of action.) This reason is valued in relation to other possible reasons for action, and these values are embedded in those structures of agency that act as conditions for the agent. What this means is that certain actions, and therefore the reasons for those actions, are privileged over other actions and their reasons, and this forms the backdrop to the choosing of a reason for an action and ultimately to the performance of the action itself.

There is a further model, which in essence is epistemological. This is that any causal model we might want to adopt is probabilistic rather than deterministic in essence. We may be unable to determine whether this model is a viable one because the world is essentially determined or because the world is too complicated to allow us to give a full account of it. However, it works (the model allows us to successfully predict within certain parameters of error), but we do not know why it works. Does it work because it is an accurate reflection of the way the world works or because in predicting the future, researchers are activating mechanisms that will bring it about? In addition, probabilistic reasoning does not account for every case being considered, but only a majority of cases; outliers are confined to the realm of either the unknowable (error at the case level) or theoretical inadequacy (the theory that is being used and that allows prediction is not sophisticated enough to account for every single case, but, though flawed, is the best there is). Thus, the empirical indicators (Wittgenstein's criteria) used to construct the causal narrative are inadequate for the task, and consequently the post-hoc theory that is developed is at fault.

A final model is that events are caused but can only be known retrospectively. Events that have taken place are caused, that is, by an intention of a human being or by the collective intentions of a group of human beings or by the conjunction of two or more mechanisms; but to say that this causal sequence can be known only after the event has taken place tells us nothing about whether events are caused or not. It tells us only whether and at what point we can identify a particular causal sequence. However, we can take this model one stage further and suggest a generative/productive view of causation. We can hypothesise a relationship and then try to work out what the mechanism might be. By mechanism I mean literally that an object has causal powers to induce change in another object, that these powers may or may not be exercised, and, even if they are, that there is no guarantee that change will occur in the targeted object, which means that we cannot safely predict how the dynamic object in the future will behave.[66] This has implications for how we construe theory–practice relationships.

Theory–practice relationships

An example of an object-relation operating at the discursive level over time can be seen in the relationship between a theory or set of propositions about objects, relations and arrangements of objects – how they might work in the world – and a set of future arrangements of objects and relations in the practice setting (from description to practice). For those concerned to provide accounts of learning, conceptualising the relationship between the theory that they produce and the practice that they are describing, and subsequently transferring to that practice setting,

---

[66] Prediction is the key to the successful use of some of these quantitative methodologies, and this is prediction in the sense that we can know at a first time point what will happen at a second time point. However, there are two principal reasons as to why it is difficult to make sound predictions: i) we may not have confidence in how we have described what has happened at the first time point, and consequently how this description can play out at the second time point; ii) our descriptions at the first time point may have influenced what subsequently happens at the second time point, thus rendering the comparison null and void. An example of this is opinion polls and the way they work. It would be unwise to trust them. This is also an example of the commodification of knowledge.

is central to their activities. In short, how this relationship is understood is important both because it affects the type of account produced and because it impacts upon the workings of practices per se. In a Wittgensteinian fashion, there are five possible positions that can be taken, with proponents of each adopting different stances as to how theories about learning practices are constructed and how they relate to those self-same learning practices.

The first of these treats science as the final arbiter of truthful accounts. There is a correct method for collecting data about learning activities. This method, if properly adhered to, leads to the creation of objective, value-free and authoritative knowledge about how teachers should behave. Teachers or practitioners but not theorists therefore need to bracket out their own values, experiences and preconceptions because these are partial, incomplete and subjective and follow the precepts of researchers whose sole purpose is to develop knowledge that transcends the local and the contextual.

Scientific theory is designated as theory because relations between educational phenomena are being expressed at a general level: they apply to a variety of situations both in the present and in the future. It therefore allows prediction, not, it should be noted, because the expression of that theory influences what will happen but because the knowledge itself is propositional, generalisable, non-particularistic and operates outside the realm of actual practice. The criteria that determine good practice in scientific research comprise in part a particular relationship to practitioner knowledge: that the former (scientific research) is superior to the latter (practitioner knowledge), and that appropriate behaviours on the part of the practitioner consist of correcting and amending errors to their own knowledge domain in the light of what is being asserted as a result of the correct scientific procedures being followed. Practice is conceptualised as the following of rules that have been systematically researched and formalised as theory. This has been described as the technical-rationality model of the theory–practice relationship in which practice is understood as the practical application of a body of theoretical knowledge. Worthwhile knowledge is understood as being located in the field of generalised propositions; practice is not conceived of as knowledge at all but as the application of theory in practical situations.

Proponents of this view make a number of assumptions: first and foremost, that theoretical knowledge can give us insights into reality; that is, it can provide adequate and meaningful descriptions of how the world works. As a result, it de-emphasises actors' perceptions of how the world works because these are partial, inaccurate, ideologically motivated or falsely conceived. Second, practice itself or practical knowledge is not in itself sufficiently robust to qualify as knowledge; that is, the criteria we apply for something to qualify as knowledge (for example, consistency, coherence, validity, reliability or generalisability) cannot be applied to practical deliberation. This privileging of theoretical knowledge over practical knowledge is not, and cannot be, conceptualised as an a priori theoretical truth.

The second viewpoint has some similarities to the first viewpoint but understands the creation of objectified knowledge in a different way. Proponents of this viewpoint would want to adopt a realist perspective but would understand that realist perspective in a different way; they might want to adopt a generative rather than successionist theory of causal relations or they might want to reconceptualise the researcher–researched relationship so that the value perspectives of the researcher are centrally implicated in the act of doing research. However, the educational text that is produced is still treated in the same way as with the first perspective, and the relationship between theory and practice is understood as being consistent with the technical-rationality mode.[67] This involves the solving of technical problems through rational decision-making based on knowledge that allows us to predict the future. It is the means to achieve ends where the assumption is that the ends to which practice is directed can always be predefined and are always knowable. The condition of practice is the learning of a body of theoretical knowledge, and practice therefore becomes the application of this body of knowledge in repeated and predictable ways to achieve predefined ends. Both of these first two perspectives, therefore – different though they are – are concerned with determining a measure of technical efficiency that will inevitably lead to the achievement of ends that are separate from the determination of means regarded as necessary to their realisation.

The third type of theory–practice relationship is multi-perspectival and multi-methodological. If there is no correct method, but only a set of methods that produce texts of various kinds, and these can be read in different ways, then the practitioner has to make a series of decisions about whether a text is appropriate or not. Theory and practice are here being uncoupled. Whether or not the practitioner works to the prescriptive framework of the theorist will depend on a number of factors, such as the fit between the values of the theorist and the practitioner,

---

[67] This was extensively criticised by Schon (2005), among others.

whether they share a common epistemological framework and, fundamentally, whether solutions are being provided by the theorist to practical problems encountered during the practitioner's everyday activity. The practitioner is here being treated as a self-sufficient producer and user of knowledge. However, there is still a sense with this perspective that the outside theorist can produce broadly accurate prescriptive knowledge, which because of the contingencies of life in educational institutions then needs to be adapted to the settings in which the practitioner works. The theorist produces general knowledge, the practitioner supplies the fine-grained detail, but in all essential respects still follows precepts developed by theorists who operate away from the practice setting.

A fourth position that can be taken is an extension of the position expressed above. This is an interpretation of the theory–practice relation in which deliberated thoughtful practice is not just the target but is the major source (perhaps the specifying source) of educational theory. What should be noted here is the rejection of a role in practice for the theorist, because the theorist operates outside of the practice. Various forms of action research fit this perspective, which understands practice as deliberative action concerned with the making of appropriate decisions about practical problems in classrooms. This cannot mean that there is no theoretical activity involved in the making of these decisions. What it does suggest is that theoretical activity does not apply only to technical decisions about how to implement theory developed by outsiders. In addition to practitioners needing to deliberate about the most efficient means of achieving certain predefined ends, they also need to deliberate about the ends themselves. Practice situations are not only particularistic, they may also be understood as complex and uncertain, and therefore actively resist routinisation. Understandings of them need to be continually formulated and reformulated by practitioners working in situ. In short, such knowledge is not propositional, which means that it always involves action and deliberation. However, operating in a non-technicist way demands that practitioners do not behave as objective theorists say they should. But this reconceptualising of the relationship between theory and practice is itself theoretical and moreover theoretical in a normative sense.

This leads to a fifth position, which is that the theorist and the practitioner are actually engaged in different activities. This more closely fits the view that the nature of theorising practice demands the identification of four different discourses, each of which has implicit within it a distinctive way of understanding a practical field such as teaching and learning, and each of which is a legitimate activity: deliberation, evaluation, science and utopianism. The deliberative discourse is understood as prescriptive and particularistic; the evaluative as particularistic and descriptive; the scientific as general and descriptive; and the utopian as prescriptive and general. The consequence of this is that the theorist and the practitioner are operating in different ways and with different criteria as to what constitutes knowledge.[68]

These five discursive formations offer alternative perspectives on an important aspect of social life. What has become a commonplace in the development of public policy over the past 20 years is the sense in which there has to be a binding relationship between theory and practice (so much rhetorical energy is given up to this); but in reality, practice in the educational and social spheres is the outcome of political deliberations and unforeseen events and occurrences. An example of this binding relationship is evidence-based practice.[69]

Evidence-based practice

Evidence-based practice, or prescriptive activity models for practitioners or teachers that are supported by evidence about how they should behave, is frequently commended and advocated within the education community. The central problem with this idea is that policymakers, researchers and practitioners disagree about what evidence is and how it can be collected. Evidence and evidence collection have a number of forms. For example, randomised control trials are used to determine whether an intervention works.[70] The rationale behind randomised control trials is straightforward: the effects of a group of students engaged in learning something or other are measured over the period of the intervention and then compared with a control group that, although equivalent in every other respect to the experimental group, has not been subject to the intervention but has continued as it normally would have. This allows the researcher to determine the actual effect size of a group's

---

[68] It hardly needs saying that these different discursive configurations can be designated as distinct objects because of how objects are arranged within them and because of the boundaries that have been established between their different objects.

[69] Whose evidence is it? and What does it signify?

[70] For a thorough critique of randomised control trials and their place in evidence-gathering practices, see Wrigley (2018). The Education Endowment Foundation is an example of a research organisation that has bought in to the idea that randomised control trials are truth-bearing methodologies.

exposure to the intervention and consequently whether or not the intervention is successful or not.

A number of variations have been developed. The first, a single-group experimental design, is where a single group of participants is tested before and after a programme of interventions to determine whether that programme has been successful or not. A variation on this is where a control group is added, so that a comparison can be made between it and the experimental group. A third approach is where the researcher accepts that more than one factor may be influential, arguing that a particular factor affects behaviour in one context, but not in another. In order to take account of this, the researcher studies a number of groups, each of which has different characteristics, and each of which is subjected to different types of interventions. Experimental researchers use methods that are essentially deductive and involve the testing of hypotheses. Furthermore, such methods allow replication, and ultimately the establishment of law-like propositions about social activities. Experimental researchers argue that as a result, uncontested and secure propositions about the way in which society works can be established.

A number of factors may have had an impact on how the old and new methods are received. For the comparison between the scores obtained by the two groups to be valid, those other factors that may affect the amount and quality of learning have to be isolated. The process of random sampling affords a partial solution to this problem. If two groups can be picked randomly (the one to act as the experimental group and the other to act as a control group), then it is possible to be fairly certain that the internal characteristics of the two groups are similar. The effect of randomly choosing experimental and control groups is that members of each group have an equal chance of being influenced by factors other than the intervention.

However, there is a significant problem, which is that randomisation is difficult to achieve in certain social settings; for example, when the researcher wishes to compare groups in schools that may have been chosen so that they are deliberately not equal. In other words, the researcher comes to a setting that is already determined beforehand and his intervention therefore relates to the teaching of those predetermined groups. There is a similar problem with matching pairs or groups, which has been described as an alternative to randomisation. In order to assign matched pairs to different groups and then to intervene at the group level, the researcher would have to be in a position to create new groups. In much social and educational research, this is simply not possible. There is a further problem with assigning students to matched pairs and this is that researchers have to be aware of, and confident in, their ability to measure those factors in order to identify appropriate subjects. In other words, they have to know before they do their research what those factors are to allow them to match one child with another.

A further iteration of this design is where the experimentalist foregoes the pre-testing process and is confident that, because he has picked randomised groups, they will be equally matched. This is known as the post-test-only randomised control group design. Measuring the abilities and aptitudes of subjects beforehand is irrelevant to the identification of isomorphic groups since the experimentalist is concerned above all with the comparative effects of interventions. In addition, there are good reasons as to why it is not possible to pre-test the various groups; for example, it is inconvenient or not practically possible. The principal advantage is that it eliminates the possibility of reactivity or pre-test sensitisation to the experiment, thus enhancing its internal validity. Randomisation allows the experimenter a measure of control over the setting, which is denied to those designs that are known as quasi-experimental.

One of the principal problems with conducting experiments is that the effects of an intervention may not show up, or the full implications of the intervention may be only partially revealed, at the moment of testing. An example is in the field of health education, where the experimenter is interested in testing for the effects of a smoking prevention programme, with the intervention comprising a teaching programme with a group of 15-year-old schoolchildren. The intervention consists of lectures, seminars, workshops and written exercises. The aim is to reduce both the number of children who start smoking after the age of 15 and the number who have already started. Because smoking take-up is heavily influenced by peer group pressure, the effectiveness of any health promotion intervention is likely to be compromised. However, in later life, when the influence of the peer group has considerably declined, learning that took place at an early age, but which had no immediate effect in terms of smoking cessation, influences later decisions to stop smoking. In other words, the experimenter has to choose the most likely moment to post-test the children, even though he is fully aware that the observed effects may be partial, incomplete and possibly misleading. Experimentalists have therefore devised a series of designs to compensate for this, although that compensation can be only partially achieved. One such design is the equivalent time-samples design, in which a series (random or regular alternation) of interventions are consecutively contrasted (over time) with a series of non-interventions. Another is a counterbalanced design, where four different experimental treatments are compared using four different groups over four different time periods. Critics of randomised control groups have focused on the reductive process of determining whether a learner has learnt something or other, the difficulties of identifying equivalent groups, the propensity of the method to ignore context and effect, the difficulties of controlling all of the variables over time, the tendency of the operation to generate simple and consequently distorting universal laws of cause and effect, and the fact that they are inherently descriptive rather than contributing to theory building. More generally, experimentalists find it difficult to give due regard to the dynamic nature of discursive, material, relational, configurational and human objects in their theories.

Essentially, this is the comparative method that John Stuart Mill wrote about at length. In *A System of Logic* he identified five comparative methods. The first is the direct method of agreement: 'if two or more instances of the phenomenon under investigation have only one circumstance in common, the circumstances in which alone all the instances agree is the cause (or effect) of the given phenomenon' (Mill, 1963–91, 7: 390). The second is the method of difference, where:

> if an instance in which the phenomenon under investigation occurs, and an instance in which it does not occur, have every circumstance save one in common, that one occurring only in the former; the circumstances in which alone the two instances differ, is the effect, or cause, or a necessary part of the cause, of the phenomena. (Mill, 1963–91, 7: 391)

A third approach he described as the joint method of agreement and disagreement:

> if two or more instances in which the phenomenon occurs have only one circumstance in common, while two or more instances in which it does not occur have nothing in common save the absence of that circumstance; the circumstance in which alone the two sets of instances differ, is the effect, or cause, or a necessary part of the cause, of the phenomenon. (Mill, 1963–91, 7: 396)

Although this is known as the joint method, the principle underpinning it represents the application of both of the methods identified above; that is, the methods of agreement and difference. Then there is the method of residue: 'Subduct from any phenomenon such part as is known by previous inductions to be the effect of certain antecedents, and the residue of the phenomenon is the effect of the remaining antecedents.' (Mill, 1963–91, 7: 398). The last of Mill's methods is the method of concomitant variations: 'Whatever phenomenon varies in any manner whenever another phenomenon varies in some particular manner, is either a cause or an effect of that phenomenon, or is connected with it through some fact of causation.' (Mill, 1963–91, 7: 401).

There are philosophical problems with this set of approaches. The first of these difficulties is conceptual. A concept is always embedded in a framework or network of other concepts (and therefore gets its meaning from that set of relationships and from how it is used in a way of life), and when we talk about the detheorisation of research, what we mean here is that traditional and reductionist forms of research separate out the concept from the framework in order for it to have the properties of a variable. Having detheorised the concept, relations are then identified between these different variables, even if the variable itself does not enter into a meaningful relationship with the world. A second problem (and I have referred to this above) is that the enumeration of meaning implicit in many of these conceptions of research is reductive and compels us to understand causation, object-relations, human capacity, free will and constraint in particular ways. What I am suggesting here is that a particular expressive mode has certain characteristics that prevent us from making true claims about knowledge of the world.[71] It is insufficient and therefore not up to the task. If we examine another example of a methodology that is in common use (the comparative survey method), we can see how its use contributes to a particular rendition of some key and necessary elements of the knowledge-construction exercise we are engaged in, such as causal relations, human behaviour and the use of particular types of object-relations.

The comparative survey method

Andreas Schleicher (2015), with regards to the Programme for International Student Assessment (PISA), uses a methodology that involves ranking a variety of countries in relation to their performance on a series of tests, and then identifying those systemic elements that are

---

[71] I have also argued throughout this book that the two expressive modes that are in common use, language and pictures, are also structured in particular ways, and thus enable and constrain the determination of meaning in particular ways.

present in high-performing countries and not present in low-performing countries. From this he concludes that it is possible to identify the optimum conditions for a system's effectiveness – a system of objects is one of our designated object-types. He is therefore able to suggest the following: children from similar social backgrounds can show very different performance levels, depending on the school they go to or the country they live in; there is no relationship between the share of students with an immigrant background in a country and the overall performance of students in that country; there is no relation between class size and learning outcomes within or across countries (the conceptual framework he works to here makes the unjustified assumption that all of the different types of learning activities are optimally performed with the same class size); there is no incompatibility between the quality of learning and equity since the highest-performing education systems combine both; all students are capable of achieving high standards; and more generally, the top-performing education systems tend to be more rigorous, with fewer curriculum items and with these being taught in greater depth.

This approach has a number of flaws in its conceptualisation and application, such as making false assumptions that tests can be culture-free, or that tests such as these can act as direct representational devices, or that they can avoid the problem of being able to test only atomistic forms of knowledge. In addition, test-makers need to acknowledge the bidirectionality of the PISA assessment process, in which washback effects on the curriculum can and do take place as a result of the testing process, and further accept that test-makers frequently use the same methods for testing dispositions, knowledge, skills and embodiments, with subsequent errors of ascription. In addition, an individual may have to reframe his knowledge set to fit the test, and therefore the assessment of his mastery of the construct is not a determination of his capacity in relation to the original construct, but a determination of whether he has successfully understood how to rework his capacity to fit the demands of the testing technology. These create serious problems for the legitimacy of such tests. Despite this, PISA is extremely influential, and an example of how simple messages can be produced by research, which lack a sense of truthfulness.[72]

---

[72] PISA has an inadequate methodology. I have written about this elsewhere (cf. Scott and Scott, 2018). For example, a false belief held is that a test can be constructed which is culture-free or free of those issues that disadvantage some types of learners at the expense of others. The extent of cultural bias in the PISA tests is unrealised and certainly under-reported. In addition, a particular technical problem with PISA relates to its sampling procedures. If different types of sampling in the different countries are used, then some of these countries will be disadvantaged compared with

There are a number of ways of identifying good practice. The first is identifying outputs from the system (these can be test scores, dispositional elements, acquired skills, ethical and moral qualities); that is, outputs that have resulted from the individual's participation in the system itself. The argument is then made that one system is better than another because it has better outputs and, further to this, that the characteristics of these national systems should be transferred to those countries or jurisdictions that are considered to be unsuccessful or ineffective in these terms. However, such types of modelling – these model types are being used to provide descriptions of the influence of Covid-19 in the world currently – depend for their truthfulness on which variables are used and how these variables are constituted.

A different way of determining quality in a system is by identifying a norm in order to allow a comparison to be made. For example, a system of learning – whether international, national or local – can be compared with, and marked against, a model of best practice, where this model is constructed to include all of the possible elements that could and should form a learning system (such as its structures, institutions, curricula, pedagogic arrangements and evaluative procedures), their arrangement in the most logical way (for example, that curricular intentions should precede pedagogical approaches and indeed derive their meaning from these curricular intentions) and the identification and enactment of logically formed relational arrangements between these elements (for instance that evaluative washback mechanisms should not be allowed to distort the curriculum as it was originally conceived). The norm that is used comparatively is constructed through sound logical and rational principles. In addition, the meaning of concepts is treated as an empirical matter, in terms of how they are used in communities or in a way of life. A reliance on outputs in the comparative process is unsafe and more importantly likely to be invalid. If we turn

others. Sampling issues are present in any test, whether this refers to selecting children from a number of grade levels and not specifying proportions from each grade, to selecting parts of countries for reporting purposes and ignoring the rest. Cultural differences take a number of different forms, such as ascribing different values, and different strengths of values to cultural items, or determining the nature, quality, probative force, relevance-value and extent of evidence, or focusing on practices that may be more familiar to people in some countries than in others. However, more importantly, cultural differences with regards to the selection of test items refer to the expression of the problem to be solved. If, for example, different national idioms, different national ways of thinking embedded in language forms and different normic values woven into the fabric of national discourses are ignored, then the presentation of the actual test items, as well as the range of possible answers that can be given, may favour students from one nation at the expense of students from another.

away from this, the methodological approach then becomes a search for mechanisms, relations and structures that are potentially causally efficacious and can be contextualised (historically, culturally and socioeconomically), but can also contribute to human wellbeing. This can be legitimately construed as a qualitative methodology.

A qualitative methodology

A qualitative methodology[73] comprises a focus on, and attention being paid to, the changing qualities or characteristics of the object or objects under investigation. If, as I have already suggested, objects, object-relations, object-types, object-configurations and persons are dynamic, then the researcher consequently has to examine the characteristics of, or qualities that inhere in, these objects. This entails a suspension of belief in the much-used notion of a dualism between quantitative and qualitative research, because strong claims can be made that these are not comparable objects and, further, that in all types of research there is necessarily a qualitative dimension. What this means is that any research or investigatory study has to address the categorising and recategorising or formulating and reformulating process that is a feature of social life.

A qualitative methodology can be understood at the levels of strategy and method as a series of steps or action-sets. The first step entails a process of reasoning that points to causal relationships as expressions of the tendencies of natural and social objects. The second is resolving a concrete event occurring in a context into its components. The third, and the most important, is redescribing these components in a theoretically significant form, where significance is understood in epistemic, rational, configurational and coherentist ways. The fourth is a retroductive move – or moving from describing the components of an event to proposing explanations about what produces or are the conditions for the event. The fifth is eliminating alternative possible explanations. The sixth is identifying a series of coherent and rational explanations and coming to some conclusions about these explanations. And finally, there is a need to explain the parameters of these explanations and how they relate to the ontology and epistemology of the world (adapted from Bhaskar, 2011).

---

[73] I am referring to the concept of quality here to indicate that all types of research should, but rarely do, refer to the categories being used in the world and in the piece of research, and to their use, reuse and reconstitution in everyday life.

In the first instance, then, researchers, who focus on learning episodes, need to examine a range of phenomena. The first of these – structural properties at each time point – may or may not have been activated in the particular circumstances, but they provide access to understanding the essential contexts of action. In doing this, researchers need to try to understand a second phenomenon – interpretations of those relations by relevant social actors. Information needs to be collected about these interpretations because they provide access to those interpretations and their effects. Instead of assuming that a structural property (in both non-discursive and discursive forms) always operates to facilitate human actions and interactions at every time point, it is important to understand when, where and how these different structures are influential; and furthermore, what the precise relationship is between them at specific moments and places during these interactions.

Researchers therefore need to gather information on those relations between different structures at each time point, and those perceived relations between different structures at each time point by the relevant human being – our fifth and most important object-type.[74] This is a necessary part of the research process for two reasons. First, it provides access for the researcher to those real relations referred to above. Second, social actors' perceptions of those relations constitute a part of them. By examining their intentions, it is possible to make a judgement about how much they know and how this influences the decisions they make.

Social researchers also need to consider the unintended consequences of actions. Some activities may be designed, and thus have a degree of intention behind them, others less so. But more importantly, all actions have unintended consequences. After each interaction, however limited, its effects on those structures that provide the contexts for future exchanges and interactions need to be assessed. This last requirement for research therefore refers to the subsequent effects of those intended and unintended actions on structural properties. Finally, there is the focal point of any investigation: the degree of structural influence and the degree of agential freedom for each human interaction. This is the crux of the matter because it allows the researcher to understand the complex relationship between agency (the willed actions of players in the game) and structure (those conditioning factors that work on agency in the world) at each time point.

---

[74] I will in subsequent pages of this book say much more about human beings.

What I have suggested here applies to learning as much as it does to other social phenomena primed for investigation. Steering a path between voluntarism and structuralism (the two dominant sociological perspectives that have been developed) in and about learning is always problematic; but if it is to be successfully achieved, then, first, a coherent meta-theory needs to be articulated and foregrounded and, second, reifying and dehistorisising structural forms needs to be avoided, as this leads to a distortion and misunderstanding of social life and educational matters. Evidence for learning, then, is a much more complicated construct than is generally acknowledged. In the next chapter I examine the important issue of values, operating as they do at both epistemological and ontological levels. Values at both of these levels are an essential part of the world and how we can know this world – in the twentieth and twenty-first centuries there are very few philosophers who subscribe to a clear fact–value distinction, although politicians, policymakers and many applied knowledge thinkers still acquiesce to this notion.

5
Values and learning theories

We are puzzled about what the world is like and how we can know what it is – a very Wittgensteinian attitude to doing philosophy. A possible solution to our puzzlement is to accept that values are central to understanding how we live and how we should live, and this valuing goes all the way down – into our descriptions of the world, into those attempts we make at creating better futures and into our relations with other people. We therefore need to work at how we do and can understand the world as it is and as we would want it to be. There are two dimensions to this claim. The first is ontological, which amounts to an assertion that objects in the world and human beings are valued in relation to each other and to other object-types.[75] Objects are arranged in the world and there could be other arrangements of these objects in other possible worlds. Indeed, objects (material and discursive), object-relations, object-formations and human beings could be differently formed. Difference therefore is understood as both dissimilarity and as the construction of boundaries between objects in the world.

A second dimension to the claim I am making that values go all the way down is epistemological, and this invariably elicits a complaint from those who assert that we can develop value-free knowledge of the world. (This is in effect a rhetorical device for claiming that one version of research or knowledge, their own, is superior to another – it is semantically empty.) If we accept that value-free knowledge is an impossibility, that we inevitably make pre-judgements about the world in our investigations, then being in the world is understood as a practice,

---

[75] In some cases, these valuations inhere in the words themselves. So, we can compare a word such as 'execution' with a word such as 'murder', and we are persuaded to understand the former as being legitimate and right because it is state-sanctioned, whereas the latter has no such legitimation. Both are in fact *killings*. And further to this, these valuations change over time.

primed for investigation, but resistant to the algorithmic and value-free methods of describing it used in the natural sciences. Again, if we accept that values are ontologically and epistemologically present in the world and in our endeavours to understand the world in its many iterations and in its many possible iterations, then we have to consider what these values might be and what their provenance is.[76] Again, in conformity to the approach I adopt throughout this book, we need to explore what these values are and what they are not – or at least what other people have construed them as being.

Virtue ethics is one of the three approaches to ethics that have a normative dimension.[77] It foregrounds the virtues or moral character of the individual and can be contrasted with approaches that focus on duties or rules, as in deontological ethics, or on the consequences of actions, as in consequentialism. Virtue ethics are different from deontological and consequentialist ethical forms in a number of ways. They are related to dispositions; what this means is that the ethical act comprises an inner state, which is already there (in some form or another), having been learnt, seeking to express itself in the world in relation to a problem in the world that requires some action. Dispositions, as inner states, precede, condition and have some influence over actions. A disposition is a character type, a habituation, a state of preparation or readiness and a tendency to act in a specified way. Dispositions, then, have this persistent quality, although they can in time be modified.[78] They have a strong affinity with a person's chosen identity.

The virtues also operate at the cultural or discursive level. In this form, they are dependent on membership of a practice, and this includes how they are instantiated in that practice. They are practice-based insofar

---

[76] Charles Taylor (1998: 27) writes about the impossibility of operating in the world in a non-normative sense: '(D)oing without frameworks is utterly impossible for us; ... the horizons within which we live our lives and which make sense of them have to include these strong qualitative discriminations. Moreover, this is not meant just as a contingently true psychological fact about human beings, which could perhaps turn out one day not to hold for some exceptional individual or new type, some superman of disengaged objectification. Rather the claim is that living within such strongly qualified horizons is constitutive of human agency, that stepping outside these limits would be tantamount to stepping outside what we would recognise as integral, that is, undamaged human personhood.'

[77] There are many ethical theories in existence, such as: axiological theories, collectivism, Confucianism, consequentialism, deontological ethics, egalitarianism, hedonism, humanism, individualism, moral realism, natural law, nihilism, normative ethics, objectivism, relativism, utilitarianism and virtue ethics. I have concentrated on the last of these and, in particular, a well-known variant of it.

[78] The argument that I am making in this book is that concepts are essentially acquired dispositions. In defence of this proposition, I have already suggested that even the most propositional of statements can be expressed as doing something in the world.

as being excellent in the practice requires a judgement to be made on what is considered to have value in the practice. This therefore implies a relation (a type of progression) between a novice and an expert within the practice.[79] The crucial issue is that any designation of an ethical virtue is always, and can only be, understood in terms of some conception of how the society is organised or even perhaps about excellence within the practice. Ethical judgements always supervene on epistemological judgements.[80]

The identification of the virtues is the hardest part of the argument to sustain because it opens up a series of unresolved issues, expressed perhaps as a series of questions: what is the virtues' provenance?; why is one set of virtues to be preferred over another?; why should one prefer a teleological account (of society, and it has to be extra-individual or broadly social, such as rationality) to a social/political value-impregnated utopian view? Aristotle in his extensive writings developed a theory of virtue ethics.

Aristotelian virtue ethics

Aristotle's view of the virtues is encapsulated in the doctrine of the mean. In any sphere of action or domain of feeling, for example, strength and health, there is both an excess and a deficiency:

> First, then, let us consider this, that it is the nature of things to be destroyed by defect and excess as we see in the case of strength and of health (for to gain light on things imperceptible we must use the evidence of sensible things); both excessive and defective exercise destroys the strength, and similarly drink or food which is above or below a certain amount destroys the health, while that which is proportionate both produces and increases and preserves it. (Aristotle, 2018b: loc. 33689)

---

[79] Alastair MacIntyre's (1981) notion of a practice in which virtue resides in the pursuit of excellence within that practice would also embrace witchcraft, iniquity, autocracy and the like, and thus there needs to be some notion of deontology or consequentialism attached to the particular goods that are being sought in the practice and which the practice is about.

[80] One of the consequences of arguing that ethics supervenes on knowledge is that one has to look in the first instance for the knowledge element in any ethical judgement one might want to make. And this epistemological and ontological object-relation is traditionally expressed as a relation between knowing the world and the world itself.

Another example concerns the sphere of action or feeling associated with fear and confidence. In relation to this there is a mean virtue of courage. For Aristotle, an excess of courage is rashness and a deficiency of courage is cowardice:

> So too is it, then, in the case of temperance and courage and the other virtues. For the man who flies from and fears everything and does not stand his ground against anything becomes a coward, and the man who fears nothing at all but goes to meet every danger becomes rash; and similarly the man who indulges in every pleasure and abstains from none becomes self-indulgent, while the man who shuns every pleasure, as boors do, becomes in a way insensible; temperance and courage, then, are destroyed by excess and defect, and preserved by the mean. (Aristotle, 2018b: loc. 33689)

Other spheres of action or feeling discussed by Aristotle in the *Nicomachean Ethics* are: pleasure and pain; getting and spending in a minor way; getting and spending in a major way; anger; self-expression; conversation; social conduct; shame; and indignation. A number of questions need to be asked about this inventory, the most important of which is whether this list of virtues is universal (that is, whether it applies equally to people across time and place) or relates specifically to a particular social formation, for example, ancient Greek society.

Aristotle's notion of a mean or middle point between two extremes has the effect of restricting the possible range of virtues. It also acts to create a hierarchy among the virtues, with some of what might be considered virtues now understood as extremes of some principal virtues. So, for example, prodigality and illiberality are understood as extreme versions of liberality and are thus deficient in some sense or another, and relative to a virtue that is considered sufficient. So, they are understood both in a negative sense and as inferior to some other ethical position. What the notion of a mean does is identify a list of virtues, with some being considered to be more important than others (this of course can be achieved by inclusions and omissions) and some being parasitic on others. Further to this, it constructs sets of relations between the primary virtues and particular strengths attached to those virtues. Aristotle's primary virtues are choices made from a list of all of the possible virtues that could be envisaged. (This list might include past, but now archaic, virtues, currently fashionable virtues or virtues that reflect the current arrangements in society and even virtues yet to be instantiated, though imagined.) Furthermore, this choice depends on the semantic content of the virtue.

An objection to Aristotle's notion of the virtues is that although this is considered to be a rule-based ethical schema, it does not always conform in this way. Aristotle is clear in the *Nicomachean Ethics* that 'the mean is not of the thing itself, but relative to us' (Aristotle, 2018b: loc. 33692). He qualifies this with regards to some of the virtues or vices, or he suggests that at least some emotions or acts are wrong per se regardless of circumstance. He gives a number of examples: malice, shamelessness and envy (these are emotions) and adultery, theft and murder (these are acts). In other words, there cannot be praiseworthy exercises of malice, shamelessness, envy, adultery, theft or murder. However, this in itself can be challenged, especially from a consequentialist ethical viewpoint; for example, if Claus von Stauffenberg had succeeded in murdering Adolf Hitler in 1944, this might have saved many lives and foreshortened the war.

However, to sustain the argument of the virtuous mean, Aristotle needed to develop a notion of difference between human beings, because, as he made clear, in determining the right action for an individual human being, it is not just the case that this person should follow the implicit rules of the already identified and learnt virtuous mean. In addition, this person must also judge the right action in relation to the details of the case, which includes above all else the actual set of dispositions she has acquired at a particular point in time. These character traits comprise tendencies towards excesses and deficiencies, and towards committing certain types of error – logical, epistemological, biases of viewpoint and the like. Thus, the virtuous act requires a prior disposition of self-regulation or self-observation that is able to identify these character flaws and allow for some type of correction. What this means is that both the identification of the mean and the identification of its excesses and deficiencies require a judgement to be made about whether those dispositions qualify as virtues and furthermore about whether there are excesses and deficiencies that fit with the virtue and with the overall and desired ethic of living. In short, the question needs to be asked: why these and not others? The doctrine of the mean cannot provide a satisfactory answer to this question.

The doctrine of the mean does not amount to the idea that emotions should always be of moderate intensity, or that strong emotions are in some sense pathologies, or that in acting the human being should always express her emotions moderately, or that human beings should seek everything in moderation, or that every virtue has faults and vices, or even that the relations between the virtues and their corresponding excesses and deficiencies are rule-based. Rather, excellence is observed by following the mean as far as this is possible.[81] Aristotle's theory of ethics was also teleological.

The telos

The telos or end point of a virtuous action was important for Aristotle. Goals are purposive and they are future orientated; the goal is by definition something that seeks fulfilment in a state of affairs (a future arrangement of material and discursive objects) that has not yet happened. Furthermore, goals require intentional activity – a sentient human being to have an intention to do some thing or other. Thus a virtue-directed activity, such as being courageous, requires both the envisaging of an end point – a better arrangement of material and discursive objects in the world – and an intention – some notion of a self-directing person and of that person having a desire or intention to do something in the world.

Virtue ethics are different from deontological and consequentialist ethics. They are related to dispositions, and what this means is that the ethical act comprises an inner state, which is already there (in some form or another), seeking to express itself in the world in relation to a problem in the world that requires some action. In the previous chapter (4) I developed a notion of non-determinacy, which is directly related to virtue ethics. The reason why this notion is important is that, first, the identification of the virtues requires a theory of knowledge (epistemology) and of being (ontology) and the identification of a relationship between the two, including a notion of causation; and second, any ethical theory (deontological, consequentialist or virtue-based) requires a theory of intention. In the next chapter, I develop a notion of difference, because in an object-epistemology, my concerns are two-fold: with knowledge – this hardly needs saying – and with the categories or boundaries between objects.

---

[81] A number of well-known objections have been made to Aristotle's doctrine of the mean, not least Bernard Williams' (1985: 36) well-known characterisation of it as unhelpful and depressing: 'Aristotle's views on [virtue] are bound up with one of the most celebrated and least useful parts of his system, the doctrine of the mean, according to which every virtue of character lies between two correlative faults or vices … which consist respectively of the excess and the deficiency of something of which the virtue represents the right amount. The theory oscillates between an unhelpful analytical model (which Aristotle himself does not consistently follow) and a substantively depressing doctrine in favour of moderation. The doctrine of the mean is better forgotten.'

6
Difference

Philosophers often understand the categories as referring to the means by which we can access the world. For example, Immanuel Kant (2007) described the categories as pure concepts of understanding. They are, for Kant, prior to experiences that we might have and are thus implicated in how we experience the world. They are the conditions of possibility for objects and not just, as some have suggested, classificatory divisions. I want to suggest here that the categories, contra Kant, set boundaries that structure our thinking and ability to access the material world, which, consequently, can be thought of as natural or constructed. Disagreement typically centres on which categories are intrinsic bearers of these qualities, and how they relate to the physical world. These arguments are significant because they are central to a proper understanding of the nature of consciousness (see chapter 9) and to the mind–world relationship.

An example of a social category, which is central to the idea of learning, is dis-ability. The underpinning philosophy of dis-abled learning has in the past drawn on three important enframings, namely the medical, socioeconomic and cultural. While the medical model suggests that problems and differences lie with the individual, the socioeconomic model places the emphasis on matters such as poor nutrition or contaminated water, whereas cultural factors refer to the ideological construction of the notion of dis-ability or difference. For example, the language used in a specific culture for dis-ability or disadvantage points to what is considered to be normal or abnormal in that culture – from a cultural point of view, the emphasis is on the need to transform the attitudes adopted in relation to, and the language used about, dis-ability and difference. This is because it impacts on how well people with dis-abilities or differences can be successfully assimilated and represented in society.

The dominant models of dis-ability (medical, socioeconomic, cultural) accentuate or prioritise one element at the expense of a multiplicity of other mechanisms, factors or influences that are involved in its formation and reproduction. For example, the social model omits the dis-abled body from the discourse by shifting the emphasis from the biological to the environmental. The medical model, in turn, neglects environmental factors by foregrounding the idea of the dis-abled body. Recent thinking about dis-ability encourages a more holistic approach and emphasises all the different levels of reality; indeed, this holistic approach has been described as a bio-psycho-social model of dis-ability.

A subcategory of dis-abled learning is the notion of dyslexia. Two strands of thinking can be identified: the first refers to a general incapacity and the second focuses on particular and specific processing functions, especially as they relate to the activity of reading. These might include coordination difficulties; hyperlexia (low comprehension but good decoding skills); language and communication difficulties; auditory processing difficulties; working-memory difficulties; information-processing difficulties; non-verbal difficulties; literacy difficulties; phonological processing difficulties; visual difficulties; and social awareness difficulties. The existence of one specific learning difficulty does not preclude the existence of another; for example, a learner can be diagnosed with phonological processing difficulties and hyperlexia.

Definitions of these terms have proved controversial. There appears to be no agreed basis for differentiating between someone who has been diagnosed as dyslexic, someone who has been diagnosed as a poor reader (this may of course refer to someone who is disinclined to learn) and a general reader. Dyslexia itself can be understood as a general term to refer to almost any form of reading, decoding and spelling difficulty. This all-embracing term, in its broad inclusivity, then becomes so general that it is not particularly useful for developing remedial programmes. However, it may satisfy a need to know which condition is afflicting someone, even if this does not in any way lead to an amelioration of the problem, with the problem being understood in normative terms so that a comparison can be made with a notional idea of how that learner should be behaving. The important question we need to ask at this stage of the argument is: are these differences between manifestations of a particular condition natural kinds or are they social and historical constructions?

Natural kinds

I identified six meta-characteristics of a discourse in chapter 1. The first of these, generality, is the designation of objects, such as dis-ability, as separate from other objects in the world. A second meta-form relating to a notion of dis-ability concerns the balance in educational and social statements between denotation and performativity, or between offering an account of something with no intention of changing the world and offering an account that is intended to change an object or create a new one. A third meta-epistemic form concerns the relative value given to an object in comparison with another object. For example, within a dis-abled discourse, one of the pair of words is given a greater value than the other, with a fairly obvious example being that abled is privileged over dis-abled. A fourth meta-structuring device refers to the bipolarity of objects, descriptions and dispositions, or hierarchical binary oppositions; that is, an object, description or disposition is defined in terms of another object, description or disposition of which it is the mirror opposite. If the abled/dis-abled binary is used as an example, it is possible to see that the positioning of the two terms as oppositional in meaning, and the subsequent valuing of one (abled) and the devaluing of the other (dis-abled) because of their oppositionality, has significant implications for the way in which the debate about relations between the two concepts can be conducted. Thus, certain words, phrases, descriptors and concepts are understood in bipolar terms, which determine how they can be used as a resource for understanding the world.

A fifth meta-principle refers to the referential value of a statement. Making an educational or social statement implies that a particular type of truth-value is being invoked. An educational statement about a category such as dis-ability is therefore implicitly or explicitly underpinned by a theory of reference embedded within a theory of truth, and this marks it out as a knowledge form. A sixth meta-principle refers to the way in which the particular ideas, concepts, phrases and descriptors are embedded in networks of ideas, concepts, phrases and descriptors, and have a history. So, for example, dis-ability as a concept is always positioned in a bewilderingly complicated network of other terms, such as: innateness;[82] trait theory;[83] genetics;[84] biology;[85] historical origin;[86]

---

[82] Once again, we are forced to confront the polysemic nature of a concept, as it is used in the world. It has been understood as that which exists naturally or because of heredity, rather than being learnt through experience; and it has been understood as having essentialist characteristics.

[83] Trait theorists are interested in the measurement of human characteristics, which can be understood as habitual behaviours, thoughts or emotions.

[84] Genetic theories are deficient because the emphasis is placed on determination and not volition.

[85] Biologists understand the categories as natural and certainly as essentialist – some biologists are also hard-line geneticists. They are also domain- or discipline-centric.

[86] A belief in historical origin demands a particular type of ontology, epistemology and causal theory.

evolutionary theory;[87] cognitive, developmental, intellectual, physical and sensory impairment,[88] and many more. I have been referring here to the relations in the discourse between different ideas and notions, and how these can vary depending on the discourse.

Strong constructivists deny that there are any natural divisions or differences between objects, social or otherwise. They argue that the similarities and differences between objects can be attributed only to the social functioning of the relevant concepts and not to any natural processes. The problem is that the social functioning of concepts and the social functioning of practices in the world that have been influenced by these concepts are what constitutes the world and therefore are real. If the natural is understood as a pre-conceptualised (before human beings have activated the world) state of being, then the issue arises of how far one should go back in history before one identifies a cut-off point between the natural and the non-natural. A conceptual division is established by the concrete actions of human beings; a boundary point is set at the conceptual level, which is neither natural nor non-natural, but real.[89] The principal argument made by constructivists is that any activity in and about the world is dependent on a human being or a number of human beings acting in the world, and this applies as much to concept development as it does to other worldly practices.

Processes of classifying and reclassifying change the nature of objects, object-relations and object-configurations. All references to the world involve the identification, manipulation, transformation and reconstruction of the categories, and we cannot avoid this. The scientific method, with its claims for the possibility of positional objectivity,[90] that concepts can be reduced to measurable constructs,[91] and that we should adopt a representational ontology,[92] is negligent of these. Another

---

[87] Evolutionary theorists are divided over how the relationship between mind and world should be conceptualised. Once again, we are forced back to some prior resolution of the argument about free will or volition in human beings.

[88] Impairment as a concept is ideological and thus has normative elements.

[89] The real is being used in this context to indicate that the object, relation, configuration or human being is underpinned by a realist ontology. This, however, is not a naive realist ontology.

[90] Positional objectivity is one of the many uses of the notion of objectivity (cf. Scott and Scott, 2018), and is used with the purpose of establishing the truth of particular assertions about the world. However, I have argued throughout that we are always positioned in some way or another.

[91] The thrust of the argument that I have made in this book is that most concepts cannot be reduced to measurable constructs, and that to do so risks the possibility of a reduction or distortion of meaning.

[92] I have situated epistemology in an ontological frame, because epistemological activity has being. This is in line with Roy Bhaskar's (2011) use of the term.

example of a discursive configuration that conforms to this way of thinking is the male/female binary.

Gender

An important binary that has had real effects in the space of learning – the area of life that is fully focused on learning – is the male/female binary, an oppositional coupling of two words or phrases, and this implies a relationship between these two descriptive terms, both of which can be problematised. In addition, the strength, type and probative force of this relationship is central to the discourse that is in operation. I therefore need to examine in the first instance the principal characteristics of this male/female dyad. Initially I will focus on the critique that radical feminists make of traditional conceptions of what constitutes true or valid knowledge about the world. Although women have been actively involved throughout the centuries in making societies, they have been marginalised when it comes to the production of knowledge about societies and social activity. Feminists therefore ask how epistemological categories are implicated in defining masculinity and femininity, how they function to define the nature of people, how they work to attach different valuations to their skills and capacities, and how gender difference is a category of analysis around which every society is structured.

These questions about how knowledge is produced and who is involved in that production underpin all discussions about particular sets of categories. They lead to a questioning of the analytic categories that are taken for granted and, in particular, how these structure outlooks and dispositions and provide the criteria for evaluating social experience. Feminist theory is not a unified or homogeneous set of ideas but rather encompasses a variety of different perspectives and approaches.

Liberal feminism is widely represented in the contemporary Euro-American world. Since the 1960s, the relationship between liberalism and feminism has underpinned the equal opportunities paradigm, which has been so influential in education and social policy. The emphasis is on removing barriers to women's participation in all aspects of public life and arguing for women to have a greater share of the rights, privileges and opportunities enjoyed by men. This variety of feminism is founded on the emancipatory impulse of liberalism, itself a significant aspect of Enlightenment thought. Its key elements are a belief in an inherent human nature, a commitment to progress and a trust in rationality.

Liberal feminism espouses an egalitarian politics, arguing that if men and women were to be treated equally in political, social and personal terms, then women's views and activities would be invested with the same degree of significance as men's. What prevents this is female subordination and oppression. This can be best understood as a problem of sexism, defined as the unwarranted differential treatment of women, which can be identified empirically and eradicated through appropriate policies and programmes.

By the 1980s, feminists were attempting to integrate their approaches into mainstream critical theories such as neo-Marxism.[93] They argued that gender inequality derives from capitalism and that men's domination over women is a byproduct of capital's domination of labour. Class is regarded as the fundamental category of social structure and gender difference, and inequality as a secondary feature of the economic exploitation practised by the control of one class over another. The site of women's exploitation is sometimes argued to be the family, while the focus is on the ideological rather than the material relations of capitalism.

A further gendered discourse is united around a position that advocates the privileging of traditional 'feminine' values.[94] Advocates for this position accept the view that women's 'nature' is different from men's and that women excel in relational and nurturing practices – if rationality is associated with domination and control of the natural world with all its destructive implications, women are fortunate not to be associated with it. They go on to argue that the characteristics associated with femininity such as caring, relatedness and community should therefore be valorised over male characteristics. In other words, they all, irrespective of emphasis, accept the rational–irrational binary and its association with masculine–feminine difference, arguing simply that the hierarchy should be reversed with a consequent privileging of all aspects of the feminine over the masculine.

From the 1980s onwards, many feminists had become disillusioned with the political project of making women equal to men as they found mainstream discourses particularly resistant to their challenge, or incapable of being broadened to include women. These experiences of being rejected and alienated led to a growing awareness of the deep-rooted patriarchal nature of such discourses. Even if sexism was

---

[93] For example, hooks (1982).
[94] For example, Daly (1992).

eliminated, with both sexes participating fully, the patriarchal nature of structures and value systems would still ensure that men and women were positioned unequally in terms of power, with female experience still defined as marginal and of lesser significance to male experience. Even if women were to be incorporated into patriarchal discourses, it would be on the basis of their sameness to men, their specificity as women not being acknowledged. In other words, women had to become surrogate men. The development of a more radical feminism therefore was a response to the perceived limitations of other approaches, which, it was argued, were based on irresolvable contradictions from which women could not escape an inferior definition and an unequal positioning.

In radical feminism, the focus shifts from equal opportunities to the phallocentric nature of all systems of representation;[95] that whenever the two sexes are represented in a single model, the feminine is always collapsed into a universal model represented in masculine terms. Theoretically, feminists have analysed how the general concepts, assumptions and categories of Western thought have been organised around hierarchies, which by association privilege masculinity and devalue femininity. Regardless of the academic discipline within which radical feminists are working, there is a widespread recognition that epistemological issues do not exist in a social vacuum but rather exert a powerful influence on concepts, ideals and values. The way we make sense of the world is through broad categories and central questions relating to the nature of reality, subjectivity, knowledge construction, morality and ethics, and political rights and responsibilities. The development of feminist theory has stimulated questions about how philosophy is implicated in defining masculinity and femininity, the values attached to men and women's skills and capacities, and how gender difference is a central analytic category around which every society is structured.

Radical feminists have added the insight that when notions such as rationality, knowledge and the self are deconstructed, their gendered nature is revealed, so that concepts which have been taken as neutral and universal are shown in effect to be masculine. The privileging of the rational is at the heart of modernist epistemology, yet this is a form of rationality that itself privileges the masculine. The claim of empirical/ analytic epistemology that rationality, objectivity and abstraction are the only guarantee of truth is actually a specifically masculine claim.

---

[95] For example, Griffin (2000); and Flax (1990).

Furthermore, each of the oppositions that structures modernist thought are derivative of the most fundamental opposition of all, that of masculine–feminine, male–female. In all binaries, the male is associated with the first element, the female with the second. In each case the male element is privileged over the female and maintains its position by its capacity to define itself as a universal norm against which the subjective, the emotional, the aesthetic, the natural and, above all, the feminine is judged and found wanting. Thus, through the very dualities of modernist thought, women's significance is defined as inferior to the rational, objective, abstract qualities of scientific method, which not only guarantees truth but positions masculinity and 'man' as a legitimate knower, capable of discovering truth. Once this kind of analysis is accepted, all of the other common-sense stereotypes about gendered identities that feminists attempt to counter fall into perspective.

Essentialists try to exalt the virtues of female nature and related notions of community, caring and relatedness, as opposed to the male virtues of control, mastery, abstraction and rationality. But these arguments are unconvincing because they have not challenged the very opposition through which the female is defined as inferior in the first place and, hence, they cannot succeed in privileging the female over the male. Equal but different simply cannot succeed in a world where knowledge is constructed hierarchically. What emerges therefore is that if particular binaries are not reversed and ultimately dissolved, oppressive structures of thought and knowledge will continue to exert their power.

All varieties of feminism try to show how gender relations operate in favour of male hegemony, and their aim is to help effect a redistribution of power towards women. This may often imply the writing of histories or giving expression to voices and views that have been suppressed or denied. Models of investigation that assume homogeneity or an economy of the same as their starting point fail to acknowledge difference and insist that women can be represented as having the same characteristics as men. However, there is also the implication that not all women have some universal experience that can be a standpoint for the building of feminist theory and practice. The category 'woman' is not unified, nor is the category of 'female' as opposed to 'male' learning: women's experience is differentiated through such factors as class, ethnicity, race, religion and many others. This means that our understanding needs to be sensitive to this diversity of female experience and to the power relations that are present among women. This also applies to female, male, trans-sex and inter-sex human beings, and to the care with which we should use these categories.

Sexuality

Another category of importance in the lifeworld is sexuality. Sexualised identities and identity formations have histories because they are socially constructed. The discussion of sexuality that follows is only one example of the process of categorisation, and the elements and processes discussed here also have affinities with the elements and processes of changing manifestations of any social object, such as the changing relations between abled and dis-abled, male and female, black and white, heterosexual and homosexual, intelligent and unintelligent, and precariat and middle-class persons.

Ideas influence human practices, which means that both ideas and practices have histories. The contemporary division of heterosexual and homosexual as terms made no sense to the ancient Greeks, although there were regional variations on understandings of sexuality. Same-sex relations, for example, were celebrated in some parts of Greece, whereas in parts of Ionia they were prohibited. Physiological differences between the sexes were considered to be of less importance than beauty in either of the sexes. What was regarded as important was whether the person exercised moderation in their sexual dealings. In addition, status had a gendered and aged dimension so that a freeman having sex with a woman or a boy was considered to be acceptable, but sexual relations between freemen were more problematic. The most important distinction was not physiological but the taking of active or penetrative roles as against passive or penetrated ones. The latter roles were appropriate only for social inferiors, such as women, slaves and male youths.

The early period of the ancient Roman Republic had similar attitudes towards sexuality. With the formation of the Empire, attitudes began to change, even before Christianity became influential. There are few criticisms of same-sex relations in the Gospels; however, early Christian Church fathers spoke out strongly against such relationships. Generally, the expression of sexuality and therefore of same-sex sexuality was not considered to be sinful. With a greater emphasis placed on marriage (understood to be between two people differentiated by their reproductive capabilities) by such renowned scholars as Saint Augustine, same-sex relations were prohibited and indeed in some parts of the now Christian world attracted horrific punishments. For example, in Emperor Justinian's code of 529 CE, persons who were caught engaging in homosexual sex were executed, though different provisions applied to those who repented. This rise in intolerance towards certain types of sexual behaviour, that is, same sex relations and sex outside of marriage, had important regional variations. As the Roman Empire weakened, to be replaced by a number of disparate barbarian kingdoms, a general tolerance towards both of these prevailed; and indeed, there were few legal prohibitions in Europe against homosexuality right up until the middle of the thirteenth century. All of this changed with the onset of the Gregorian reform movement in the Catholic Church, which argued for licensing natural kinds of sexuality and therefore for prohibiting unnatural kinds, such as homosexuality, extramarital sex and non-procreative sex within marriage.

This appeal to natural law[96] became a defining feature of the spread of ideas concerning sexuality over the next six hundred years and is only now beginning to be played out. However, we should be careful about these distinctions in the early and late medieval periods, because, for example, a sodomite was understood in a different way from our modern conception of the notion of being a homosexual or even in some circumstances a heterosexual married person. It was not so much being a certain sexual type but engaging in acts of a same-sex nature that was of concern. And in addition, if the person repented, then they could be excused punishments that were reserved for sodomites. Gender again is not significant here.

Despite the risk of severe punishment, homosexual cultures flourished in many European cities in the nineteenth century. In addition, there were significant reductions in legal penalties for sodomy (not just homosexuality), with the Napoleonic Code decriminalising it. However, there were moves, supported by new frameworks of ideas, to reinforce strong boundaries between the sexes, and this in turn meant that same-sex relations between people of roughly the same age became or at least were becoming the norm. Scientific accounts of sexuality at this time, based as they were on notions of mechanical causation, led to views of sexuality as biologically given or innate to the person. Medieval views that, for example, sodomy was freely chosen by the individual, were giving way to ideas of the passive homosexual, and that as a consequence it became possible to portray homosexuality as defective or even pathological, with all the authority that the medical model could muster. In the twentieth century, sexual roles were transformed. Premarital intercourse became an acceptable norm, as did the association of sex with pleasure, in opposition to some sections of the Catholic Church, which

---

[96] 'Natural law' is a term much favoured by jurists, who argue that human beings have certain natural rights and protections.

still understood sex as exclusively procreational. Gay sex became increasingly celebrated. The American Psychiatric Association removed homosexuality from its list of deviant sexual acts, and legal equality for gays and lesbians became permanent features of European and North American life.

In addition, lesbian, gay, bisexual, transgendered, queer/questioning and intersex (LGBTQI+) identities were being recognised and accepted. What is distinctive about these moves is, first, the fluid nature of gender and sexuality (though resisted by many who would position themselves at the extremes of the political spectrum), with people moving between different sexual identities over time. Second, and perhaps paradoxically, newer forms of sexual identity are being created and for some these are becoming well-defined markers of identity and lifestyle. Third, it should be noted, because this has consequences for public policy, that many of these new forms of sexual identity are deliberately crafted as oppositional and transgressive. For example, the recent revival and use of the word 'queer' denotes an oppositional stance in the politics of sexuality. Sexuality is different from other forms of difference because it is essentially and fundamentally embodied, although learnt in the first place. This has a number of implications: first, this means that it may be learnt without any conscious decision being made by the person concerned; second, it persists over a long period of time; and third, the actual desires are powerful and generally resistant to change.

Here is a list of distinct and normalising sexualities, ineluctably framed by time and space: heterosexuality, where the sexual attraction is between members of the opposite sex; homosexuality, where the sexual attraction is between members of the same sex; bisexuality, where the sexual attraction is to both the opposite and the same sex; asexuality, where there is a lack of sexual interest in others; polysexuality, where there is sexual attraction to more than one gender, but this is different from bisexuality as the latter implies that there are only two sexes; pansexuality, where there is a sexual attraction towards other people regardless of gender, and where gender is thought of as insignificant in determining whether they are or are not sexually attracted to other people; and transsexuality, where a person identifies themselves with a gendered position that is different from their own biological one, and this has profound implications for their sense of sexuality. A different list would include paraphilic desires, such as towards non-human objects, the suffering or humiliation of oneself or one's partner, children and non-consenting persons. Indeed, one source has listed as many as 549 different paraphilic behaviours.[97] What this illustrates is that these different lists are valued; that is, they have values embedded within them. In this case, these values comprise notions of deviance, difference and normalisation.

The key concept that I have focused on in this chapter is difference – the type and extent of dissimilarity between different manifestations of a category, such as abled and dis-abled, men and women, or heterosexual, homosexual and others. Crude versions of these relations are ever-present in modern societies. However, difference can be understood in a number of ways. There is the common use given to the term, where difference is understood as not being or as being opposite to something else. Then there is the meaning given to the term by Jacques Derrida. In his essay 'Différance' (Derrida, 1982), he suggested that the term points to a number of ways in which textual meaning can be produced. The first of these relates to the idea that words and signs have meaning only within other arrangements of words and concepts, from which they differ. This is the predominant way in which I have used the idea of difference in this book so far – a use that has been neglected in most discussions of the social world. Meanings are thus forever deferred. The second way in which Derrida uses the term is to refer to a notion of espacement or spacing, so that what we should be concerned about is the force that differentiates social elements from other social elements, and in the process engenders binary oppositions and endlessly reiterated hierarchies of meaning.[98] These processes, then, are essential elements in an object-epistemology and in an in-depth understanding of the notion of learning. Two other binary categories are scientific/practical and educative/training knowledge, and these are the focus of the next chapter.

---

[97] cf. Aggrawal (2008).

[98] Derrida's (1982) characterisation of difference is derived from an idealist perspective. Furthermore, Derrida's embrace of Heidegger meant that in general terms he equated ontology with language: 'language is the house of being' (Derrida, 2016: 1).

7
Knowledge dualities

In this chapter I will be examining two important binary categories: scientific/practical and educative/training. These are important because they act as cultural conditioning agencies for many of the institutions and systems that exist in the field of education and learning. The strength of the boundary between two contrasting manifestations of a concept influences how learning institutions (buildings, pedagogies, curricula, environments and the like) are constructed; for example, if a strong boundary between vocational and academic education is in place, this can mean that children are assigned to different types of schools, are taught in different ways, follow different curricula and learn in different environments. For instance, in Germany, at the secondary level, there are three types of compulsory educational institutions: Hauptschule, Realschule and Gymnasium schools. The Hauptschule (grades 5–9) has the same curriculum as the other types of school but teaches that curriculum at a slower rate. Students generally enrol in a vocational school combined with apprenticeship training at the end of grade 9. The Realschule (grades 5–10) in most states provides a technical education, although some students are able to switch to a Gymnasium school at the end of grade 10. Those students who are assigned to a Gymnasium school at the beginning of grade 5 follow an exclusively academic curriculum, with in most cases a university as the destination at the end of the twelfth grade.[99] The point of this example is to suggest or show how in the real world difference is constructed. The first of these binary categories is the scientific/practical divide.

---

[99] The claim has been repeatedly made that Germany, despite the difficulties of reunification, is a better-educated and trained society than many other countries in the world. I am using this set of divisions as an example in the real world.

Scientific/practical

In the first instance, scientific knowledge (broadly knowledge that is propositional in form) and practical knowledge (broadly knowledge that allows us to go on in life) can be compared, and this involves identifying the constituents of each and the relations between them, and then showing how they are different or the same. This mirrors the dichotomous relation between the sacred and the profane developed by Émile Durkheim (1995), which can be expressed in many different ways: nomothetic–idiographic, abstractive–concrete, generalisable–particular, objective–subjective, factual–valued and universal–disciplinary. These are all specific renditions of a distinction that can be made between scientific knowledge and the type of knowledge that circulates in the lifeworld.

For example, it has been suggested that scientific knowledge is nomological – the knowledge claim can be couched in a language of rules and invariant happenings – whereas everyday or practical knowledge is idiographic – the focus is on the meaning of contingent, unique and perhaps subjective phenomena.[100] There are four possible approaches that can be taken by a researcher or investigator: inductive, deductive, retroductive[101] and abductive.[102] These four strategies are nomological in kind in that they seek to identify laws or make propositional rule-bound claims to knowledge, which persist over time and/or place; whereas practical knowledge makes no such claims, or so the argument goes.

Another way of framing this argument is by contrasting abstract knowledge with concrete knowledge (knowledge of particulars); an abstraction being understood as a construct in the mind[103] in which new ideas are formed if a number of these ideas are analysed together and those features that are different are then omitted. If we consider a range of so-called sharp objects, we can abstract from them their different qualia and thereby come to a notion of sharpness. The object itself is initially conceptualised in its concrete form. The claim is then made that practical forms of knowledge do not engage with these processes of abstraction.

---

[100] The word 'subjective' is being used here to refer to an internal process and not to the antithesis of any notion of objectivity.

[101] cf. Bhaskar (2011).

[102] cf. Harré (2011).

[103] I prefer to use the term 'in the mind' rather than 'mental' because of the latter's pejorative associations.

A third way of framing the argument is to invoke a notion of generalisation. The defining property of this is that the knowledge claim being made can accommodate more than one instance of a concrete event. There are two problems here. First, how do we identify, and in the process come to understand, the boundaries of an object, a concrete event or happening in the world? And second, how do we reconcile this identification of the object with it being manifested in a number of ways? For example, in order for the object to be manifested quantitatively – so that there are a number of instances of it – there has to be some measure of generality already present in the object itself; the words, concepts and ideas used can then embrace a large number of instances or manifestations. The intention, however, may not be to accommodate a number of the object's manifestations, but to give a detailed account of a mechanism[104] and how it might have worked in the world. In both cases, knowledge of the object is not isomorphic with the object itself.

Another attempt at distinguishing between the two forms of knowledge understands scientific knowledge as knowledge that is not tainted by values, interests, preconceptions and so forth, whereas practical knowledge is ontologically valued knowledge.[105] Generally, knowledge is said to be objective when it is not influenced by personal values and emotions, whereas subjectivity refers to knowledge that is based on personal opinions, feelings and interpretations. However, as I suggested in chapter 1, the concept of objectivity (as it is used in the world) contains multiple rather than singular meanings. The distinction between value-free and valued knowledge cannot be directly read into the distinction being made here between scientific and practical forms of knowledge.

In a positivist/empiricist philosophy, a distinction between facts and values is usually made. This received its first explicit representation in 1738 in David Hume's (2000) *A Treatise of Human Nature* and was subsequently taken up by Durkheim (1939) and Weber (1964). Common sense would suggest that description and evaluation are separate activities, although the idea of common sense is here being stripped of its ideological meaning. This distinction has been criticised on the grounds that any fact is inevitably a value judgement in some way or another and involves a selection process, which in turn can be made only from an epistemological perspective or position. Facts are only facts, and thus

---

[104] The term 'mechanism' is frequently used by critical realists. However, they are not using the term to denote a mechanical and deterministic ontology.

[105] I have already argued that all types of knowledge are valued, despite attempts by many people to make a claim for value-free objective knowledge.

truth-bearers, under some type of epistemic frame or another. This distinction therefore cannot serve as a marker of difference between scientific and practical forms of knowledge.

A further justification for scientific knowledge is that it is produced in specialised places or locations for the production of knowledge (in most cases the disciplines or domains).[106] A counterargument that supports a notion of interdisciplinarity or transdisciplinarity is predicated on the idea that a multiplicity of causes and theories is always involved in the explanation of any event or happening. However, in order to move from a set of disciplines or domains to interdisciplinarity and then to transdisciplinarity, an acknowledgement has to be made that the knowledge required can no longer be generated by combining the knowledge of the various disciplines concerned but requires a real integration.[107]

A number of suggestions have been made above, which would allow us to distinguish between scientific and practical knowledge: nomothetic–idiographic, abstractive–concrete, generalisable–particular, objective–subjective, factual–valued and universal–disciplinary. Each of these in turn, as concepts, has been shown to be problematic, although they do point to some differences between the two types of knowledge.

Everyday practical knowledge

I now need to develop a theory of practical knowledge, knowledge that allows me to go on in life and is an essential element of the lifeworld. Andrew Collier (2003) used an example of repair work – this is a form of practical knowledge. If I am riding a bicycle and the bicycle breaks down, I stop. In order to repair the bicycle, explanatory knowledge – and not just embodied knowledge of how to ride the bicycle – is needed. However, in order to make that repair, I do not need to understand the physics of stability such as that there is enough forward velocity, or know about the two parameters of stability (the lean angle and the steering angle) that describe the orientation of a bicycle as it travels in a forward direction, the role played by gyroscopic effects, leaning orientations to compensate for the effects of centripetal acceleration, and the degree of force that propels the bike forward and especially when going up a hill. What I would

---

[106] The arguments for some form of transcendental knowledge are set out in chapter 2.

[107] This is a position that Roy Bhaskar et al. (2010) take.

normally do is look at the various parts – chain, gears, handlebars, saddle, riding capacities and so on – and compare them with a template that seemed to operate when the bicycle was functioning properly and then try to adjust the one so that it works more like the other. This is a very different process from starting from first principles (as scientific knowledge does), then working out from these principles that the concrete application of them in the form of a damaged bicycle does not conform to them, translating these deficiencies in the theoretical model into concrete actions of repair, and then effecting the repair. This argument would suggest that we do not need first-principle knowledge to diagnose the problem and effect the repair. In some cases, it may be positively harmful – as in training to be and acting as a teacher, where too much theory may actually impede in various ways both learning to be and performing as a teacher.

However, Collier (2003) maintained that theoretical knowledge is necessary because it can act as a repair to breakdowns in practical knowledge. Theoretical or first-principle knowledge allows us to replenish the store of practical knowledge we hold. The issue then becomes that practical knowledge is always in this symbiotic relationship with theoretical knowledge, so that practical knowledge grows, even tacitly, in line with theoretical knowledge. An alternative is to understand it as a process, whereby practical knowledge grows and becomes more sophisticated in response to experience, practice and learning (the pedagogical element). Most practical knowledge, whether tacit or otherwise, is learnt in the practice itself, through trial and error, or by imitation or through other means, and therefore, always has a pedagogical element. What this means is that theoretical knowledge is not just an addendum to practical knowledge, appropriate for thinkers, theoreticians and academics, but is essential to the development of practical knowledge and in turn is partly generated by it.

The central question becomes: do these differences allow us to determine that one of these types of knowledge, and specifically scientific or theoretical knowledge, can be shown to be of greater worth than the other, insofar as acquiring it is better in some specific way than not acquiring it? This would require a fuller answer than space allows for here, and in part would require an empirical investigation. However, what it is possible to suggest is that those differentiating principles, if translated into forms of knowledge held by significant numbers of people, can in principle contribute to the eudaimonistic society[108] (see chapter 5). This

---

[108] The eudaimonistic society or way of life is a very general idea or concept.

is both a conceptual and a practical problem, and it has implications for how we form and reform teaching and learning practices in educational institutions, as does the conceptual division between training and education. One of the complications of using this binary divide and of identifying how it is used in the world is that at times the two words are used as equivalents and at other times as opposites.

Training and education

In order to make sense of the training and education binary and resolve the difficulties of operating through this binary, one way of proceeding is to suggest that one of these concepts is superior to the other. So, we can say for this or that reason or this or that set of reasons that an educative model gives a better account of learning than a training model. We have to be careful here about how we conceptualise these two terms for two reasons. The first is that the account we give may not capture the subtleties of the concept at work in the world, and the second is that to treat them as oppositional constructs may distort the reasonable argument that some aspects of learning are better captured by the term 'training' and other aspects by the term 'education'.[109]

The first task is to try to show how these two terms as concepts are used in a way of life. In this instance, as we have seen in chapter 1, this comprises, for Wittgenstein, a determination of the possibilities of the phenomena. This is complicated by the fact that we are dealing here with two phenomena that can potentially enter into a number of different types of relationships; for example, that one of these concepts is correct and the other is false; or that one of these concepts is a more adequate account of learning than the other; or that one of these concepts is a better descriptor of some aspects of education and the other is a better descriptor of all of the other aspects of education that are not covered by our first concept. If we want to sustain the first of these suggestions then we have to show[110] in relation to our criteria for truthful knowledge (epistemic adequacy, coherence, rationality and referentiality)[111] that our understanding of these terms meets the demands of these criteria. And

---

[109] There are some politicians, policymakers and academics who want to treat all learning activities as training activities and abandon altogether those characteristics and attributes that have been associated with education. This would seem to be a matter of operative power.

[110] This form of words denotes a logical relationship.

[111] For a fuller discussion of these criteria for true knowledge, see chapter 1.

second, we have to provide an argument, which suggests that it is possible to say that one is better than the other. In the second case, we have to show, in addition to meeting the criteria for truthful knowledge, that the issue is not one of true or false judgements about the two phenomena being made but of one being a better and more useful descriptor than the other. The third is qualitatively different insofar as our concern is now with the concept of learning itself, and that some activities that can come under this concept can be better delivered through a training model, while others can be better delivered through an education model. What this requires is an inclusive model of learning and a way of showing that training and education models can subsume all of those activities that we want to attach to the notion of learning.

An example of an attempt at drawing a distinction between the two is Basil Bernstein's characterisation of a particular form of learning and being. Pedagogisation is understood as the development of processes of social and symbolic control (Bernstein, 2002: 366) and as inter-changeable with a notion of training: '(t)he concept of trainability places the emphasis upon "something" the actor must possess in order for the actor to be appropriately formed and reformed according to technological, organizational, and market contingencies'. It is also understood as a performance activity rather than as a competency. The performance model, for Bernstein, clearly emphasises marked subject boundaries, traditional forms of knowledge, explicit realisation and recognition rules for pedagogic practice, and the designation and establishment of strong boundaries between different types of students. Bernstein compared this with a competence model, in which the acquirer has some control over the selection, pacing and sequencing of her curriculum (and much more besides). For Bernstein (2000: 65), performance modes are seen as the norm, whereas competence modes are understood as interruptions to this normality. Regardless of whether this is so or not, I want to suggest that these basic categories (competence, performance, trainability and pedagogisation) are not well formulated and thus are unable to perform the roles assigned to them.[112]

Knowledge and knowledge development always have a pedagogic form. Knowledge is transformed at the pedagogic site, which could be

---

[112] Some of these terms, such as 'competence' or 'competences', are used in different ways now from the way Bernstein sought to use them. 'Performativity' is another example, although Bernstein was more circumspect in this regard.

a formal classroom in a school, an informal meeting between friends or an inadvertent and barely noticed encounter with an object in nature. The difference between these pedagogic sites is not that they do or do not contain pedagogising influences, but that their characteristics are differently realised as conditions for learning. These are: the simulation of the learning object; the representational mode of the object; its degree and type of amplification; control in the pedagogic relationship; progression or its relations with other learning objects; the type of pedagogic object; relations with other people in the learning process; the organisation of time (temporal relations) and types of feedback mechanism; and they are fundamental components of any pedagogic transformation[113] (see chapter 12 for a fuller explication of these key properties). What this means is that in the learning process, the learning object takes a new form as a result of changes to its properties, with these properties being more or less influential in the pedagogic exchange or learning sequence; that is, in all and every pedagogic exchange or learning sequence. Bernstein's notion of a totally pedagogised society does not take account of this. The second problem with the notion of a totally pedagogised society is its totality. This is an attempt by Bernstein to suggest that at certain historical moments, it is the only pedagogic form being used. However, trainability is only one manifestation of pedagogic relations, and it therefore competes with and operates alongside other forms of pedagogy.

Relations

The first set of relations or connections between training and education is that the object of learning and the arrangement of its characteristics at a particular moment in time are the prime determining factors in whether a training or educative model should be used. This argument makes sense only if we accept that training and education constitute two different forms of learning – they have distinctive approaches to learning and how learners experience activities associated with learning. In chapter 12, I show how it is possible to distinguish between different models of learning: observation, coaching, goal-clarification, peer learning, trial and error, hypothesis-testing, reflection, meta-cognitive

---

[113] This does not refer to Bernstein's pedagogic device, but to the way in which knowledge is transformed in specific pedagogic settings.

learning and practice. The argument that I am making here is that each of these approaches is appropriate only for certain types of learning object (either cognitive, skill-based, dispositional or embodied).[114]

A second set of possible relations between training and education suggests that the determining factor in distinguishing between a training pedagogy and an educative pedagogy is the function or purpose of the learning activity. This requires the identification of a set of differences between the two and then the initiation of a process whereby different functions or purposes are matched to these different models of training and education. So, for example, a teacher is trained to become a teacher because what she is required to learn is a set of behaviours and mechanistic actions. In this scenario there are no reflective, self-reflective, meta-cognitive, meditative and imaginative elements that we might want to describe as educative.

A third set of possible relations refers to the learning approach that is being adopted. In chapter 11, I discuss five possible learning philosophies: behaviourism, phenomenology, cognitivism, construc-tionism and materialism. Each of these learning philosophies has different characteristics. For example, behaviourists focus on how human beings behave and not what is in their minds, and thus they argue that if these terms are used as descriptors then they should be replaced by behavioural terms or, at least, those mind-dependent constructs should be translated into behavioural descriptors. This has implications for whether one should adopt a training or educative model, although a decision such as this also depends on which characteristics are given to a notion of training and which characteristics are given to a notion of education.

A fourth set of possible relations refers to the values we hold. Such values are embedded in a worldview, with the characteristics of a worldview being: a person's dynamic capacities and affordances, and the environments within which the person is situated; relations between a person and her environments; accounts of understanding, learning and change; and inferences from these premises and conclusions about representations, media for representations, learning environments and practical actions. A training model has a particular view of these characteristics and capacities, as does an education model, and they are significantly different.

------

[114] Cognitive, skill-based, dispositional and embodied forms of knowledge do not have equal status in the pedagogic transformatory process.

A final set of possible relations between the two models comprises their manifestations as power stratagems.[115] There are different trajectories of power (in history) and consequently different power arrangements are now associated with the use of each concept. Educative models give greater amounts of agential freedom to the learner, and these are sometimes denied to learners in training models. Consequently, training models are generally more popular among state bureaucrats and policymakers; the reasons for this are clear – a training model acts to reinforce the strength of the hierarchical arrangement of goods and people, and it provides a greater degree of control over its workforce. In addition, each of these concepts has a different history. Fundamentally, the various valuations given to each of these concepts change over time. Many of the activities that were previously thought of as educative are now thought of as training activities. We can see how these different arguments play out in different conceptions of teacher training or teacher education.

Models of teacher training

I have been concerned, then, with professional learning environments and processes of professionalisation *and* how we can construct these within the constraints and enablements of the teacher training system. Inevitably we are making judgements about a number of issues, such as the pedagogic mode (the type of relationship between the teacher-trainer and the student teachers), the learning mode (the type of learning approach that underpins the work of the teacher-trainer), the resources and technologies needed to allow that learning to take place, formative feedback mechanisms by the teacher-trainer (the modes, approaches and purposes), where the learning environment is, timings of different activities during the teaching sessions, the tasks that the student-teachers are expected to complete, and how the learning can be transferred to other environments. Learners here are student teachers and teachers already in service, and their learning environments are university

---

[115] Training and educative models have different types of object-relations attached to them. To reiterate from chapter 4, these relations are one-to-one or one-to-many, strong or weak, vertical or horizontal, corrosive or developmental, endogenous or exogenous, enabling or constraining functionally, feed-back or feed-forward, convergent or divergent, framing or reframing, categorising or recategorising, and subsumptive or contiguous.

and higher education institutions, schools and in-service training institutions.[116]

There are perhaps three dominant models of teaching and preparation for teaching: craft worker, executive technician and professional learner. The first two of these have greater affinities with training models, with the last being more akin to an education model. Craft knowledge has the following characteristics: it is rooted in practice and in the routines that shape practice, and this rules out certain types of learning or pedagogic approaches. This means that imitation and scaffolding various attempts to perform the activities are key to the development of this type of knowledge. The teacher or facilitator is the expert practitioner, and knowledge is derived from exposure to the performances of the expert. The expert is therefore not primarily a skilled pedagogue but a skilled practitioner. The emphasis is placed on observing and imitating the practice. The justification for this is that the nature of the practice is better understood in these terms: that the learning object, becoming and being a good teacher, is a craft activity.

Craft knowledge values situated understanding and downplays the importance of technical know-how and critical reflection. This leaves little room for what might be called research-based knowledge, even if this is understood in a non-technicist way and as having a non-binding quality to it. Though advocates of craft-based knowledge accept that there may be a role for systematic propositional knowledge, this is confined to what is taught, or subject-based knowledge, rather than to the processes of teaching and learning in which the teacher or student teacher is engaged. Furthermore, this entails a clear separation between content and process knowledge, or between the learning object and the pedagogic process. In addition, this focus on practical judgements as the essence of the teaching activity fails to account for ethical and epistemological elements in the judgements teachers make. These judgements as a consequence of their lack of reflective critique and adherence to external expert judgement may be inherently conservative and potentially unreliable, based as they are on observations of existing practice and common popularisations.

The second of our teaching models is the executive technician.[117] This requires the teacher to perform in a particular way; to have, and be able to execute, a repertoire of preconceived actions. In this model,

---

[116] Teacher-training models are framed historically as training activities, and this is not just about what they are called. Recent UK government reforms have reinforced this tendency.
[117] cf. Winch (2017).

teaching is a rule-based activity and learning is understood as the assimilation of these rules and ways of enacting them, without recourse to critical reflection or situated understanding. The executive technician model recognises the value of research findings, which means that it is not thought to be appropriate for teachers to interpret those findings for themselves. Educational researchers generate findings that can be expressed as protocols for action, and the role of the teacher is to implement these protocols in the most efficient way possible given that there are always situational constraints. One consequence of this is that the knowledge being transferred tends to lack a sense of change, emergence, immediacy or relevance. This positions the learning object, these rules and protocols, outside space and time and effectively reifies the learning object. This also applies to the assimilative and performative functions of learning.

These rules are identified by researchers and practical policymakers as external to the setting. They are not situation-specific or even sensitive to the particularities of the setting in which they are being applied. Educational research is understood as the making of nomothetic statements about educational activities; educational disputes about how teachers should behave in the classroom are settled by atheoretical and value-free empirical inquiry; and theoretical knowledge of educational matters is thought of as superior to practical knowledge, with the result that practice is understood as the efficient application of theoretical knowledge constructed by professional experts. Learning at pre-service and in-service levels, then, is reduced to the assimilation of these rules and to ways of following them in concrete situations such as classrooms. A more refined version of the executive technician model is that educational propositional knowledge should not be understood as being applicable in every possible circumstance and as having a certainty of outcome, but that it can act as a guide to practical action. This brings back a measure of interpretative activity into the proceedings.

Both the craft and executive technician models can be contrasted with a professional learning model. Professional learning emanates and is derived from an understanding of the characteristics and functions of being a classroom teacher in the context of where that teaching takes place. Apart from the content and methodological knowledge that teachers need in order to plan and teach a lesson, they also have to take a variety of other factors into consideration and integrate them in a coherent, efficient and pedagogically effective way. Among these are the previous knowledge, schooling biographies and expectations of their students, the individual differences between them (such as capabilities, interests and motivations), the objectives of the programme and the overall institution, as well as their own pedagogical aims, theoretical assumptions and values. Teachers have to make a considerable number of instantaneous and ad hoc decisions – they need to react to and take the lead in classroom interactions and modify their plans and methodological procedures according to the needs of students at specific points in time during the lesson. Ideally, they should create an atmosphere that encourages learning and communication and make sure that the task level is neither too high nor too low. In addition to this, institutions as well as classes have their own particular norms and patterns of interaction and communication. Teachers play a key role in mediating between this institutional culture and their students. They usually determine the content of classroom talk, organise the distinct phases of the lesson, determine the behaviour that is expected from students, select who is permitted to respond to a question or contribute to a discussion, decide what kind of answers are regarded as valid, and so forth.

Teachers need to take a multitude of sequential and simultaneous decisions that have to take account of personal, interpersonal, interactive, disciplinary, pedagogic and institutional factors. Imposing a predefined and fixed innovation on teachers (and students) in diverse institutional and regional contexts in a coercive, top-down fashion is counter-productive and likely to make them revert to safe and routinised practices. It seems more promising to encourage practitioners to try out new ideas in their classrooms, to make adjustments and then justify their decisions. To this end, an awareness of the contexts in which teachers work and their own behavioural and communicative patterns can be developed. Participants analyse their own classes, strengthen their communicative competences and classroom management strategies, and amplify their pool of teaching resources. In this discussion of training and educative models, a key issue has been that of power and authority and how these two important concepts play out in training environments and educative settings. In the next chapter I address this issue.

8
Institutional/systemic power

In chapter 1, I identified five types of object: discursive objects, material objects, relational objects, institutional/systemic objects and people – the point is that they have different characteristics and, in particular, that they generate different types of object-arrangements. Objects and object-arrangements have powers, although these are not always realised. They are also sometimes naturalised as objects and object-configurations. What I mean by this is that they are understood as natural, and thus beyond reproach. An example of an institutional/systemic object is a school system. Comparative educationalists have traditionally studied national education systems, with a notion of comparison among systems or within individual systems being the dominant knowledge-development device. The field was first developed in the early nineteenth century in parallel with the rise of national education systems, and it took the national system as its main object of inquiry.[118] Some have argued that this approach is now redundant, since nation states are in decline and national systems are consequently becoming obsolete.[119] Indeed, the very idea of a system is anachronistic in a world of global markets, multinational, transnational or even stateless corporations and cross-national comparative systems of evaluation and control. However, I want to suggest that nation states and national systems of education are far from redundant and, furthermore, that even in single nation studies, comparison[120] still has a role to play.

Education systems change over time and experience transformations to both their internal and external structures and relations. Whether

---

[118] cf. Noah and Eckstein (1969).

[119] cf. Reich (2015).

[120] Comparison is a key notion in any methodology. I have identified one way in which it is used in chapter 4, about which I have significant doubts.

change occurs or not depends on the capacity within the system as well as the condition of the change-catalyst or set of reforms. These in turn are structured in particular ways, and this determines their ability to act as change-agents. Certain types of catalyst are more likely to induce change in a system than others; for example, changes of personnel, new policies, events in nature, external interventions, new arrays of resources, new arrangements of roles and functions within a system, new financial settlements and so on. In short, some of these change-catalysts are more powerful than others, or at least have the potential to be more powerful. Even here, though, the capacity of the catalyst to effect change within a system cannot guarantee or determine whether change actually occurs. Even the most comprehensive of reform processes cannot guarantee or determine the degree and type of change within the system, how long-lasting the reform is and any unexpected consequences there may be. Furthermore, some types of change-catalyst are more likely to be successful in inducing change within the system than others. This is not only because some interventions in education systems are more powerful than others but also because their capacity to induce change better fits the change mechanism within the system being reformed.

What I have been doing here is categorising an education system as a set of institutions and relations between its parts, and even perhaps as a coordinating body for a number of subsystems, which have a particular relation to the central authority and a particular position within it. However, this does not mean that the relation between the central authority and the schools remains the same over time. These object-relations may change for a number of reasons; for example, the invention of new ideas, natural progressions, structural tensions in open activity systems[121] and so forth. In addition, it is possible to characterise education systems along a series of continua: restrictive control by the central authority over its constituent parts as opposed to loose control over these parts, or centralised as opposed to decentralised system-relations; strongly defined notions of expertise as against weakly defined notions; specialisations of functions and roles within the system rather than general capacities; and clearly defined external relations with other bodies and systems as against weakly defined externalities.

It is fairly easy, then, to understand an education system as a coordinating body that directs a number of subunits, so that if the central authority demands action of a particular type, then these subsidiary

---

[121] cf. Engeström (2001).

bodies will implement its directives. The cohering element in the notion of a system being used here is that one body commands a series of other bodies, although all are considered to be elements of a system. However, it is rare for any actual system to function in this way. Within the system, the extent and type of power that the coordinating body can exercise over the other elements may be delivered in a different way. Thus, a system's coordinating body may have more or less direct relations with different parts of the system. Indeed, it may be that some of these relations become so attenuated that it becomes harder to include them in the system. Institutional/systemic objects then have powerful characteristics, or at least they have these potentialities – power flows operate through the identification and use of these objects.

Institutional power

The use of new educational technologies is another example of power-relations operating in and through education systems.[122] For Michel Foucault (1975), the introduction of the examination in France in the eighteenth century combined the techniques of an observing hierarchy with those of a normalising judgement.[123] Knowledge of persons was created that had the effect of binding individuals to each other, embedding those individuals in networks of power and sustaining mechanisms of surveillance, which were all the more powerful because they worked by allowing individuals to govern themselves. The examination introduced a whole new mechanism that both contributed to a new type of knowledge formation and constructed a new network of power, all the more powerful once it had become established throughout society. This is the objectification of the individual as a branch of knowledge, so that the individual could now be described, judged, measured and compared with others.

For the first time, the individual could be scientifically and objectively categorised and characterised through a network of power whereby the most important factor is the differences between people and objects. Hierarchical normalisation becomes the dominant way of organising society. Foucault was suggesting here that the examination itself, seemingly a neutral device, in reality acts to position the person

---

[122] The issue of what a technology might be is taken up in chapter 13.
[123] *Surveiller et punir* (Foucault, 1975) is an extraordinary book. There is only a brief mention of education within it, where Foucault refers to the examination.

being examined in a discourse of normality,[124] so that for people to understand themselves in any other way is to identify themselves as abnormal and even as unnatural.[125]

Roy Bhaskar (2011) distinguished between three types of power.[126] The first type refers to the capacities of human beings to act in the world, that is, to speak a language, teach, reason or communicate. These power(s) exist even if they are not theorised, perceived or actualised in events. Power can also have negative characteristics, referring as it does to relations of subjugation, control, oppression, domination, exploitation or specific forms of master–slave relations. Bhaskar identified a third type of power, which he developed through his philosophy of metaReality.[127] This type of power is intertwined with the notion of in-the-world spirituality, and this should not be confused with religious practice. Power is enframed in all individuals as a capacity or potential that can be transformed in action. From this standpoint, any form of action, including empowerment, liberation and emancipation, pivots on its fundamental qualities. Catholic education over a long period of time can serve as an illustration of how this happens.

Catholic education

Advocates for Catholic education need to provide answers to two potentially damaging objections.[128] The first of these is that, as with all faith-based programmes of learning, it is indoctrinatory and not educative. In order to sustain this argument, those critics of faith-based programmes need to be able to show that the educational programmes they support (whether explicitly or implicitly) have pedagogic elements that are superior to those within faith-based programmes.

---

[124] Normalisation is another example of the atomisation of identity and, in a general sense, of reality.
[125] The notion of unnatural desires has a long and sad history.
[126] Being powerful is a characteristic or attribute of a discursive object, or a material object, or a relational object, or a configurational object, or a human being. Power can be possessed, exercised or actualised.
[127] MetaReality focuses on the self, human agency and society. Roy Bhaskar (2002) showed how the world of alienation and crisis we currently inhabit could be transformed by the ground-state qualities of intelligence, creativity, love, a capacity for right-action and a potential for human self-realisation or fulfilment.
[128] Catholic education and Catholic pedagogy are generalisations, which would suggest a disregard for the variety of forms inherent in the two concepts. The reason for including this case is to suggest that power, power dynamics and powerful practices are ever-present in the construction over time of a discourse.

A second objection focuses on the idea that the framework of Catholic values, which underpins the curriculum content of Catholic education, is in some sense fallacious or insufficient. And attached to this is a belief that as a consequence of this deficiency, Catholic pedagogy in schools generates persons who cannot experience a fulfilled life. The problem, as critics of faith-based programmes have pointed out, is the insistence on a strong coupling between spirituality *and* ethical behaviours and dispositions. Indeed, there may even be a problem with identifying distinctive Catholic pedagogical styles and techniques, although I argue below that many of these styles and techniques of learning were the originators of common and secularised forms of pedagogy that are now in common use. In the Gadarene rush to secularisation, secularists have simply borrowed or taken over pedagogies that could be called Catholic in origin.

The first objection, then, is that Catholic education is not educative at all but indoctrinatory. The enlightened person seeks at all times to be educated rather than indoctrinated. Catholic pedagogy therefore must on this account be a practice that subscribes (in a deontological sense) to those features we think of as belonging to an educative practice and in addition as engendering, if it is successful, persons who in their lives outside the formal education setting are educated and thus live in ways that conform to this state of being (and I have to say here, these are not lives that conform to an indoctrinated state of being).

There are two meanings that can be given to the idea of the indoctrinated person. The first focuses on the arbitrary nature of what is being imposed and the second on the effects that it may have, so that the indoctrinated person now cannot think, act and behave in an autonomous fashion (where autonomy is understood as that human quality a person possesses that is most opposed to those qualities associated with an indoctrinated person and comprises in part the capacity to will one's own actions). In the first instance, what this requires, as part of the argument, is the development of a basic premise that Catholic pedagogy, indeed Catholic education, is in some way different from other forms of education or from an ideal model of an educational practice. This requires the development of some notion of non-arbitrariness, with regards to both the content of what is being taught and the end result, so that the person has some measure of autonomy in the judgements he makes as he lives his life.

If a distinction is to be maintained, then, between indoctrination and education, where the latter is understood as involving some measure of autonomy, then an argument to justify this distinction has to be provided. Before I do this, a further objection should be noted. This is that an argument could be made for the indoctrination of young learners on the grounds that it is a necessary imposition because it allows them to exercise their autonomy after they have grown up and left school. Clearly, there is a sense in which both processes – learning how to be autonomous and being autonomous once one has learnt how – involve specific actions by the learner. If autonomy, then, is defined as the capacity to make sound judgements about the consequences of one's actions, this does not just happen, but results from a series of actions on the part of the learner, with the result that the learner is better able to make those sound judgements after the learning experiences than before. Thus, the learner is provided with experiences, which, if they have positive effects, enable the learner to become autonomous, and he would not have become autonomous unless he had actually had those experiences. In short, for his own good as an educated person, and if it is accepted that the optimum state of affairs is that he should exercise his autonomy, he should be inducted into this way of life, which some might want to call indoctrinatory.

Further to this, it is not at all clear that a notion of education involving the imposition of a particular state of mind on a child does in fact lead to the development of dispositions that in later life we might want to call, in a Catholic sense, conscience-driven and thus autonomous. In part, this is an empirical matter, and yet even then we have to be sure that a causal relation that we have identified from an examination of what has gone on in the past can allow us to predict what will happen in the future. We can make a judgement from knowledge of what has happened in the past that certain experiences do not in fact allow the individual to lead a full, holistic and autonomous life when he grows up because those experiences have in some sense damaged him. I am thinking here of child abuse in which children have been so badly affected by their experiences that they cannot lead fulfilled and happy lives. In addition, it is difficult to identify those experiences that might lead to the desired state of being after the child has experienced them. It is tempting, however, to suggest that experiencing autonomy or being allowed to make those choices that constitute an autonomous life as a learner is a better way of learning to be autonomous than being told what to do.

The second area of difficulty revolves around the extent to which we can make sense of the idea of a non-indoctrinated child. Various attempts have been made to identify such a child and these have focused on the type of imposition afforded to the child. Hand (2006) defines indoctrination as the imparting of beliefs so that they are held non-rationally. Non-rationality is further defined as without regard to evidence. We should note here that the definition focuses not on the justification for imposing such a state of mind but on the imparting of those beliefs to the child. So, a child can have a religious faith, having been inducted into such a belief during his time at school, but he has been indoctrinated if he holds such beliefs without regard to the evidence. If this is put in this way, then a problem with religious belief immediately comes to the fore; which is that it is hard to see what might constitute good reasons for such a belief, and the belief, if this is accepted, would then be categorised as irrational, and the learning of it would be consigned to the realm of indoctrination.

Two points need to be made here. The first is that an indoctrinated state is being construed as a psychological state in which the person is impervious to changing his mind or his belief system. The second is that the test for whether the arguments and evidence for changing the person's mind constitutes a public assessment to determine whether those arguments or the evidence amount to a sufficient reason for that person to change his mind. There may be a less stringent test, which we can call the weaker argument, and this is that the public test is discarded and replaced with a test involving the strength of the argument. If good reasons are provided as to why the person should change his mind, and this argument accepts that the capacity to change one's mind is a precondition of an autonomous state of being, then though the person may choose not to change his mind, he does so because the reasons provided do not constitute sufficient grounds for his doing so. He is therefore still acting autonomously. This, however, leaves us with a dilemma, which can be expressed in the form of a question: what might constitute a good reason for changing one's mind?

One possible answer is that we are committed to some form of coherence of argument about what we should do, and we might want to change our mind to produce in our belief system a greater sense of coherence. Another reason might be that our present state of being has led in the past to certain unhappy consequences, and we are seeking to develop a set of beliefs that in our judgement will produce happier consequences for us. A third set of reasons might focus on the notion that we are simply wrong to hold to the particular set of beliefs that we presently have and that we should therefore amend our beliefs so that they are more correct. A fourth set of reasons might focus on a desire to live our lives free from the dictates of reason; and we are thus committed to acting irrationally. In this last case, it should be noted that although we choose to act irrationally, all we are in fact doing is the mirror opposite of what the rational person might choose to do. Thus, the criteria for determining what we do are in fact based on a system of rational thought and action, and we could not go on in life without accepting that there is a system of rationality. Finally, we might actually be confused about why we do this rather than that, and thus the choices we make are essentially arbitrary. To equate autonomy with the making of choices is therefore potentially problematic.

What is also problematic is defining the person acting in a non-autonomous way as someone who is not open to rational persuasion. And this is because of the difficulty with identifying what a good reason for changing one's life or making choices might be. The argument made by Catholic philosophers is that it is possible to induct a child into a religious way of life without at the same time indoctrinating them. The counterargument is that inducting a child into a religious faith is per se indoctrination because that person is now less open to changing his mind about his belief system, and the purpose of a liberal education is to open the mind to further possibilities rather than close it. However, in effect this is the same for the learning of all types of beliefs, and education of whatever type cannot be sustained without some notion of imparting a belief system to an initiate. Once again, we need to remind ourselves that the person may still be acting autonomously, even if he chooses not to exercise this facility. The problem with the dichotomous nature of the pair of words, 'indoctrination–education', is that any prescription about education involves the development of a set of presuppositions about how the child and the future adult should behave, and consequently is essentially normative. It is to this argument that we now need to turn our attention. What I have sought to do here is place in suspension the idea that there is an indoctrinated way of life and a non-indoctrinated way of life and furthermore that being a Catholic and learning to be a Catholic necessarily involves leading an indoctrinated way of life.

And the reason I have chosen to do this is because, if autonomy is to provide the underpinning rationale for what should constitute a curriculum, then first there is a need to be clear about what an autonomous life might be, and second, there is a need to be clear about why leading an autonomous life is better than leading a non-autonomous life. If education, and certainly formal education, is defined as an intervention in the life of the child, then though that intervention may have unexpected and unplanned consequences, it is still designed to initiate the child into a form of life. This operates at the level of knowledge as well as at the level of skill or disposition. We cannot avoid the prescriptive nature of education, and this is because by choosing an array of skills, or a particular knowledge agenda, or a set of embodiments, or a set of dispositions, we are necessarily putting to one side other knowledge or skills or embodied or dispositional agendas. We might have good reasons for doing so, but the act of curriculum-making per se comprises the inclusion of some activities and the exclusion of others.

We now come to the main part of the argument, which is that those experiences that should be incorporated into the curriculum can be derived only from a notion of what the good life is (and this of course is given a particular definition by the Catholic discourse community), insofar as the skills and knowledge children need to acquire as they grow up are necessary for living the good life. Is it therefore possible to identify what that good life might be? We have already suggested that it is more than making choices or living the autonomous life, for two reasons. First, there may be moral or ethical reasons for sanctioning some forms of behaviour and supporting others. Second, individuals in being autonomous may make choices, which do not lead to fulfilment in their lives. However, we have established the principle that however hard it is to define what the good life is, this end can be the only logical raison d'être for determining what is in the curriculum, whether we understand this as Catholic or secular.

It may be possible to anchor this prescriptive activity in some notion of human nature. In effect, there are three possible scenarios. The first of these is that human nature has a plasticity, which does not allow us to say that human beings have dispositions that should be fulfilled. Human needs and wants are infinitely flexible and, beyond the basics of survival, can be construed as irremediably social. They are in a sense therefore manufactured, or at least the human need, want or desire comes about because of the way society is structured. The second scenario suggests the opposite, which is that the natural can be identified and this natural state of affairs persists and has persisted through time; and though we do not always know what we want – for example, because we have misled ourselves or are confused about what we want – we can understand these false beliefs only in terms of a pure consciousness that seeks fulfilment. The third scenario is a variant on the second, in that there is an innate and natural sense of completeness built into human beings, which needs to be achieved in order to lead the good life, and though in most cases human beings do not achieve this, it does provide a criterion for judging the state of affairs that we might want to call the good life. If we are to accept either or both of these last two scenarios, then further arguments or evidence would need to be provided to support such assertions.

And these assertions always have a backstory, which in the case I am focusing on here is Catholic in orientation. This backstory has a number of features: a language for understanding the educative process; a capacity for analysing this process (identifying and separating out the various elements and the relations between them); an ontology and an epistemology, and the relations between them; a way of turning all of these into a coherent whole that prescribes what is needed for an educational setting; and fundamentally a set of Catholic values.

Values

The second objection to Catholic education revolves around the issue of what it is that Catholic education wishes to convey, and this is also bound up with processes of modernisation and secularisation that are taking place. There are two possibilities. The first is what could be called the liturgy of the Catholic faith and, in particular, the observances of the Eucharist, obedience to Church law and confessional practices. In short, the liturgical Catholic education process is one in which the child is, as a result of various pedagogical processes, affirmed or reaffirmed in the specific activities of the faith, which include those systems of belief and those practices that the Catholic Church deems to be suitable expressions of that faith. The second possibility can be called Catholic virtues, where the trait that is most valued is moral excellence. The child is deemed to have achieved moral excellence when he has acquired those virtues, which in their application lead to the good life.

A distinction needs to be drawn between two types of Catholic virtues, which can be understood as religious values and ethical values. This distinction is important because, as the story goes, the latter, logically, are not dependent on the former. A person can live the good life without in any way subscribing to what I am calling religious values. The counterargument is that these secular values are dependent on and can be achieved only through immersion in religious values; what is meant by this is a full and sincere affirmation of the religious life and, to some extent, its embedded behaviours.

The second type of virtue, then, is that of moral excellence, where religious virtues (our first type) are neither a prior condition nor a necessity. These are virtues associated with acts of kindness, charity and care for the poor, and are socialistic and communitarian in kind. Here, the story goes, the particular ethos and pedagogy of a Catholic school leads to learning (understood in its widest sense) in which the person, who of course might be an unbeliever, behaves in all essential respects as a Catholic, even if he does not attend to the rituals of the Catholic Church.

There is an alternative viewpoint. This is the reformist pathway, where an attempt is made to secularise Catholicism. Charles Taylor (2011) identified three types of secularism. The first of these is what he called 'secularity in terms of public spaces' (educational, political, cultural, professional, recreational, and so on), with the understanding that these have now been emptied of references specifically to God or even to some ultimate reality – in other words, some notion of a metaphysical being. The second of these senses of secularity is a falling away of religious belief and observances, so that, for example, fewer people go to church on Sundays. And the third sense that Taylor gave to this notion of secularity is where the idea of God or some ultimate reality is challenged at every moment of life and understood as an alternative choice among many others; the authority of God (and the Church) has been superseded by other forms of authority. Taylor's point is an empirical one: this is what has happened and is happening. However, the problem still remains for Catholic education, which is that the educative process may still embrace a set of ethical precepts that would be approved of by the Catholic Church, but they do not include religious values or taking part in the Catholic liturgy or conforming to Catholic rituals. There is a further avenue to explore, and our concern here is with the pedagogic transformatory process rather than the values (forms of knowledge, skills, embodiments and dispositions) that have occupied our attention so far.

Pedagogical approaches

Broadly, seven major Catholic pedagogical styles and techniques can be identified. These are events. Each has different emergent pedagogical properties. The styles flex and overlap with each other. The first is exegetical. This is fundamentally organised around a holy book or books and the associated commentary and interpretation. The modal inspiration is perhaps the educational parts of the sixth-century Rule of Saint Benedict, based as it is on humility and unhesitating obedience. The curriculum is holy reading and prayer.

More subtle and non-dogmatic processes of exegesis abound in the history of Catholic education.[129] For example, in Maximus the Confessor's

---

[129] cf. Louth (1996).

Ambigua ad Joannem and in his *Ad Thalassium*, two traditions of monastic spiritual pedagogy are described: the exegetical aporial tradition, a hermeneutic process that seeks to resolve difficulties posed by certain biblical passages; and the quaestio-responsio. This last comprises a series of steps: asking the question; formulating objections that the teacher will eventually have to provide an answer to; the making of the sed contra, which consisted of the reading of a passage from the scriptures suggesting the position the teacher would have to defend; the responsio, or the giving of an interpretation of the passage by the teacher in relation to the question originally posed; and finally, there is a resolution of the difficulties and objections raised at the beginning of the proceedings by the teacher. This suggests that the *Ad Thalassium* and the responsio were in essence a form of spiritual catechism leading the learner to a mystical contemplation of the logoi and logos of creation. The Scriptures are revealed in this exegetical approach to be windows to higher, spiritual realities. The implication here is that the path to the good life requires more than the adoption of secular ethical values, however Catholic in orientation they are.

Reflection on the world is a third type of pedagogical approach. An example would be a pedagogy developed within the tradition of Saint Ignatius, the founder of the Jesuits. The thrust of this pedagogy was that in performing the spiritual exercises (in order to know the will of God), this would transform the individual so that he would make appropriate decisions about how he should act in the world. Note the order of activity in the pedagogic sequence: understanding the spiritual is a prerequisite of acquiring those values, ideals and attitudes that allow one to behave in an ethical way in the world. Without this sense of spirituality, the subsequent ethical precepts held by the individual that compel him to behave in this rather than that way are empty and moreover are likely to be misguided and wrong. Reflection, then, in this sense also embraces action in the world. The individual behaves in a reflective manner.

There are a number of models of reflection based on specific philosophical approaches (for example, John Dewey, 1938; Jurgen Habermas, 1981; or Saint Ignatius, expounded in Duminuco, 2000) that are in common use. To facilitate critical reflection, a range of tools and practices have been developed, which include the use and analysis of critical incidents and the much-used Kolb learning cycle. The idea of a learning cycle, developed by David Kolb (1984), is based on a belief that deep learning (learning for real comprehension) comes from a sequence of experience, reflection, abstraction and active testing. Reflection is a form of evaluative thinking. It is applied to ideas for which there is no obvious solution and is largely based on the further processing of knowledge and understanding and possibly emotions that the learner already possesses. It is thus a second-order internal activity, which can in certain circumstances be transformed into a learning strategy. In addition, in Catholic theological terms, the focus of the reflective process should always be on the 'forming and informing of conscience' (Grace, 2013: 105). This has some affinities with Michel Foucault's (2010) notion of 'care of the self'. (For Foucault, this is an ethical precept.) For some, including Gerald Grace, this requires spiritual work, with the reflective process dovetailing between Catholic social teaching and the 'teaching, practice and mission of Jesus Christ and the Saints' (2013: 105). It should be noted here that the education of children is in some sense deficient if both elements of Catholic pedagogy – the teaching and learning of those knowledge sets, virtues and embodiments that are perhaps Catholic in origin but which would now be shared by most liberal educators, *and* a sense of spirituality, which is manifested in one of its forms as contemplation of the life of Jesus Christ and the saints – are not included in the overall programme of learning.

In using an instructional pedagogy, the teacher needs to: gain the attention of the group of learners; inform the learners of the objectives of the learning exercise; stimulate recall of prior learning among the group of learners, so that the new information is related productively to previous and current learning; present content to the learner; implement appropriate scaffolding processes; stimulate a performance by the learner; provide feedback to the learner that is a comment on their performance and allows corrective action to take place; and evaluate the corrected performance. Catholic pedagogy in schools has for a long time depended on instructional approaches, with compliance as the dominant metaphor.

Meanwhile, as an essential part of a Catholic liberal, emancipatory, theory of education, a pedagogical approach has been developed that could be called individual self-discovery. The goal here is for the individual learner to achieve an independent point of view, and a personal Catholic voice. For a long time, the key lay in a close personal reading of the classics (religious and secular) – of great books in general and the Bible in particular. This can perhaps be described as a form of spiritual apprenticeship.

A more organised form of external engagement reached its height of popularity in the North American enthusiasm for service learning, using the resources of the surrounding community for learning scenarios.

At one end of the spectrum lies volunteering (whether or not from an expert base); at the other lies the educational goal of deep but temporary immersion in the dilemmas of particular groups in civil society. Service learning in Catholic schools has a long tradition, and also involves the learning of some ethical virtues that are Catholic in orientation, although originary claims are made for these by secularists. Finally, in Catholic education, there has been an emphasis on another long-standing approach, much favoured by the philosopher John Dewey (1938): learning by doing, which has some affinities with service learning but also comprises a notion of phronesis or practical wisdom.

The story goes that Catholic education can uniquely provide human beings with a gestalt that can act to frame their subsequent life and behaviours. The Catholic child grows as a person as a result of an individual and cultural maturation, or *Bildung*. And, so the argument goes, this sense of leading the good life cannot be adequately fulfilled without subscribing to doctrinal as well as ethical precepts of Catholicism. Despite the efforts to secularise or disenchant the religious life, some elements of this enchantment[130] and some adherence to Catholic rituals are still required to lead the good life. This, of course, is in opposition to a view of Catholic education, which simply argues for the inculcation of those virtues (and the subsequent capability to instantiate them in the world) that are derived from Catholic theology and doctrine. The two are not the same and may be in opposition to each other and, in addition, at the pedagogical level may be fundamentally in conflict.

I have suggested above that the claim that Catholic education (and I suppose any faith-based education) is indoctrinatory cannot be satisfactorily made, insofar as the various possible ways of making this claim are not up to the task. In general, this involves a repudiation of the sharp distinction between prescription and non-prescription with regards to both pedagogy and curriculum. The second dilemma that I have explored here revolves around the emphasis that the Catholic educator places on spirituality as well as on ethical values. I have suggested above that a compelling case can be made for both as being part of a Catholic pedagogy. However, what this does is establish strong insulations between Catholic education and other forms of education.

The final issue that has been addressed here is whether it is possible to identify a distinctive Catholic pedagogical form. Given that all and

---

[130] Charles Taylor (2011) writes about disenchantment and re-enchantment, and makes the point, among others, that a strong evaluation of the world is still possible, even if the pictures we now paint of the modern world are predominantly scientistic and reductionist.

every pedagogic form has evolved in some way or another from faith-based educational practices, with many of them being Catholic in origin, this does suggest a historical connection. These practices change over time, and processes of secularisation have contributed to their current forms. If spirituality is considered to be a significant feature of a Catholic educational practice, then this claim is fairly easy to make. Without a sense of spirituality as part of the mix, it becomes much harder.

In this part of the book, I have focused on some important ideas in the history of thought: what concepts are; the relationship between knowledge and learning; the possibility of universal knowledge; excellence in a practice; what evidence is; the distinction between epistemology and ontology; the role and place of values in our descriptions of the world and in the world itself; the notion of difference; different epistemic categories; and powerful practices. I also need to relate all of these to a notion of human identity.

9
Identity and consciousness

In this chapter I will be addressing the issue of personal identity (and thus, collective identity), which refers to the way in which a person identifies with a particular social object, such as a nation, a collection of nations, an ethnic trait, a racial classification, a geographical entity, a personal history, a sense of heritage, a sporting club, an abstraction such as goodness or love (for example, Philip Larkin's *An Arundel Tomb*: 'What will survive of us is love'), a social unit such as the family, a religion or a sexual orientation. Whatever the social object, this identification comprises a preference for that object over other objects of the same type – for example, identifying with a nation such as Britain over and above a collection of nations such as the European Union, or identifying with a particular racial grouping and not with human beings in general. These social objects can be nested in some type of identity grouping, so one can identify with an area within a country ('I am a Londoner'), a country ('I am English'), a nation ('I am British'), a union of countries ('I am a European') or even the world ('I am a world citizen'). Belonging to all five of these identity groupings is not in itself incoherent or irrational.

What is pivotal here is how a person constructs her personal identity – how she gives more importance to one particular social object or even to a number of objects and consequently less importance to others. A person's identity refers to certain properties of the social world to which a person feels a special sense of attachment or ownership; that is, in all her deliberations about the world and with regards to her activities in this world, she prioritises some reasons for action over and against others. As a result, she sees the world in a particular way, although she may share that world with other people who subscribe to the same or similar markers of identity. All of these identity markers are imagined conceptualisations of the social object, so racial, spatial, historical, ethnic, religious, sexualised, embodied or familiar attachments comprise imagined and constructed narratives about race,[131] geographies,[132] histories,[133] ethnicities,[134] religions,[135] sexualities,[136] bodies[137] or social groupings.[138] Frequently, human beings reify the properties of the social object to which they are attached, treating them as natural or as common sense and thus beyond reproach.

A person's sense of identity, then, consists of those features of the imagined object that define her as a person or even that make her the person that she is. They give that person a sense of belonging, and they focus that person in a particular way. Fundamentally, personal identity is a matter of what human beings care about in the world. Since they are what they are, human beings interact with the three orders of reality: the natural, the practical and the social.[139] If human beings are going to flourish, they have to sustain relationships in all three. As a result, they cannot afford to be indifferent to the concerns that are embedded in each of these three orders.

These are also markers of difference; that is, they refer to the type and extent of dissimilarity between different manifestations of the social object, for instance, abled and dis-abled, male and female, black and white, heterosexual and homosexual, intelligent and unintelligent, precariat and middle class, *and* British and European. Crude versions of these relations are ever-present in modern societies. However, difference can be understood as not being or as being opposite to something else, and in addition, that ideas and concepts are part of a network of words and signs, which have meaning only within other arrangements of words and concepts, from which they differ. However, difference can become pathological if different sets of values, usually in opposition to each other, are attached to different manifestations of the social object.

Being a woman, liking poetry and living in London may be characteristics of a particular person, but they do not constitute identity markers for that person, if that person has not invested enough feeling and commitment in them to trigger actions. In addition, it may be possible

---

[131] An example of which is Hall (1980).
[132] An example of which is Jensen and Richardson (2004).
[133] An example of which is Foucault (1969).
[134] An example of which is Malesevic (2004).
[135] An example of which is Taylor (2011).
[136] An example of which is Foucault (1978b).
[137] An example of which is Shilling (2016).
[138] An example of which is Giddens (1986).
[139] These three types of relationships are ill-characterised here and may not be of the same logical order. However, broadly they are three different types of relationships that are central to the concerns of human beings.

for a property to belong to a person's identity, in that it is a central defining belief that she has (ethnic purity, for example), with at the same time that belief being false. A person's sense of identity may be changeable, fragile, focused on different social objects at different times and contingent. However, for most people, social attachments that are acquired at an early age persist over time and are extremely difficult to reverse – although they may take a different form at different moments in that person's life and indeed involve denials and repudiations, such as in ethnic or racial identities.

Identities and identity formations operate at different social levels and therefore in different ways. These different levels can be categorised as: the sub-individual or psychological level; the individual or auto-biographical level; the ordinary level of living our lives; the functional level at which we are concerned with relational roles such as capitalist and worker or shop owner and customer; the structural level as in the functioning of whole societies or their parts (such as the economy or the political sphere); the mega level of whole traditions and civilisations; and finally the planetary or cosmological level where the person's immediate concerns are with the planet (or cosmos) as a whole (cf. Bhaskar, 2011).[140] At these different levels, then, different forms of identity and agency are constructed, causing in some cases deep-seated dislocations, anomic frames of mind and unhappinesses.

What sort of things then are people or persons? What are their fundamental properties? What, for instance, are they made of? Are they substances wholly or partly formed and reformed by material, embodied and discursive features of society or is each person able to shape her own life course? And, fundamentally, how do human beings construct their sense of self? These are difficult questions to answer, but the answers that are given and the subsequent identities that are assumed have consequences – some trivial, some serious.

Identity is being used here to indicate a sense of wholeness and thus persistence across time. All discussions of a person over time require some understanding of change; that is, a notion of change is built into the conception of the human being. If there was no cohering element between time moments, so that every moment entailed a change of person, we would not have a sense of personhood, which therefore has to include a notion of persistence over time and, in addition, has a notion of emergence. And this is emergence understood in its two modes: as

---

[140] These are examples of spatial geometries; see chapter 21.

a temporal phenomenon, and ontologically as a response to the stratified nature of reality. Identity and consciousness are homologous concepts; that is, they operate in the same way and have similar properties. In saying this, we still need to understand what consciousness is, as it is a polysemic concept.

Consciousness

It is possible to identify those elements of consciousness that cannot as yet be replicated by artificial intelligence (AI): intentionality, non-deontological ways of being, reflexivity, meta-reflection and referential reflection, identity formation and acting in a virtuous way. The question that needs to be asked is: can a machine ever act in intentional, non-deontological, meta-reflective, identity-forming and virtuous ways? I do not think that a machine could ever replicate all of the functions of a human being, although I suppose it is just possible to imagine new material and substance inventions that replicate (or are superior to) human bodies, brains and of course minds, with the proviso that these machines would not be able to act intentionally and virtuously.

I am making a comparison between a human being and an artificial replication of a human being in an attempt to show that a human being has different characteristics from a machine, and that this is directly relevant to answering questions such as: do human beings have a conscious mind? If they have a conscious mind, do they have free will?[141] If we are asleep or if our minds are working at a subconscious level, can we say that we are conscious at these moments? Our brains may be active during moments of sleep or inattention, even if this does not point to a notion of consciousness generally, and even if subsequently we intuit or work out that something has changed (subconscious activity can affect conscious activity later on).

Philosophers have proposed a number of theories of consciousness[142] – what it is, how it operates and why we need a theory of consciousness at all. General theories of consciousness largely divide between standard mind–body operations, such as dualist theories, and physicalist

---

[141] The relationship between consciousness and volition is indeed complicated. Understanding it rests on the argument that one cannot be conscious unless one also has some control over the operation of one's mind, and that volition or the exercise of free will requires as a minimum condition that a person (though this idea is of course problematic) can influence in some way or another the conditions through which individual agency is manifested.
[142] cf. Van Gulick (2018).

theories. Those who believe in dualist theories argue that some operations of the mind fall outside the realm of the physical and cause–effect–cause relations, as they are generally understood. Substance theorists, taking their inspiration from René Descartes (1988), suggest that there are both physical and non-physical substances, and minds are examples of the latter, with these minds embracing a notion of consciousness. Property dualists suggest that minds cannot be reduced to physical properties, but nonetheless causal relations can be instantiated by the same things that trigger the operation of physical processes. Fundamental versions of property dualism accept that consciousness consists of operative physical processes, but ontologically a claim is being made that properties of consciousness do not and cannot be derived from physical properties. Emergent property dualists introduce into the equation a notion of emergence so that even though they accept that consciousness and conscious processes come about through the operation of physical processes, the result cannot be understood or expressed in physicalist terms (or, it needs to be said, in how language and semantic structures currently operate). Monist property dualists understand both the properties of the mind and physical properties as being derived from a more basic level of reality. This clearly has some affinities with medieval conceptions of transcendentals (see chapter 2). Panpsychism would suggest that all properties of objects have mindful and thus non-physical properties attached to them. This allows a form of consciousness to be realised. These dualist theories mark out a clear distinction between the properties of the mind and the properties of a physical reality; and it is hard to see how any theory of consciousness could be anything other than vacuous if a purely physicalist theory was endorsed.

In particular, physicalist theories of consciousness cannot embrace a notion of free will, which means that in every aspect of our lives we cannot be sure that we are not being radically deceived. Physicalist theories vary enormously in their scope and direction.[143] For example, some type–type identity theories (in which each type of mind-state is a type of brain-state) deny the notion of consciousness altogether, whereas others argue that since the conscious property and the neural property are of the same type, then there is no need to explain how the one can cause the other or give rise to it. Most physicalist theories of consciousness are not of this type but aim to understand the world in terms of some form

---

[143] Such as: higher-order theories, reflexive theories, representationalist theories, narrative interpretative theories, cognitive theories, information integration theories, neural theories and quantum theories.

of psycho–physicalist relation, in which the two are not identical. All of these theories come up against the existence of free will, and all of them are essentially deterministic.

A key issue, then, that relates to identity and consciousness is free will, that is, volition. John Searle (1984) endorsed a physicalist position – all forms of conscious life involve the interaction of molecules – and thus implicitly accepted a mechanical causal view of the mind–body relationship, and from this he concluded that any idea we may have of free will is merely an illusion. This means that for Searle an activity of the mind is also physical (and therefore has to abide by the laws of physics), and if it is, any notion of intentionality influencing our actions or even causing further actions in the mind is simply the operation of prior molecular processes, with their commitment to a notion of cause and effect. However, again for Searle, we have a strong sense that in life we subscribe to a notion of having a state of mind, which in some way causes (not in a Humean sense, see chapter 4) other states of mind or physical actions. However, this cannot – if we subscribe to the notion of the operation of the mind being in no fundamental sense different from the operation of physical objects outside the mind – be anything other than an illusion. There is no such thing as free will, only a thought in our heads that we freely choose some action or some other thought from a range of possible thoughts and actions. This is of course not just a criticism of anti-physicalism but also a sceptical position per se. Unless we can establish some certain point outside of the particular case that we are considering, by which we can judge our original claim to knowledge, then we are forced to withhold assent to it being a valid claim of knowledge. Further to this, if we cannot find good grounds for suggesting that the basis for having any conscious function in the mind at all is not illusory, then we are forced to accept a sceptical position with regards to knowledge of anything, if and only if we construe all processes in the mind as conforming to the principles of physicalism. What this means is that everything is literally physical or at least that everything supervenes on the physical, and further to this that these principles of physicalism – all events, including events in individual minds, are the product of the play of molecules at a lower level – cannot save us in this regard.

Scepticism, further, is necessarily false. For if we support a notion of scepticism, then we additionally have to show why it is true. If we do this, and we are, I think, committed to doing this, then at least one item of true knowledge exists, that is, that we should be sceptical about knowledge, and this of course contradicts the original premise. We cannot be sceptical about knowledge in its entirety. For any theory of learning there needs to be some reconciliation of the persistent problem of the relationship between mind and matter. The reason for this is that one element of the learning process may be conceived as a transfer of a material object, an entity, to what some think of as a non-material object, a mind.

Thomas Nagel (2012), coming from a dualist position, suggested that substances in the mind and processes cannot be directly subsumed into physical substances and processes – there are significant differences between the two; however, we do not have at present, and possibly never will have, a language for describing states of the mind, even if we can provide good grounds for suggesting that they are different. What this means is that we cannot provide a convincing account of what these states are and what the relation between states of the mind and physical states might be, although we can deduce that differences exist between them. Causal explanations in science are necessary. Given the theory, the observed effects must follow. For example, we can deduce from the molecular composition of H_2O certain properties or features, such as solidity or liquidity at a given temperature. However, no necessary connection exists between the physical body and the mind. No matter how much we know about the brain, we could never deduce from our understanding of it a single predicate of the mind.

The problem with a physicalist notion of consciousness is that not everything can be explained by this view of the mind–body relationship – every action of the mind cannot be explained fully by an identical movement in the brain. It is this missing knowledge that constitutes the core of consciousness. Consciousness under this conceptualisation is more than what we already know about the mind and the brain, and more than we can literally ever know. Nagel (1974) in his famous essay on bat consciousness asked the question: What is it like to be a bat? Even if we knew everything physical there is to know about a bat, it would still leave us in a state of ignorance about one key aspect of consciousness: what it is like to be a bat. Even if we used our imagination, we would still not understand the bat's subjective or first-person point of view. If this is correct, then any physicalist theory (and there are many of them) is inherently flawed. Consciousness is thus too complicated to explain through the methods of physicalism or neurophysiology.[144]

---

[144] A friend of mine recently remarked that neurophysiological approaches and methods held out the possibility of fully understanding how the brain works and thus for him how the mind works. My argument here, and it is long and complicated (it has taken up most of the book so far), would suggest that he may have a long time to wait, and even then, any answers that are given to this philosophical problem may prove to be unsatisfactory.

Two issues are relevant here to learning. The first is that there is a real sense of intention behind every act of learning, and the second is that the missing ingredient in consciousness is this sense that each and every learning act is intentional and that this constitutes it as a conscious act. This is an essential part of the general theory that I am attempting to formulate in this book.

10
The general theory

In this chapter I set out the general theory within which I am positioning the concept and practice of learning. Theory or theorising is a concept. Thus, in line with the argument that I have set out in this book so far, *theory* should be understood as an acquired disposition, so that as a concept it takes the form of *theorising*. Theory is not just a type of propositional knowledge, but an active, engaged and committed activity in the world. Again, as Wittgenstein proposed, in the first instance we should 'call to mind the *kinds of statement* that we make about phenomena' (Wittgenstein, 1953: §90, his italics). Any and every methodological approach that I adopt in this book points to the possibilities and, as importantly, limitations, of a word, word-set or linguistically structured concept, such as theorising(s), with the purpose of determining meaning.

There are different meanings that can be attached to and inhere in the word-object of theorising, and the list is long and varied.[145] For example, Theory$_1$ understands the concept of theorising as a set of tentative hypotheses about the relations between objects in the world and about the types of relations that inhere in a discursive configuration. Theory$_2$ suggests that this concept might consist of a set of hypotheses about the past, present and future behaviour of a configuration, that is, whether this theory comprehensively applies to all of those cases that are relevant in the past, in the present and in the future; in other words, it refers to all of the possible cases that have been and could be. A third possible interpretation (Theory$_3$) is that it is an account of a configuration of objects, which is underpinned by meta-theoretical constructs that can

---

[145] Theory also has a sense of incompleteness. It is used as a way of indicating that what is being proposed is tentative, needs to be corrected and is only a first attempt at explaining something. This is a common use.

successfully be used in relation to past, present-past and future cases. Another possibility (Theory$_4$) is that it is a set of truth-bearing propositions – the theory of truth that is subscribed to here is simpliciter coherentist or rationalist or empiricist or logical. And given that, in chapter 1, I argued that there needs to be some form of reconciliation between these judgemental criteria, a fifth possibility (Theory$_5$) is that a theory is a set of abstract truth-bearing propositions that successfully fuses coherentist, rationalist, empiricist and logical criteria.[146]

In distinguishing between different semantic conceptualisations of theorising, I am engaging in a theoretical exercise – I am using a theory and I am theorising. And thus, I need to continue with my long list of possibilities that inhere in the concept. Theory$_6$ is where a general sense can be given to a set of relationships between a series of propositions or to a logically connected system of general propositions, which allows us to say something about an activity, event or discursive object-configuration in the world. Theory$_7$ is an explanation of a phenomenon, where this phenomenon presents itself in the world as an object, object-relation, object-configuration, person or set of persons. An example might be the referendum vote in 2016 in the UK and the intention here would be to theorise about its cause or causes and what factors might be included in the theory that one is trying to develop. Theory$_8$ offers an original interpretation or reading of an aspect or aspects of the world and is located in and is about the past or the present-past (see chapter 20). Theory$_9$ has a different focus to Theory$_6$, Theory$_7$ and Theory$_8$, in that it points to the making of an interpretation, a reading, an exegesis, a critique, or a hermeneutical reconstruction of a text produced by someone else, and this text or texts has a sense of being in the past or present-past. Theory$_{10}$ is a *Weltanschauung*,[147] or a unique worldview, held by a community in place and time. Heidegger's (1962) notion of enframing has this meaning, as does the injunction that all events, empirical happenings and life workings are enframed in some way or another. This type of theory or theorising brings it closer to the sense that I have used in this book – that of meta-theorising or using transcendental notions such as truth and knowledge.

Theory$_{11}$ invokes the argument that a normative position underpins any and every aspect of the lifeworld and the way in which we can describe it. For example, history can be written from a Marxist

---

[146] In this book I have not proposed a means of combining these four criteria, although one method, employed by Haack (1993), is to reconfigure the various processes through elimination and reformation so that one criterion emerges, foundherentism.

[147] From the German word-complex *Welt* or 'world' and *Anschauung* or 'view'.

perspective[148] or from a feminist perspective,[149] and both of these can be designated as theory. Four additional meanings can be given to the notion of a theory or what one is doing when one theorises, and these are essentially epistemological. The first of these (Theory$_{12}$) is where the construct is abstract, discursive and meta-theoretical as opposed to empirical. The second (Theory$_{13}$) is general as opposed to particular, so that the particular is not thought of as theoretical, whereas the general is. The third meaning (Theory$_{14}$) that can be given is to contrast the contemplative with the practical – where once again the practical is not thought of as theoretical but the contemplative is. Finally, there is a functionalist sense (Theory$_{15}$) where the exegetical is contrasted with the heuristic, and the former is designated as theoretical while the latter is non-theoretical. And there are many more.

Theory or theorising has a stratificational orientation and consequently it can refer to different strata of the lifeworld: the psychological level; the autobiographical level; the ordinary level of the lifeworld; the functional level at which we are concerned with roles such as capitalist and worker or shop owner and customer; the structural level; the mega level of whole traditions and civilisations; and finally the cosmological level where the person's immediate concerns are with the planet as a whole.[150] The question then becomes: which of these uses of the concept of theorising makes better sense in relation to the world as it is presently constituted? This general theory of objects and object-relations is an attempt at answering this question. An initial step might be to examine two constructs that are generally thought of as theories, Maynard Keynes' *General Theory of Employment, Interest and Money* and Albert Einstein's *General Theory of Relativity*.

Keynes' general theory

Maynard Keynes' (1936) *General Theory of Employment, Interest and Money* suggests that in times of economic depression, governments should put in place measures to increase consumer demand and this will lead to enhanced economic growth.[151] In times of economic expansion, however, governments should put in place measures to reduce or

---

[148] For example, Hobsbawm (1988).
[149] For example, Pedersen (1993).
[150] cf. Bhaskar (2011).
[151] cf. Skidelsky (2013).

stabilise demand and growth. Keynes believed that consumer demand and all that it is related to is the driving force of an economy in all and every socioeconomic set of circumstances – in the past, in the present-past and in every circumstance that will occur but has not yet happened. This focus on consumer demand manifests itself in supporting an expansionary fiscal policy because government spending has an effect on: infrastructure (building and creating the means for socioeconomic expansion); on rates of unemployment (the fewer people out of work, the greater resource there is for other spending projects, and an expanded workforce in this set of circumstances contributes to economic growth); and on education (a better-educated and skilled workforce contributes to the possibility of further economic growth in the future). It may also lead to inflationary pressures, although as we can see from the current Covid-19 crisis and the UK government's implementation of fiscal expansionary measures, circumstances may mean that inflation does not occur (for example, the low cost of oil, the reduced use of energy sources and reductions in the cost of raw materials).

What should concern us here is the future behaviour of a number of mechanisms (price ratios, consumer demand, imported costs of materials) in a particular set of circumstances. If the theory works and can be shown to work in every possible circumstance, then it is a general and not special theory. Keynes' theory was developed in the 1930s after governments round the world failed to implement economic policies to end the Great Depression, and indeed the USA employed Keynesian economics to develop its New Deal programme; for example, the President, Franklin D. Roosevelt, as a response to the depression, increased the debt by $3 million and instituted programmes such as the Works Progress Administration to create 8.5 million jobs.

Government spending, even if it came from borrowing rather than taxation, was considered to be the most important factor in increasing aggregate demand and, in addition, it was an important spur to maintaining full employment. In contrast to classical theories of economics being propagated at this time, Keynesian economics argued for government spending on infrastructure and unemployment benefits, because the unemployed could have a role in increasing demand and thus contribute to the expansion of the economy, which would lead to more jobs. This was opposed to the idea that in times of depression, at the bottom of the business cycle, attention should be given to supporting business activity in the private sector, and that governments should play a limited role in the recovery and focus their efforts on companies rather than consumers.

Classical economic theorists argued that government interference in the economy was counterproductive and that markets should be allowed to operate through the supply and demand mechanism, even in an economic downturn. Eventually the business cycle would revert back to conditions of boom and expansion. They argued for a large private sector, which should be allowed to own the mechanisms that lead to growth: entrepreneurship, capital goods, including capitalisation, natural resources and labour. The principle is that successful economic practices should be allowed to develop ways of working that maximise profits. Classical economics,[152] in contrast to Keynesian economics, advocated a limited role for governments. Too much government spending restricts private investment, especially when the economy is doing well. Monetarists claim that monetary policy and not fiscal policy is the real expansionary driver of an economy, and that, anyway, trickle-down economics will in the end benefit everyone.

One of the components of the general theory is the Keynesian multiplier.[153] This is a measure of how much demand is created through government spending. So, Keynes suggested that £1 of government spending creates £1 of increase in gross domestic product (GDP), a multiplier of 1, in times of depression. Because government spending is a component of GDP, it must have this impact, and perhaps more than this. Likewise, a cut in government spending has at least the possibility of resulting in a 1-to-1 reduction in GDP. The general theory described here then can be called general because it applies in all circumstances, including the world economic depression caused by the spread of the Covid-19 virus in the 2020s.

Einstein's theory of relativity

In a similar fashion, Albert Einstein's theory of relativity comprised both a special theory and a general theory, and this mirrors Keynes' special theory of employment, interest and money, and his general theory.[154] The difference between a general theory and a special theory is that the latter

---

[152] Adam Smith and David Ricardo are examples of classical economists.

[153] At the time when Keynes proposed the multiplier, it was heavily criticised for its false sense of precision, and for other reasons.

[154] Both Keynes and Einstein were criticised at the time of publication for not making the distinction between a special and a general theory clear enough; cf. Howard and Giovanelli (2019).

can be applied only to a specific set of cases and circumstances, whereas a general theory can be applied to all of the possible cases that have already occurred, that are in the dimension of time that I am calling the present-past, and that, perhaps most significantly, have a bearing on the future. Special relativity is a theory or theoretical construct that attempts to explain how *spacetime* works. Einstein first developed it in his paper (originally published in 1905, republished in Einstein, 1923), 'On the Electrodynamics of Moving Bodies'. There are two underlying postulates of this theory. The first is that the laws of physics, as laid down by Isaac Newton, are equivalent for everyone in any inertial frame of reference relative to each other; and the second is that the speed of light in the particular circumstance of a vacuum is equivalent for everyone, regardless of their relative motion or of the motion of the light source. What this means is that two events experienced by an observer may not be operating in the same timeframe for another observer if they are in different motion settings. In addition, objects are shortened in their direction in relation to someone who is observing them. Maximum speed is finite, and mass and energy are equivalent and transmutable.

Einstein's general theory of relativity was developed between the years 1907 and 1915 and published in 1920 (reprinted in Einstein, 2010). An underlying principle is that states of accelerated motion and stasis in a gravitational field are in all respects the same. Free fall under this conception becomes equivalent to inertial motion, and things do not only fall because of gravity, as classical theories of physics and mechanics suggested they did. Einstein's initial response to this and to his postulate in the special theory – this was in effect a correction to it – was to suggest that spacetime is curved. He developed this further to incorporate a relation between the curvature of spacetime and mass, energy and internal momentum. Some of the consequences of his general theory are gravitational time dilation, orbital precessions, rays of light bending in a gravitational field, rotating masses exerting a force on spacetime, and the metric expansion of space. Both the special theory and the general theory described here operate as epistemological constructs and not ontological ones, although there is a sense in which all epistemologies are a subset of ontology, because they have substance and are potentially causally efficacious. However, they exist outside of the physical universe and are attempts to make sense of it. In order to bring the discussion closer to my principal concerns in this book, I need to show how theorising is relevant to two important issues: causation and learning.

A general theory of causation

Causality[155] can be understood in the same way as employment, interest and money or relativity. As I discussed at length in chapter 4, in a generative-productive model (Theory$_a$), causality is understood as a property of objects, and this has implications for how we should act, and whether it is possible and appropriate to use descriptions of current learning environments as a basis for predictions about future ones. Scientific empiricists and statistical positivists ordinarily subscribe to a Humean theory of causality as spatiotemporal contiguity, succession and constant conjunction (Theory$_b$), and this is founded on the idea that relations between events are associational and not directly causal, although the claim is then made that one can infer a causal relation from a persistent association.

Another theory of causality (Theory$_c$) is that there are only apparent regularities, and therefore what is understood as a causal relationship – a first event has led to a second event on every occasion on which they have interacted – is a product of chance. A more radical solution, then, is to argue that there are different types of causes (Theory$_d$) and they are different in kind because they operate in different ways; a person with a reason for doing something that also causes him to do it, such as painting the walls of the sitting room, is different from that person not being able to go outside his house because the door to the garden is locked. This type of causal sequence is different from a causal sequence (Theory$_a$) in which an object with its potential powers and liabilities comes into contact with another object, which both triggers a change in these objects and creates a new object with new powers and liabilities.

A fifth theory is that the world is not random but is caused (Theory$_e$) – the universe is a closed system of objects, and this includes the actions of individual human beings. These objects have causal powers that may or may not be activated, and, if they are activated, they behave mechanically, so that when an object comes into contact with another object, then a new object is formed, and this is what constitutes a causal sequence. It takes place regardless of whether it can be or is described or theorised about, and therefore notions of probability are not relevant at this level of explanation. The important point to note about this model is that human intentionality is ignored or peripheralised. One substance in

---

[155] My preferred version of causality works better in the social domain than in the physical domain.

conjunction with another substance necessarily causes a new substance to be formed. This ineluctably implies determinism and necessity.

Theory$_f$ is different, and is predicated on the idea that reasons can be and are causes; however, this needs to be qualified by the adoption of a further supposition, which is that reasons are not causes in the same way that events have antecedent conditions which necessarily have to be present for that event to take place. A final theory (Theory$_g$) is that events are caused but can only be known retrospectively. However, we can take this theory one stage further and suggest a generative/productive view of causation (back to Theory$_a$). We can hypothesise a relationship and then try to work out what the mechanism might be – an object has causal powers to induce change in another object, these powers may or may not be exercised and, even if they are, there is no guarantee that change will occur in the object, and this means that we cannot safely predict how the dynamic object in the future will behave. This applies to learning, as a theory.

A general theory of learning

The concept of learning is potentially polysemic and can be understood only in relation to how it is used in the world. A key determination of the meaning of this concept is whether and in what way it relates to a meta-theory, which invokes a relation between mind and world, and which has transcendental elements. Earlier I suggested that concepts cannot be fully determined with regards to their meaning in definitional and essentialising ways, but only in terms of how they are used in a way of life (see chapter 1). I then argued that a distinction could be made between knowledge of the world and meta-knowledge, which refers directly to knowledge of this world and not to the world itself. And further to this, all knowledge, including knowledge of learning, is in part constituted by criteria of excellence, whether these criteria are implicit or explicit.

As I argued in chapter 1, learning as a process has a set of pedagogic relations – it incorporates a relationship between a learner and a learning object. A theory of learning pivots on the idea that there is an entity called, for the sake of convenience, a human being, and this entity has a relationship (both inward and outward) with an environment. Knowledge and learning are homologous concepts. Knowledge is fundamental to the three types of learning that I have identified: cognitive, skill-based and embodied. Prior to each of these is a set of dispositions, without which cognitive, skill-based and embodied learning would be unsustainable. Acting in the world requires the use of, and is underpinned by, conceptual frameworks of one type or another. Propositional knowledge or making a claim that this or that is the case is, in common with the other two forms of knowledge, a process of doing and thus of knowing how to do something or other. And this results in all of these types of knowledge having the same general form, which allows them, in this form, to be understood as learning actions or acts of learning.

This learning theory is underpinned by a number of axioms. The first of these is that there is a logical connection between the learning object and its pedagogic form, and thus its learning mode. Theoretical and contextual considerations impact, then, on how elements of teaching and learning are realised. Acknowledging this allows the identification of a number of learning models; for example, observation, coaching, goal-clarification, peer-learning, trial and error, hypothesis-testing, reflection, meta-cognition and practice (see chapter 12 for a fuller explanation of these models). Choosing between these models depends on the nature and constitution of the learning object; in other words, the former is logically dependent on the latter. A second axiom is that boundaries and categories used at the discipline or domain level, temporary as they are, cannot be translated, without serious distortion, into organisational principles for the development of a learning programme. And a third axiom is that this work is enframed in epistemological, ontological and relational arrangements.

In this part of the book, I have focused on a number of important theoretical elements: what concepts are (see chapter 1), the relationship between knowledge and learning (see chapter 1), the possibility of universal knowledge (see chapter 2), excellence in a practice (see chapter 3), the nature of evidence (see chapter 4), epistemological and ontological concerns (see chapter 1), the role and place of values in our descriptions of the world and in the world itself (see chapter 5), the notion of difference (see chapter 6), different epistemic categories (see chapter 7), powerful practices (see chapter 8) and the possibility of consciousness (see chapter 9). In the second part of the book, my focus is learning as a concept and a practice.[156]

---

[156] And, in addition, the relationship between concept and practice is an important consideration.

Part Two
Learning as a concept and as a practice

The second part of this book focuses on the concept and practice of learning. Anything and everything that I say here about the concept and practice of learning is ineluctably underpinned by the general theory set out in the first part of this book. To reiterate: this general theory is an account of discursive objects, material objects, relational objects, structural-institutional-systemic objects and people (chapter 1), transcendental knowledge (chapter 2), judgements and criteria (chapter 3), objects and object-relations (chapter 4), ontic and epistemic values (chapter 5), difference (chapter 6), knowledge dualities (chapter 7), institutional and systemic power relations (chapter 8) and identity and consciousness (chapter 9). The book borrows ideas, insights and arguments from two seminal books by Ludwig Wittgenstein: *Philosophical Investigations* (1953) and *On Certainty* (1969). His work provides the inspiration for the general theory that I set out in the first part of this book and summarise in chapter 10, and his influence continues through this second part.

In this part I focus exclusively on learning in its two guises: as a concept and as a practice. These need to be analysed separately because they are different types of object, and what this also requires, then, is an explanation of how they are connected or how they can be connected at both ontological and epistemological levels. This key relation in the lifeworld is between the world itself and our knowledge of it. I start off by examining five important philosophies of learning: behaviourism, phenomenology, cognitivism, socioculturalism and socio-materialism (chapter 11). Theoretical and contextual considerations impact on how elements of teaching and learning are realised. Acknowledging this allows the construction of a number of learning models: observation, coaching, goal-clarification, peer-learning, trial and error, hypothesis-testing, reflection, meta-cognition and repetition. And each of these in turn is underpinned by a particular theory of learning. What this means is that any model of learning that is used in the world is constructed in relation to a particular view of how we can know the world and what it is. These models or learning sets give different emphases to the various elements of a learning process (chapter 12).

In chapters 13 and 14, I examine four important concepts that relate to learning: technology, artificial intelligence, literacy and numeracy, treating each of them in socially semiotic ways with regards to their meanings and their possibilities. A key dispute in the field of learning is whether learning is a concept and indeed whether a concept such as this is useful and meaningful. I suggest in chapter 15 that this is a false argument. In chapters 16 and 17, I examine two concepts that have a direct relationship with learning: progression and pedagogy, and this discussion allows me to develop the idea of a play-pedagogy. In chapter 18, I consider a particular theory of curriculum knowledge (cf. Young and Muller, 2007; 2010; Young, 2005). Despite its imperfections, it has been enormously influential. I suggest in this chapter that it is incorrect or at least imperfect in a philosophical sense. This leads on to the development of a history, archaeology and genealogy of learning and a discussion of some key episodes in these timeframes: learning processes relating to disengaged reasoning, curricularisation, scientism, atomisation, innatism, bureaucratisation, naturalism and representa-tionalism (chapter 19). I then focus on two of Kant's[157] universal categories as they relate to learning: time (chapter 20) and space (chapter 21).

I conclude the book with a brief discussion of doubting and certainty in knowledge, and consequently learning, and return to an examination of Wittgenstein's ideas and philosophies (chapter 22). This book is a rejoinder to: empiricist and positivist conceptions of knowledge; detheorised and reductionist conceptualisations of learning; regressive and degenerative notions of curriculum; the propagation of simple messages about learning, knowledge, curriculum and assessment; the employment of punitive forms of power in the management of people; the use of bureaucratic power mechanisms in new public management strategies; and the denial that values are central to understanding how we live and how we should live, with this valuing going all the way down – into our descriptions of the world, into those attempts we make at creating better futures and into our relations with other people.

---

[157] Kant (2007).

11
Philosophies of learning

Five theories of learning are examined in this chapter: behaviourism, phenomenology, cognitivism, socioculturalism and socio-materialism. These can be construed as framings or enframings of the concept of learning; however, they are not equally coherent, relevant or epistemically correct. The representational problem is also present here, since it is the dominant metaphor in behaviourist, cognitivist and socio-materialist theories of learning. In the last of these cases, representationalism is explicitly repudiated – this is the central argument made in its development as a theory of learning. However, by denying the possibility of both an agent and a referent in the process, this in itself means that the type of relation that constitutes the connection between mind and world can never be properly examined and given expression to (as an activity in the world).

As I suggested in chapter 1, a philosophy of learning has a number of elements: an account of a person, including her capacities and affordances, and the environments within which she is situated; an account of the relationship between a person and her environments; knowledge about understanding, learning and change, with regards to the person and the environments in which she is located; inferences from these premises and conclusions about appropriate object-appearances, media for these representations and learning environments; and a set of practical actions that emanate from these claims. There are many such philosophies.[158] I cannot examine all of them for reasons of space and

---

[158] Here are some more theories of learning: adult learning theory, algo-heuristic theory, anchored instruction, andragogy, aptitude-treatment interaction theory, attribution theory, cognitive dissonance theory, cognitive flexibility theory, cognitive load theory, component display theory, conditions of learning theory, connectionism, constructivist theory, contiguity theory, conversation theory, criterion referenced instruction, double loop learning, drive reduction theory, dual coding theory, elaboration theory, experiential learning, functional context theory, genetic epistemology,

time. So, as a proxy activity, I will provide brief accounts of the five most prominent ones: behaviourism, phenomenology, cognitivism, socioculturalism and socio-materialism. I need to do this because any act of learning, however insignificant and trivial it might seem to be, is enframed in various ways, and, in this chapter, I want to consider some of these enframings. At this stage in the argument that I am making in this book, I am unapologetically reintroducing the notion of correction, or at least the possibility of correction. The claim I am making therefore is that these five philosophies of learning are flawed (they do not meet the criteria I identified for determining truthful knowledge in chapters 1, 2 and 3), sometimes in a partial sense and sometimes in their entirety. The first philosophy that I want to consider is behaviourism.

Behaviourism

Behaviourism is a philosophical theory that has been used within the discipline of education to provide an explanation for the play of social and educational objects in history. Behaviourists make three interrelated claims. The first is that if investigators are trying to understand the psychology of a particular human being, they should not be concerned with what is in this person's mind but with how she behaves.[159] The second claim is that human behaviours can be fully and comprehensively explained without recourse to any form of construct or event in the mind. The source of these behaviours is the environment and not the mind of the individual. And the third claim that behaviourists are likely to make, and which follows from the first two claims, is that if mind-specific terms are used as descriptors, then they should be replaced by behavioural terms, or, at least, those mind-dependent constructs should be translated into behavioural descriptors.

---

gestalt theory, general problem solver theory, information pickup theory, information processing theory, lateral thinking, levels of processing theory, mathematical learning theory, mathematical problem solving, minimalism, model-centred instruction and design layering, modes of learning, multiple intelligences theory, operant conditioning, originality theory, phenomenography, repair theory, script theory, sign theory, situated learning theory, social development theory, social learning theory, stimulus sampling theory, structural learning theory, structure of intellect theory, subsumption theory, symbol systems theory, triarchic theory and transformational learning. Some of these theories can be incorporated into the five overarching theories being considered in this chapter.

[159] John Watson (1930: 11), one of the originators of behaviourism, wrote as follows in relation to the purposes of investigating human behaviour: 'to predict, given the stimulus, what reaction will take place; or, given the reaction, state what the situation or stimulus is that has caused the reaction'.

Behaviourism has its roots in British empiricism and in particular in the associational theory of David Hume.[160] Observed or experimentally induced associations allow the investigator to uncover causal structures on the basis of processes of spatiotemporal contiguity, succession and constant conjunction. Learning is therefore understood as associational without recourse to states of or events in the mind, with an emphasis on the reinforcement histories of people. Any reference to experiences (especially if couched in the language of states of mind) should be replaced by observations of events in the environment; and references to thoughts, ideas or schemata should be replaced by references to overt observable behaviours and responses to stimuli.

Behaviourism as a theory of learning, then, suffers from a number of misconceptions. Because of its strictures against immaterial substances, and against agents endowed with the capacity to operate outside of embodied, socially derived or genetic causal impulses, it is now rarely thought of as a coherent or convincing theory of learning. A number of problems with it have been identified – perhaps the most important of these is the claim that a theory of human learning is flawed, in part or in its entirety, unless reference is made to non-behavioural states of mind. In particular, this refers to the way in which an individual represents the world, and how this is conditioned by institutional, systemic, embodied and discursive structures, stories, narratives, arguments and chronologies, and structures of agency.[161] A second reason for rejecting behaviourism is the existence of internal or inner processing activities. We feel, intuit, experience and are aware of our own inner states in the learning process. To reduce these phenomenal qualities to behaviours or dispositions to behave is to ignore the immediacy and instantaneous nature of those processes that condition learning. Finally, it has been suggested that reducing learning to individual reinforcement histories[162] is to develop an impoverished or incomplete theory, and consequently marginalise pre-existing structures, developed schemata, complex inner lives, prior representations, and structural enablements and constraints that allow learning to take place.

Behaviourist frameworks have implications for learning. The argument is made that positive reinforcement leads to the replication

---

[160] As I suggested earlier, Hume's theory of causation is associational and not generative-productive.

[161] By structures of agency I mean those material, discursive, configurational, relational and human constraints and enablements that act to shape the agential possibilities for the individual and collectivities of individuals during their life course.

[162] The obvious example of a theory such as this is operant conditioning theory (Skinner, 1953).

of desired behaviours if the person comes to associate them with the receipt of rewards, such as merit marks or special privileges. Furthermore, knowledge is conceptualised in relation to the principles of behaviourism and as a result has a restricted content and form. Again, this has implications for the construction of learning programmes, curricula and learning environments, and indeed for wider issues such as identities, subjectivities and representational modes. Behaviourists use feedback – or in their terms, reinforcement – to modify behaviour. This is in contrast to cognitivists and sociocultural theorists who understand feedback as a guiding, supporting and strengthening mechanism to facilitate change within the conscious minds of learners.[163] The second of these educational philosophies that I want to consider is phenomenology.

Phenomenology

In contrast to behaviourist perspectives on learning, there are phenomenological approaches. Phenomenology is a meta-philosophy that focuses on the three key aspects of learning: the relationship of the individual to and with the world involving a process of change; the subsequent conception and activation of being in the world; and how our descriptions, words, schema and theories can provide us with some purchase on that world. The focus is on the givens of immediate experience, and phenomenology is an attempt to capture that experience as it is lived, both by the individual herself and the external observer. This knowledge-making activity is directed in the first instance to the things in themselves that are the objects of consciousness, and that try to find 'a first opening' (Merleau-Ponty, 1945) on the world, free of those presuppositions brought to any learning setting. This entails a learning methodology that foregrounds subjective experiences and understands them in their own terms, both linguistically and conceptually, while at the same time treating these two modes separately. This presupposes that the experience of others is accessible to us, even if with the greatest of difficulty. And this points to the break with behaviourism that phenomenologists generated. Whereas behaviourists are concerned above all with the behaviour of individuals and ignore the inner workings

---

[163] The issue of consciousness – what it is and how we can know what it is – is discussed in more detail in chapter 9.

of the mind, phenomenologists understand consciousness as essential to any theory of learning.

This is consciousness as it is experienced from a particular person's point of view. It is thus intentional or has intentionality – it is directed towards something such as an object in the world. It refers to how we experience objects in the world and the meanings things have in our experience, that is, the value of objects, the values given to objects in the world, the flow of time and evolving constructions of the self and events in the world; in short, the experiences we have in our lifeworlds. When we are conscious, we are conscious of something. For Edmund Husserl (1973),[164] the concern was with the experiences we have, and these include those experiences as they are framed through particular concepts, thoughts, ideas, images, and so on. They are mediated. There are also enabling conditions of intentionality, such as our embodiment, our cultural context, our language and much more.

Being conscious is uniquely about experiencing things in the world, living through them and performing them; characterised as the three stages of learning, these are: accessing objects in the world, internalising those objects and then externalising them. The internalisation process includes processes such as evaluation, reflection, familiarisation, recategorisation and reformulation. There is a time component in that when we are angry or joyful, the intensity of the experience is such that the reflective elements are either downplayed or postponed. What this means is that these reflective processes can take place at different time moments during the learning sequence and in different ways; so, for example, a learning action can be performed at the site of sensation or at the site of internalisation.

Husserl (1913) drew a sharp distinction between noesis and noema. Noesis refers to the intentional element of consciousness; noema refers to what the intention is directed towards. Phenomenological analyses of our desires, intentional states and actions always involve a consciousness of or about something, usually an object in the world, with this being a semantic activity. Husserl advocated the method of epoché (bracketing out the natural world around us), with the intentional act of consciousness being conducted without reference to the object. Consequently, this becomes a highly artificial process. Martin Heidegger (1962) disagreed

---

[164] Edmund Husserl is sometimes cited as the founder of phenomenology. Regardless of whether he was or not, much of what he argued for has been criticised by philosophers such as Jean-Paul Sartre and Martin Heidegger, although both are sympathetic to some of his basic tenets, such as intentionality and volition.

with this notion of bracketing out the world from our investigations, and in particular our investigations into the conceptual framing of that world, because *being (Dasein)* is always in the world and thus requires a methodology that takes account of this. He understood our relations with the world as being essentially practical, and certainly not enframed by a representationalist epistemology. Intentionality is a process of meaning-making and a typical act of consciousness is enframed, which means that it has a background of meaning – in place and time, political, social and epistemological. These various phenomenological perspectives have contributed to a distinctive theory of learning.

Phenomenological approaches, then, reconceptualise the pedagogic relationship so that learning is now understood as a responsible, precarious and uncertain relationship between the teacher and the learner, and fundamentally as an unplanned and personal existential experience. What this means is that phenomenologists support a different conception of pedagogic relations from those embedded in preformed curricula, standardised learning programmes and summative forms of assessment and control. Feedback mechanisms are understood as those mechanisms that are used to support pedagogical relationships and that allow the learner to uniquely realise her potential (although there are serious philosophical problems with this notion[165] – see chapter 16), without specifying in advance, or throughout the process, what that potential is. Potentiality is a difficult notion to make sense of, and it has been used as the prime signifier in eugenic notions of education, intelligence and learning. The third philosophy is cognitivism.

Cognitive theories of knowledge

Cognitive theories of knowledge[166] focus on structures and processes in the mind, and on internal representations of reality by the learner.

---

[165] Potentiality can be understood as an inbuilt and mind-dependent ceiling for certain human attributes. The example I have used in this book is intelligence, where some people have a greater capacity for performing in the world than other people, and this is either genetically endowed or socially determined. In the latter case, this capacity relates to what the individual has learnt so far in her life; in the former case, it relates to an inherited characteristic, which cannot be changed during the life course. Geneticists, eugenicists and the like have exploited this idea and, in addition, the idea itself is conceptually and empirically flawed.

[166] Albert Bandura (1977), in his social cognitive theory of learning, identified three basic models of observational learning: i) a live model involving an actual individual demonstrating or acting out a behaviour; ii) a verbal instructional model involving descriptions and explanations of particular behaviours; iii) a symbolic model involving real or fictional characters displaying particular types of behaviours. This learning model has been extensively criticised by sociologists and philosophers alike, though it still has some credence among social psychologists.

Knowledge therefore has both external and internal referents. The central issues that interest cognitivists are the internal mechanisms of human thought and the processes of knowing. They are concerned to find answers to questions such as what and how knowledge is stored, and how the integration and retrieval of information operates. Many of these ideas and assumptions (perhaps formally expressed, and in philosophical terms understood, as representationalist) can be traced back to the early decades of the twentieth century – for example, to the cognitive learning theory of Edward Tolman (1932)[167] or Jean Piaget's (1962) cognitive development theory.[168] These theories of learning identify the basic mechanisms of learning in terms of stages, and the representation and storage of information.

Jean Piaget suggested that there are a number of interactive learning mechanisms located between the stimulus and the person. The first of these is accumulation; this is where there is little schematic formation in the individual (usually due to age) and learning consists of recall and applications in situations that are similar to those in which the knowledge was originally received. The second is assimilation; this is where a new element has to be addressed and made sense of by the individual, but this process is still essentially passive. The new elements are easily absorbed, indeed assimilated, into the existing schema of the individual. The third element is accommodation; this is where the new element does not and cannot fit the new schema and thus a process of transformation of both takes place, involving the original stimulus or object of learning and the schema that is attempting some form of accommodation with it. In Piaget's terms, it has been internalised.

Piaget (1962) proposed that children and young learners progress through an invariant sequence of four stages: sensorimotor, pre-operational, concrete operational and formal operational. Those stages reflect differences in children's cognitive abilities. The learning process is therefore iterative, with new information being shaped to fit the learner's existing knowledge, and existing knowledge itself being modified to accommodate the new information. Piaget's theory has a variety of implications for learning and instruction, such as that the learning environment should support the activities of the learner. Learners acquire knowledge through their actions. As a result, a learning

---

[167] Tolman (1932) used experimental (animal-based) methods to determine understandings of human behaviours.

[168] cf. Donaldson (1978) for a thorough and convincing critique of Piaget's theories of child development. She provides a plethora of reasons for suggesting that there are errors in his approach and in helping children move beyond egocentric thought.

environment is created that encourages learners to initiate and complete their own activities. This is an active, discovery-oriented environment. Feedback is considered to be an essential requirement for the actions of the learner, and this relates fundamentally to future learning experiences. In addition, learners' interactions with their peers are an important source of cognitive development – peer interactions are essential in helping children move beyond egocentric thought.[169]

Learners need to adopt instructional strategies that make them aware of conflicts and inconsistencies in their thinking; they must experience disequilibrium, or an imbalance between their current cognitive structures and the new information to be assimilated, in order to move to a new stage of development or to a state of equilibration. Content is not introduced until the learner is cognitively ready to receive it. As a result, the instructional design focuses on the development of a method to facilitate the process of organising schematic structures, and to make meaningful connections between what the learner already knows and the learning object. Feedback mechanisms in cognitivist terms are understood as corrective, with the expert or teacher engaged in providing information to the passive recipient. In contrast, facilitative feedback is more closely associated with a socio-constructivist viewpoint, where feedback is understood as a dialogic process that takes place within a learning environment to help learners gain new understandings, without determining what those understandings are. The fourth of these philosophies is constructivism.

Constructivist theories of learning

A particular iteration of sociocultural or constructivist theories is cultural-historical activity theory. That there is now a three-generation model of cultural-historical activity theory is part of its formation as an established theory. This and each generation of activity theory can be understood in two distinct ways. The first is in terms of its historical trajectory, so it is possible to understand Lev Vygotsky's (1978) theory of mediation as a reaction against what it emerged from – it sought to replace the stimulus-response model of the behaviourists; or it can be understood as an attempt to frame the concept as a universalising category. Both of these explanations have meta-theoretical and thus universalising elements – insofar as the first requires a theory of history

---

[169] cf. McLeod (2018).

and the second requires a theory of social psychology – but these universalising elements are framed in different ways.

Lev Vygotsky (1993) inspired the first iteration of cultural-historical activity theory, and as its centrepiece positioned the well-known triangular model of subject, object and mediating artefact. When people engage in a learning activity (and in a sense this constitutes the principal activity of consciousness), they do so by interacting with the material world around them (although here the material world is embodied, structured and discursive). What they are doing is entering into a social practice, which is mediated by artefacts. This needs to be qualified in two ways: there cannot be an unmediated practice – so, for example, a discursive practice cannot be atheoretic – and as a consequence it is not possible to have direct access to the practice itself; indeed, it is difficult to understand the idea of a practice that is separate from the way it is mediated for us. Vygotsky (1978) therefore suggested that artefacts, such as physical tools, technologies or social norms, mediate relations between people and the environment. This in turn led him to a preoccupation with the notion of meaning and thus to the development of a notion of semiotic mediation, and in particular to a rejection of the behaviourist paradigm, which posits a passive object-to-subject relationship.

Learning can be seen as adaptive rather than transformative, and Vygotsky's (1978) work has always been associated with the latter rather than the former. However, the notions of adaptation and transformation are complex. The idea of adaptation would suggest that what is learnt conforms to those sets of behaviours, norms and strategies that constitute the social world, and which are external to the learner. The learner enters into a state of equilibrium, so that what is inside the mind of the learner (this changes) is now synchronised with what is outside the mind of the learner (which has not undergone any change at all). On the other hand, a transformative approach would suggest that both the mind of the learner and the object in the environment have changed. What this implies is not that one theory is misguided and should be replaced by another – a better account of a practice – but that there is a need to build into the theory being developed the possibility that some learning is adaptive and some is transformative.

Four issues are of concern here. The first relates to whether meaning resides in the object itself or is created in conjunction with or through the interaction between subject and object. The second relates to the idealist tendencies in Vygotsky's thought and the potential they have for misappropriation and misrepresentation. The third issue is that all of these mediating devices are expected to work in the same way, even though they have different grammars and constitutions. And what follows from this, specifically in relation to learning, is that it is hard to believe that every interaction has an equal possibility of influencing and thus changing the zeitgeist or at least the learning environment. For Vygotsky (1978), the focus of his analysis was tool mediation and the activity system where these mediations occurred, rather than focusing on the individual per se. However, what is being suggested here is that this activity can be transformational both for the system (or learning environment) and for the individual, but not in every circumstance.

The second generation of cultural historical activity theory is usually, though not necessarily, associated with the development of the original theory by Alexei Leontiev (1978) and, in particular, with his elaboration of the concept of activity, with a distinction now being drawn between an action and an activity. An action is said to be motivated by the intention of the person – the person has an object or objective in mind; an activity is understood as undertaken by a community and thus has some of the characteristics of that community: a division of labour, various means of production and so forth. This still leaves many unanswered questions about both the mind–world relation and the way in which both of these and the relationship between them is transformed.

Five principles underpin the third iteration of cultural-historical activity theory (cf. Engeström, 2001). The first principle is that the activity system is central to the process of learning: with that activity system being collective, artefact-mediated, object-orientated and networked with other activity systems. This constitutes the primary focus of analysis. The second principle emphasises the way in which the activity system is stratified, historicised (traces of other human activity are present) and multiply layered. The third principle is that activity systems are in a state of constant flux and thus are transformed as they are shaped. The fourth principle is that a notion of contradiction is central to the transformation of the activity system. These contradictions are both internal and external to the activity system under examination. The fifth principle suggests that activity systems move through long cycles of change, as the internal and external contradictions lead to and indeed cause individual and collective changes.[170]

---

[170] For Engeström, contradiction is at the heart of the transformation of the activity system. These contradictions are both internal and external to the activity system being examined, and, as Engeström (2001: 137) reminds us, they are 'not the same as problems or conflicts. Contradictions are historically accumulating structural tensions within and between activity systems ... Activities are open systems. When an activity system adopts a new element from the outside ... it often leads to an aggravated secondary contradiction where some old element ... collides with the new one. Such contradictions generate disturbances and conflicts, but also innovative attempts to change the activity.'

Vygotsky's central arguments about development and instruction have a number of implications. Cognitive development is better achieved through the use of dialogic pedagogies, in which the learner develops her ideas and understandings in discussion with her teachers and peers. This means that learning progresses better when the learning objects are scaffolded by a learning expert or at least by someone with more experience of the learning object and the learning process than the learner. In addition, learners need to be given tasks that are focused on what is developing within their minds rather than in relation to knowledge already developed, and they need to develop conscious mastery of the learning objects rather than reciting facts that may have little meaning for them. The development of principled knowledge is not subject-specific, but involves general principles of learning, such as that it is important not to teach something until the learner is able and ready to make sense of it. Programmes for learners should not be limited or constrained by the use of diagnostic or summative forms of assessment or by learning environments that do not allow help and support from teachers, parents and other students. The knowledge framework that structures the learning experience is understood as propositional, skill-based, embodied and dispositional, and is socially conceived both in origin and in individual development. As a result, arrangements within the learning environment need to be made that allow collaboration, collaborative learning, flexible learning and meta-forms of learning. This pedagogy involves a rejection of strong insulations between different types of students and is in opposition to essentialist notions of intelligence and ability. In addition, feedback mechanisms from a socio-constructivist viewpoint are understood as facilitative, with feedback seen as a process that takes place within a learning context involving a dialogue between the teacher and the learner to help the learner gain new understandings. We also need to consider post-human, actor-network and complexity philosophies of learning.

Post-human, actor-network and complexity theories of learning

What distinguishes a complexity theory of learning from conventional theories is the different focuses of researchers and investigators, so that it is now the flows and relations between objects rather than the objects themselves that are the focus of attention. Society is characterised by notions of continuous emergence, flux and change, which though non-predictive, can be adequately captured in language. Objects in the world cannot be characterised by their essential qualities, but only through their interactions with other objects. Complexity resides in all of these various interactions that produce new objects (characterised as different forms of structure), which results in complicated arrangements of material and human objects and object-relations, and, because they are difficult to characterise, rarely allow definitive accounts of what is going on to be produced. It is the complexity of these object-interactions and their subsequent and temporary coalescences that makes it difficult to provide complete descriptions of them. The epistemic level is unsynchronised with the ontological level because researchers and investigators have not sufficiently developed their instruments and conceptual schema for capturing something that is both ever-changing and has too many elements to it – it is too complex. However, this does not categorically rule out the possibility of providing more complete descriptions of events, structures, mechanisms and their relations in the world, and this suggests a notion of human fallibility that means our actions (which correspond to learning episodes) are corrigible. The twin elements of complexity and temporal emergence (where systemic formations are understood as not incommensurable) do not rule out correct descriptions being made of activities in the world, only that these elements can create considerable difficulties.

Many of these theorists go further than this and hold to a version of emergence in which there is a radical incommensurability between different formations over time (whether material, embodied or discursive). Furthermore, it is impossible to predict what interconnections, new formations and iterations of the object-system will be realised because the principles of the new mechanism are not given in the current arrangements. In other words, the relations between objects, and the objects that make up activity systems, are not patterned in any meaningful sense – there is a radical incommensurability between these different iterations. What this also suggests is that any attempt to describe even the basic outline of the system and the way it works is incompatible with this idea of radical incommensurability.

It is possible to focus on the formations, but not on the way they were formed. This operates at the ontological level. Although one formation, it is acknowledged, has emerged from a concatenation of others (prior to it in time), this process cannot be codified or captured symbolically (using words, numbers or pictures) except by using words such as 'chance', 'non-linearity' or 'non-predictability'. However, each of these is contested conceptually. Because something is non-predictable at the time it operates does not mean that it cannot be described after it has happened – a post-hoc theorisation of the object or arrangement. Non-linearity implies that the sequence of events has not followed the accepted pattern whether this has been deduced from previous occurrences or from logical and normative investigations. Chance, by virtue of what it is, precludes a causal explanation of it.

Actor-network theorists[171] (Latour, 1991, for example) argue for a symmetricality of human and non-human elements, which means that at the level of analysis they should be treated in the same way. This has the effect of marginalising the hermeneutic dimension of learning and fits better with a structuralist or materialist ontology. The intention is to understand history not as the outcomes of originary actions by individuals or collectivities of individuals, but as sets of material objects (human and non-human) coalescing and working together. It is the networks, confluences and collective action-sets that produce the conditions of action. What follows from this is that the contents of these networks and the inevitability of flux and change as essential elements are likely to mean that our descriptions of them are incomplete and fragmentary. However, what applies to the networks and assemblages themselves and to the relations between them also applies to the meta-theory itself. Thus notions of symmetry, translation, problematisation, interessement, immutable mobility, delegation, multiple-perspectivism and actor-networking (all terms used by Bruno Latour, 1991; Michael Callon, 1991; and John Law and John Hassard, 1999) should be understood as incomplete and undeveloped as the theorist tries to plot what is happening and what has happened.

Actor-network theorising cannot, then, amount to an argument in favour of social patterning or systemic predictability. Actor-network theorists have argued against treating those traditional educational constructs and forms – such as curriculum, learning, leadership, management, and standards – as stable, expressing their opposition to the conventional understandings of these terms by pointing to the emergent and unstable ontology of material, discursive and human

---

[171] Fenwick and Edwards (2010: 9) suggest that: 'Actor Network Theory's (ANT) unique contribution is first, to focus on the individual nodes holding these networks together, examining how these connections came about and what sustains them. These include negotiations, forces, resistances and exclusions, which are at play in these micro-interactions that eventually forge links. Second ... Actor Network Theory (ANT) accepts nothing as given, including 'humanity', 'the social', 'subjectivity', 'mind', 'the local', 'structures' and other categories common in educational analyses. What we usually take to be unitary objects with properties are understood as assemblages, built of heterogeneous human and non-human things, connected and mobilised to act together through a great deal of ongoing work.'

objects, and the need to move away from prioritising intentionality and therefore human agency over other objects in the world. This creates a particular aporia in the theory of actor-networking, for which the notion of the actant is barely able to compensate. By disprivileging the agential and giving it equal status to other objects, actor-network theorists are making a point about what happens in the world. They are implicitly if not explicitly arguing not just that as theorists they should foreground something other than human agency – the relations between different networks of human and non-human material objects – but that this allows a better purchase on the world than theories that privilege an essentialised version of the human being and their relations. What actor-network theory essentially does is dissolve the boundary between material and human objects; to, in a sense, argue that there are no real differences between them, with the effect of discounting ideas of distinctively human characteristics, such as intentions and the capacity to operate in the space of reasons.

This sense of agency, structured in different spatial and temporal ways, allows and conditions the various acts of learning. In characterising the field, I have been concerned with epistemic differences between the principal theories of learning, and therefore inevitably with the strength, probative force and attached value given to those relations and entities. This is the way the field is constructed. There are two implications of this. The first is that because the field has been constructed in a particular way, this does not then preclude choices being made between these different theories. And second, these choices are underpinned by a particular theory of knowledge, which also has implications for the development of a theory of learning in which knowledge plays an important part. My attention now shifts to how learners learn, what the role of learning environments might be and how what is intended determines how it should be learnt. In the next chapter I pursue these strands of the argument – the task as it has been throughout is to examine the boundaries between different objects and different object-formations in the world.

12
Learning theories and models

Theoretical and contextual considerations impact, then, on how elements of teaching and learning are realised. Acknowledging this allows the realisation of a number of learning models: observation, coaching, goal-clarification, peer-learning, trial and error, hypothesis-testing, reflection, meta-cognition and practice. And each of these in turn is underpinned by a particular theory of learning. What this means is that any model of learning that is employed is constructed in relation to particular views of how we can know the world and what it is. These models or learning sets and their properties give different emphases to the various elements of a learning process.

A first type is an observational model (cf. Bandura, 1977). There are three types of teacher-led stimuli: acting out the behaviours to be learnt; describing and explaining a set of behaviours; and offering up a set of scenarios and expressive performances. The learning process consists of the following: observing a performance by the teacher; comparing this performance with an embodied form of that display already held by the learner; adjusting what they currently have through modification or substitution; practising while being supported within the artificial environment; practising without support within the artificial environment; transferring the skill to the real environment while being supported; and consolidating without support through using it in this real environment. This model is underpinned by a cognitivist theory of learning.[172]

A second type is a coaching model. Here the focus is on a series of steps: modelling by the expert, coaching while the learner practices,

---

[172] Bandura (1977: 43) suggested the following about learning by observation: 'Most human behaviour is learned observationally through modelling: from observing others, one forms an idea of how new behaviours are performed, and on later occasions this coded information serves as a guide for action.'

scaffolding where the learner is supported during the initial stages, with that support gradually being withdrawn as the learner becomes more proficient (coaching here involves the teacher in identifying deviations from the model in the performance of the learner, and then supporting the learner as he makes attempts to correct his mistakes), articulation by the learner of that process, reflecting on those processes by comparing them with the expert's reasons for action, and exploration where the learner undertakes the various activities without support. Coaching can be understood as a one-to-one activity, or as a collective exercise within a community of practice. This model better fits a sociocultural theory of learning.[173]

A third model involves the teacher clarifying and sharing learning intentions and criteria for success with the learner over a period of time. To this end, teachers provide learners with explicit statements and explanations about the instructional objectives in a lesson or series of lessons. Goal clarity has three elements: explanations about how learners are expected to undertake the tasks assigned to them; opportunities for them to grasp what is expected of them; and reflections about their capacity as self-directed learners in the completion of the tasks.[174]

A fourth model of learning is peer-learning. Here an assumption is made that the learning relationship is between equals. Examples of this type of learning include: being offered emotional support if learning proves to be difficult; confrontational exchanges between learners so that

---

[173] Muijs and Reynolds (2011: 80) suggest that: 'Coaching is a process of motivating learners, analysing their performance, and providing feedback on their performance. Great teachers help the pupils while they are solving problems independently or in a group, which will motivate and support them. One form of coaching is called cognitive coaching. Cognitive coaching is designed to make pupils more aware of their own thinking processes, which will help them to be more reflective about their learning. This will build up their problem-solving skills, by giving them tools they can use in a variety of situations. This type of coaching helps pupils think about the way they are solving problems. It involves them in self-reflection, internalising and generalising.'

[174] Again Muijs and Reynolds (2011: 39) explain one of the principles behind goal clarification, without seemingly being aware of its technicist orientation: 'The lesson should have a clear structure, so pupils can easily understand the content of the lesson and how it relates to what they already know. Many researchers recommend starting the lesson with a review and practice of what was learnt during the previous lesson, for example by going over homework, as this will allow the teacher to find out to what extent pupils have grasped the content of the previous lessons, and therefore to what extent this content will need to be retaught. The objectives of the lesson should be made clear to pupils from the outset ... During the lesson, the teacher needs to emphasise the key points of the lesson, which may otherwise get lost in the whole. A certain amount of repetition will certainly do no harm here. At the end of the lesson, the main points should once again be summarised, either by the teacher or, preferably, by the pupils themselves, such as through asking them what they have learnt during the lesson. Subparts of the lesson can usefully be summarised in the same way during the course of the lesson ... This emphasis on explaining the goals of the lesson – not just what was to be done during the lesson, but how that related to what pupils could learn longer term – was found to be typical of effective teachers ...'.

each individual can test his theories, ideas and constructs against those held by other learners engaging in the same type of learning; cooperation between two learners of roughly equal standing, so that in a problem-solving exercise, better solutions are forthcoming because there are two problem-solvers rather than one; non-expert tutoring between equals, which has the advantage of each person being able to make his own evaluation of the advice being offered unencumbered by status or hierarchy; and the joint production of a script, artefact, performance or text so that alternative and new interpretations/readings can be made.[175]

A fifth model is trial and error. Here, the learner makes repeated attempts to solve particular problems, with these solutions being tested in real-life situations. If these solutions prove to be deficient, then the learner tries out different solutions until he is satisfied that he has found the correct one. In adopting a trial-and-error approach, the learner is required to engage in a series of interrogative processes with regards to texts, people and objects in the environment, and come up with solutions to problems.

Hypothesis-testing is a form of learning in which the learner develops an idea of how something in the world works and then does something in the world with the express intention of confirming, disconfirming or partly confirming the original idea. This starts with some tentative view about how an aspect of the world works and could work in the future. A method is then chosen to verify the truth or otherwise of this conjecture. The method is then applied, and some conclusions are drawn. The important principle that has to be observed is that the method chosen is an appropriate way of testing the actual theory being investigated. In many cases, especially in some tests of statistical significance, this principle is misapplied.[176]

Another model of learning is reflection. There are perhaps three types of reflective practice: intensive action reflection, which is understood as tacit, implicit and occurring on a daily basis, where individuals use intuitive tacit knowledge to inform practice (reflection-in-action); reactive or reflective learning (knowledge of action) involving immediate reactive reflection on events that have already taken place; and deliberative reflection (knowledge for action) involving the conscious management of thoughts and activity and the deliberate setting aside of

---

[175] cf. Topping (2001a; 2001b; 2003) and Topping and Ehly (1998).
[176] This form of learning is discussed in greater detail in chapter 17.

time to ensure that judgements are based on a deep understanding of a particular issue (see chapter 17).[177]

Meta-cognitive learning refers to learners' awareness of their own knowledge and their ability to understand, control and manipulate their own cognitive processes. Most meta-cognitive processes have three elements. The first is meta-memorisation. This refers to the learners' awareness of their own memory systems and their ability to deploy strategies for using their memories effectively. The second is meta-comprehension. This refers to the learners' ability to monitor the degree to which they understand the information being communicated to them, to recognise their failures to understand what they are being presented with, and to employ repair strategies. And the third is self-regulation. This refers to the learners' ability to make adjustments to their own learning processes. The concept of self-regulation overlaps with meta-memorisation and meta-comprehension – its focus is on the capacity of the learners to monitor their learning (without external stimuli or persuasion) and to act independently. These regulatory processes may be highly automated, making articulation of them difficult for the learners.[178]

Finally, there is practice and repetition. Practice is the act of rehearsing a behaviour over and over again or engaging in an activity again and again. This reinforces, enhances and deepens the learning associated with the behaviour or activity. Choosing between these models depends on the nature and constitution of the learning object – the former is logically dependent on the latter. (For a fuller explanation of, and justification for, this important claim, see chapter 19.) It also depends on the choice of learning theory that is made. These learning models have an important role to play (whichever one is chosen) in processes of learning and constitute elements of a pedagogic process. We also need to examine the relationship between two of the most important concepts discussed in this book: knowledge and learning.

Knowledge and learning

Knowledge is transformed at the pedagogic site, so it is possible to suggest that properties such as the simulation of the learning object, the representational mode of the object, its degree and type of amplification,

---

[177] David Kolb (1984) extended his theory of reflection to encompass different types of reflectors. These were: accommodators, divergers, convergers and assimilators.
[178] cf. Butler (2015).

control in the pedagogic relationship, progression or its relations with other learning objects, the type of pedagogic text, relations with other people in the learning process, the organisation of time (temporal relations) and types of feedback mechanism are fundamental components of this pedagogic transformation. What this means is that in the learning process the learning object takes a new form as a result of changes to its properties. In contrast to some other frameworks – for instance, Bernstein's sociolinguistic code theory (2002) or Maton's (2014) knowledge and knowers thesis – the sheer complexity of the possible pedagogic knowledge forms that this allows means that relations between pedagogic arrangements and social arrangements, and between these pedagogic arrangements and notions of identity-formation and social positioning, can be sketched out only tentatively.

The first of these properties is the degree and type of simulation. In a simulation, a new medium is chosen that gives the learning object a new form, with these media being virtual, graphic, enumerative, enactive, symbolic and oral. Indeed, depending on the new form, there is a gap between the formation of the original object and the mediated object. This does not mean that the object is better or less well represented in its new form, only that it takes on a new guise – it is pedagogically formed. And this means that its potential impact is likely to be different. A simulation might involve, for practical purposes, a virtual representation of something in nature that cannot be experienced by the learner. Inevitably, the properties of the object and the relations between those properties are changed in the simulation; and what this means is that any reaction or response to the object by a learner is influenced by its new media as well as the shape and form it now assumes. The response is always to the mediated object. And the implication of this is that the pedagogical relation between the learner and the world is never direct but is realised through the mediated object, with the process of knowing the unmediated object having a retroductive orientation, although this may be understood in a different way by the learner.

A second property is the type of truth criterion that the knowledge constructor adopts. As I suggested in chapter 1, there are five conceptions of truth: truth as correspondence, truth as coherence, truth as what works, truth as consensus and truth as warranted belief. This property refers to a determination of the relationship between knowledge and the world, although it should never be assumed that this relationship is straightforward, linear or easily understood.

A third property, which is subject to transformation during the learning process, is amplification. Amplification is a central term in the field of rhetoric, and stands for all the ways in which an argument, explanation or description can be expanded and enriched. In addition, amplification refers to the capacity of the pedagogic object to increase in size, in extent, or in effect, as by the addition of extra material. The use of a microscope in a science laboratory, or the use of the internet to extend the reach of the learning object, or the taking of a deliberate and alternative position from the accepted norm for the sake of debate or to further the argument but always to deepen the learning process, are typical examples of amplification.

A fourth property is control in the pedagogic relationship. Framing refers to the message system of pedagogy. Do teachers and pupils control its content, its organisation, how it is sequenced and so on? A syllabus with rigid topics, to be completed in a predetermined order, within a specified time, is strongly framed. Weak framing occurs when the teacher is able to select topics on the basis of a rational principle and organise the sequence and pacing of material according to pupil readiness. Two control pathways can be identified. The first refers to the relationship between the teacher and the learner *and* the curriculum organisers of knowledge (these organising processes may be formal or informal), so that a teacher or facilitator of the message system has either a restricted or extended control over the way it is received in the pedagogic setting. The second refers to the relationship between the teacher *and* learner, and again this refers to the amount of control either one or the other has over the constitution of the message that is central to the pedagogic or learning process. Clearly, in this last case, the one varies in relation to the other.

A fifth property is curriculum integration or the types of relations between learning objects. Progression is one manifestation of these relations. Curriculum standards, or learning objects, are written at different levels of difficulty. Most forms of progression between levels or grades in curricula around the world are based on a notion of extension, that is, at level one a student should be able to do this or that, at level two the student is expected to be able to do more of this or that, and at level three the student is expected to be able to do even more of this or that. However, there are other forms of progression between designated knowledge sets, skills and dispositions besides extension, such as prior condition, maturation, intensification, abstraction and articulation. Indeed, some knowledge sets, skills and dispositions cannot be appropriately placed at some lower-level or even some higher-level grades. For example, many governments around the world have chosen not to start formal reading processes until at least seven years of age, and consequently reading does not feature in the curriculum standards at pre-primary levels in these countries. (For a more detailed discussion of the notion of progression, see chapter 16.)

A sixth property is the constitution of the task given to the learner in the pedagogic setting. There are a range of learning tasks or activities that take place in classrooms, such as: working with other people, individual study, sharing, debating, playing games and so forth. Learning tasks have a number of constituent elements, and how they differ in kind allows us to determine and identify these different elements: media of expression, the logic of this mediated expression, its fit with a learning model, its assessment mode and its relation to real-life settings. Media of expression include oral, graphic, pictorial and enumerative modes. Each of these media has an encompassing logic to it, so that a task requiring a written response to a request is of a different order as a learning experience from one that requires an oral response. A further component of a pedagogic task or activity is the mode of assessment that inheres in it, with these modes of assessment being understood broadly as formative or summative. Finally, there is the authenticity of the task, which refers to whether and how the task relates to real-life settings.

The activity or learning task has a logical relationship with the learning model being employed. Frequently there is a mismatch between them so that the task or activity (such as an oral response to a question, a written analysis of a text, a reading exercise, an argumentative response, a feedback loop and so forth) and the type of learning model that is being adopted are incompatible. For example, a meta-cognitive exercise that is focused on propositional knowledge rather than process knowledge would be inappropriate. A dialogic peer-learning exercise that asked each participant to grade other participants' work on a five-point scale again would be inconsonant. Feedback that failed to engage the learner in a conversation would not work.

Questioning, for example, sets up a choice situation between a finite range of possible answers. The type of answer that can be given legitimately has to be implicit in the grammar of the question, both in its form and content. For example, open-ended questions offer an extensive range of answers; that is, the restricting and enabling quality in the question is weakly formulated. What this means is that there is a greater range of possible answers to the problem. This has to be qualified in the sense that some questions, by virtue of their propositional content, have a greater facility for generating appropriate answers, whereas other questions have fewer possibilities for generating appropriate answers. However, this does not nullify the original proposition, which is that the form a question takes restricts or enables the type of correct answer that is appropriate. The reason for designating both an enabling and restricting function is to indicate that any action performed by an individual is located in discursive and material contexts and that these contexts exert an influence on the action itself.

A seventh property is the relationship between the learner and other people in the pedagogic setting. One way of characterising the relationship between the text, object in nature, particular array of resources, artefact, allocation of a role or function to a person, or sensory object *and* the learner is by determining its strength along a continuum ranging from a diffuse mode to a concentrated mode. What this means is that the message being conveyed is embedded in a relationship between a stimulus and a recipient, which is either diffuse or concentrated, or could be placed on a continuum between them. An example of a diffuse strategy is an instructional mode of learning where the stimulus is being shared by a number of people. An example of a concentrated strategy is a one-to-one coaching relationship. Since the relationship is both from the catalyst to the learner or learners and also from the learner or learners to the catalyst, this is going to influence the type of message received by the learner. We model the world as a sequence of messages passing from one to the other. The stimulus is clearly of a certain type. These are message conveyance systems or processes of semiotic transmission that operate with a particular stimulus.

Learning is always embedded in temporal arrangements of one type or another. (For a more detailed discussion of the notion of time and learning see chapter 20.) A curriculum is an arrangement of time given to different items of knowledge, so any learning episode is going to be embedded in these arrangements. For example, pace of learning is important; that is, the pace at which a student works in completing a learning activity, or the pace at which he is expected to work against some norm – in other words, the average or mean of a population. Pace can be understood as a performative construct, so it is not meant to provide an empirical description of how a person has performed but is designed to act as a stimulus to increase the pace of learning for the general population – it thus has an explicit normative function. That there are eight properties of the learning environment means that there is potentially an extensive range of possible environments as there is considerable variation within each dimension. In the next chapter, I want to examine three key educational concepts: technology, artificial intelligence and the concept of learning as it relates to these two ideas.

13
Technology, artificial intelligence and learning

The first of these concepts is technology. In the last chapter I suggested that knowledge, in what could be called its originary state, is transformed at the pedagogic site. The simulation of the learning object, the representational mode of the object, its degree and type of amplification, control in the pedagogic relationship, its progression or its relations with other learning objects, the type of pedagogic text, relations with other people in the learning process, temporal relations and types of feedback mechanism are all fundamental components of this pedagogic transformation. Technology is a part of that learning environment. It can be understood in two principal ways: as an object-artefact and as a discursive configuration.

It is possible to argue that artificial intelligence in the guise of a computer, robot, machine, mechanical algorithmic accessory, electronic device set up for the purposes of storing and processing binary data, abacus, Turing-like device, electronic brain or sense enhancer, as in sight or sound extension, allows certain activities to be performed in more efficient or more timely ways than if those activities had been performed by human beings without these devices. If we take the game of tennis, for example, it is possible for us to have more confidence in a line judgement performed by a camera linked to a set of enhancement devices than in a judgement made by a human being, however capable she is, sitting in the umpire's chair.[179] Again, if we take a large database and our intention is to find common patterns within it, then a computerised device can do this more quickly than a human being, although this can be done only if all of the elements of this complicated operation are reduced to mechanisms

---

[179] Another example might be the video assistant referee (VAR) system in football.

that conform to algorithmic procedures.[180] A further set of technological devices comprises different kinds of artificial intelligence, where this is understood as an inanimate object having the capacity to trigger a limited number of operations without recourse to human intervention. These operations range from the relatively simple (for example, some video games, such as electronic chess) to the moderately sophisticated (for instance, lane assist or collision avoidance as options for cars on a motorway) to the highly sophisticated (as in an iterative learning system embedded within a robot, providing medicalised care and monitoring to help an older person cope alone at home). These, I would have thought, are uncontentious claims: that certain operations can be performed more efficiently by machines than by human beings.

Artificial intelligence can currently replicate, and indeed make more functionally efficient, a limited range of human capacities and processes. These include: supervised learning, analysing and storing large amounts of data, hyperlinking to other sources and some forms of self-repair. Currently, the impact of artificial intelligence is limited to data being inputted at one moment in time and producing a simple response at a second moment in time. Examples of this include: human facial recognition;[181] collecting and using biometric data; tracing individual histories of consumer use and targeting this information; transcribing spoken to written text; translating from one language to another; and the use of sensors in equipment such as hard disks or plane engines to determine functionality. These cause-and-effect systems are what we mean by supervised learning, and it seems reasonable to suggest that human intelligence does far more than this at present. Indeed, these deep neural networks are expanding their reach, such as in the creation of technology-saturated classrooms. What these supervised learning processes require, however, are large amounts of data. For example, a photo tagger in a passport control process requires anywhere between hundreds and millions of pictures as well as appropriate labels or tags attached to them. Building a language translation system requires the use of a large vocabulary store and grammatical system in both languages, plus recognition software to bridge the gap between them. In addition, artificial intelligence can act to enhance human functions and senses; for

---

[180] As with all knowledge-producing technologies, we should be aware of their propensity for changing the type of knowledge being developed and not just their capacity for making a process more efficient. In cricket, football and tennis, these technologies are changing the way in which these games are and can be played.

[181] As with all of these technologies, there are always ethical and social consequences to their use.

example, with sight as in a telescope, with hearing as in a loud speaker, with taste as in taste-enhancer molecules, with touch as in a synaptics touchpad driver, with access to data as in a data analysis function on a computerised device, and so on. However, there are functions and capabilities of human beings that cannot as yet be replicated by artificial intelligence, such as higher forms of thinking, many self-repair processes, imaginative recreations[182] (the claim has been made that computers can write poetry, although the quality of this poetry is poor) and the like.

The issue of whether or not a machine or, generically, artificial intelligence, can replicate the human brain depends on how the brain, and consequently the mind, of an individual is conceived. The relation between brain and mind is complicated, with the difference between the two resting in the first instance on the difference between determinism (following a set of predetermined rules and causes) and volition (not being determined by a variety of cause-effect relations). If a physicalist position is adopted, with the implication that free will is merely an illusion, then it is not hard to imagine that in time artificial intelligence will be able to replicate the functions of the human mind. However, if we understand the mind as a volitional learning instrument, then it is reasonable to suggest that artificial intelligence will never, and indeed cannot, have or acquire every capacity of the human mind.[183] We also need to consider how the concept of technology can be understood in a wider sense, for example, as technical-rationality thinking.

Technical-rationality thinking

Herbert Marcuse (1964) argued that the end result of capitalist forms of life was the decline of the individual. For him, the metaphysics of the human subject had been superseded by technology and by the way the human subject always has to face up to a one-dimensional technical world. What is dominant is instrumentality and efficacy. Technology is not merely the application of techniques or gadgets; it is also a social process of production, distribution and exchange, and it constitutes the

---

[182] I recently gave a talk at the University of Buckingham about technology in educational settings and failed to convince one member of the audience that there are limits to the powers of artificial intelligence objects because they are essentially rule-bound and cannot be driven by a human-like intentionality. I think that the rest of the audience agreed with the arguments I was making.
[183] The debate between physicalism and human volition underpins every argument that I make in this book.

totality of how we organise society.[184] This can be seen most clearly in, for example, those neoliberal institutions central to modern societies, such as universities, schools and hospital systems, and how we can give an account of them. Human work is disvalued in this technical-rationality process; for example, phenomena, such as domestic work, are not reported in accounting processes.[185]

Mariana Mazzucato, in *The Value of Everything: Making and taking in the global economy* (2018), insists, and rightly so, that both the economic structures that we have set in place and the means by which we give value to objects within those structures are valued in themselves. For her, these valuations are skewed in our current social, political and discursive arrangements. Mazzucato further argues that this is where we should start from when we debate issues that are economic (or, of course, educational, social, taxonomic and the like) and the systems of measurement and valuation that inhere in them. For example, she suggests that over the past 150 years we have been in hock to understandings about economic affairs that exclude any economic activity that does not have a market value. An example of this is gross domestic product (GDP), seemingly an objective indicator, but in reality, an ad hoc assemblage of valuations and disvaluations of economic goods with no reasonable or rational basis to them. And so, for Mazzucato, these calculations reward the wrong types of work (understood in a wide sense), discourage those workers whose work is not officially recognised and thoroughly mislead naive politicians and policymakers. New modes of social control are exercised through technological, consumerist, administrative and bureaucratic means.[186]

Michel Foucault and his anti-humanist perspective

The French philosopher Michel Foucault used the terms 'technology' and 'technique' in his various writings, and these were in time transposed to 'technologies of power' and 'technologies of the self'. Foucault typically employed these terms to refer to methods, approaches and procedures for

---

[184] And how learning is organised and arranged in modern societies.

[185] In accounting and accountability systems, the key is to understand how the object being measured is framed – what its boundaries are. These accountability systems thus have built into the way they work processes of atomisation, reduction and potentially distortion.

[186] It sometimes surprises me that educational administrators, while actively advocating notions of social justice and fairness, employ methods that produce the opposite effects. Perhaps I should not be surprised.

governing human beings. This raises the issue of Foucault's use of the word 'technology', and in particular, the use of terms such as *'technique'* and *'technologie'*. The distinction between technique and technology, more pronounced in English than in French, can be said to lie with the difference between an abstraction at the level of culture or ideas and a set of tools for achieving some limited purpose at the level of practices. There is also the sense in which technique applies to practices concerning the production and use of objects, with technology obtaining its meaning from those theoretical domains that underpin these practices. More modern usage has resulted in an elision of these two meanings, with the result that reference is now ineluctably made to political and social concerns. Foucault at times took the view that these two terms could be used interchangeably. In a lecture given in 1978, he explained that his 'research deals with the techniques of power (psychology's "techniques of retraining" or the anatomist's "technique of the corpse"), with the technology of power' (Foucault, 1978a: 532).

These technologies of power, sometimes referred to as technologies of truth (Foucault, 1969), were attempts by Foucault to examine notions and practices that related to power. He used them to make four central points: i) the same procedures that were being used to control nature, production and time were being used to manage human beings in institutional settings, an example of which is current UK university management practices;[187] ii) power should be understood in a productive sense as that which shapes, moulds and more importantly enables human behaviour, rather than in a purely negative or repressive sense; iii) so powerful are these positive forms of power that they can operate to override moral ordinances and beliefs about appropriate conduct held by powerful people in neoliberal institutions, such as universities; and iv) in the field of education it is striking how psychology as a discipline, in conjunction with other disciplines that share its epistemology, have now assumed an ascendency even with people who do not profess to be psychological theorists.[188] Technology was seen by some as the solution to many of the ills of twentieth-century life – social stratification, industrial alienation, environmental despoliation, economic recession, nationalistic warfare and so forth.

---

[187] Some academics in universities in their writings use Foucault and endorse his notions of normalisation and bureaucratisation, and then behave as traditional bureaucrats always have in other parts of their working lives.

[188] Psychology as a discipline or domain of knowledge has embraced, but not in its entirety, an empiricist epistemology and a naive realist ontology.

Debates about industrial management, human relations at work and the role of artificial intelligence (although this constitutes an extreme form of technologisation) indicate an extension of the original meaning of the word 'technology' to embrace forms of social organisation and control. In *The Order of Things: An archaeology of the human sciences*, Foucault (1970) made the point that the human sciences, such as psychology, criminology and education, are deeply implicated in modern forms of power and, in particular, in the control mechanisms that constitute modern subjectivities. In education, for example, dealing as it must with the development of these subjectivities, notions of what research is, how it can be assessed and how one can make judgements about texts and people have been technologised through such devices as the Research Excellence Framework (REF), rule-based hierarchies of control, and technicist and reified understandings of educational and learning practices. Even the soul, and consequently the self, is understood by Foucault as being the consequence of powerful punitive structures and thus is a concept that can be understood only through the genealogical method[189] (see chapter 19).

Foucault argued that humanism, and its ethical variants, far from being a solution to the ills of technology was in fact the problem: the modern conception of human beings had the same epistemological antecedents as modern technological applications of power. Examples of this are the various iterations of the discourse of school effectiveness in the field of education, which provide the conditions for making judgements in educational settings, and the technologies of power, positive and negative, that are pervasive in the modern academy. This cannot conceal the ambiguity in his thinking about technology, which is that, despite being fully aware of the way in which technology might work in a negative sense, he never proposed, indeed he deliberately downplayed, humanist solutions to technological ills or suggested an alternative to a technologically saturated world.[190]

For Foucault, his whole work was a reaction to the then dominant phenomenological perspective (for example, Jean-Paul Sartre's *Being and Nothingness*, 2003). Phenomenologists argue strongly that human consciousness comprises the apprehension of phenomena in the world and thus focuses on how the world appears to the individual. And further

---

[189] This is a philosophical technique in which one questions the enframings of various discourses attached to different objects over time. An example is tracing the lineages of certain key concepts. I have attempted to do this with a number of key concepts that are related to learning.
[190] During his lifetime, Michel Foucault advocated prison reform in a traditional liberal way.

to this, consciousness is never a passive mechanism but is always directed in the world in a particular way – for example, in memory, in imagination, as objective truth and so forth. Thus, it has intentionality. Phenomenology has as its principal focus consciousness and intentionality and through these two important processes constitutes itself as volitional. For Foucault, this reified notion of self and therefore of subjectivity is one to which he was implacably opposed, in particular to the 'moral claims of humanism' (Foucault, 1970: 34).

An important metaphor for Foucault in his later period was the *dispositif*, which can be translated as apparatus, machinery or deployment; or, as Foucault intended it, a totality of means for the exercise of power, or procedures for the technical management of human beings. In his *History of Sexuality*, volume 1 (1978b), he used the notion of *dispositif* to explain negative and productive techniques of power; for example, the way a number of discrete practices, bodily functions and institutions are linked and thus forms of sexuality are created. We are a part of the deployment of power in understanding and practicing our sexuality; we are not just required to repress our sexual urges: '(t)he *dispositif de sexualité* functions by using mobile, polymorphic, and circumstantial power techniques' (Foucault, 1978b: 140). The *dispositif* is fundamentally a technique or technology of power and of truth, and, for Foucault, this would also apply to those ideas and sets of ideas related to artificial intelligence in education. Martin Heidegger was also concerned with these matters.

Martin Heidegger and concernful dealings

In *Being and Time* (1962), Martin Heidegger argued that the meaning of the word, and the concept of, 'technology' cannot be confined to the means of achieving certain well-defined ends, especially and as in the natural sciences, but that it also encompasses implicit understandings about human activity. And further to this, he suggested that the detached and objective attitude that this encompasses restricts our understanding of the world: 'science flattens the fullness of our concernful dealings' (Heidegger, 1962: 32).

Heidegger's most important work that explicitly relates to technology is his lecture 'The Question Concerning Technology', published in 1954, which was a revised version of part two of a four-part lecture series he delivered in Bremen in 1949. In this lecture he observed that technology contributes to 'all distances in time and space shrinking', and yet, he went on to suggest, that this 'hasty setting aside of all distances brings no nearness; for nearness does not consist in a small amount of distance' (1977: 34). Here he is focusing on only two dimensions of technology, time and space, although other possibilities exist; for example, how technology relates to different types of thinking such as technical-rationality thinking and theory–practice rationalisations. For Heidegger, all things increasingly present themselves to us as technological, thus artefacts merge with knowledge constructions. In the classic Marxist assertion, the worker becomes nothing more than an instrument for production, with the consequence that forms of anomie and alienation result. In human resources terminology, we become objects to be arranged, disarranged, rearranged and disposed of. In workplace education, personalised online learning programmes are thought of as appropriate substitutes for face-to-face cohort learning. These are three examples of technical-rationality thinking.[191]

Instrumentalism is at the heart of technical-rationality thinking: the desire to treat all means simply as stepping stones to predefined ends. For Heidegger, this critique does not 'show us technology's essence', and this is because it cannot signify how technology is a way for all human entities, not just machines and technical processes, to show themselves in the world. He argued that representational epistemologies (including correspondence theories of truth) are deficient (cf. Heidegger, 1962). This therefore requires the adoption of epistemologies that in essence and appearance are not representational or disciplinary-focused, and indeed what this means is that the whole concept of epistemology, as it is generally understood, becomes redundant. This is the route that Heidegger took. He wanted to replace it in the first instance with a notion of textual reading that insists on reading as an interpretive activity involving processes of fore-having, fore-sight and fore-conception. This therefore requires a disclosure. The second move that Heidegger made is even more crucial and this involves a repudiation of the disengaged self and the punctual self (cf. Taylor, 1998). We are beings (*Dasein*) always in the world, agents engaged in realising a particular form of life. This is what we are about, as Heidegger put it, *first* and *mostly*. The third move is to locate all of this within a metaphysical notion of Being (being in Being). Heidegger famously identified a form of thinking, calculative thinking, that is wholly injurious to the world and in tension with

---

[191] I have addressed this issue in chapter 4.

his notion of being in Being. Heidegger argued that it is not through science but through an ontological understanding, revealed through mood, that the totality of Being is unconcealed.

In the Bremen lectures (2012) and his article, 'The Question Concerning Technology' (1977), Heidegger set out the four components of his critique of technology. First, the essence of technology is not artefactual; it is a mode of being or of revealing. Technology, then, is an event, which we take part in, and it involves the structuring, ordering, reordering and requisitioning of everything around us. The second point he made is that technology is everywhere, refers to everything and even has metaphysical connotations. The third point is that technology has become more pervasive – our lives are technologised. The fourth point, and this is perhaps the most important, is that we can understand nature scientifically because it has now become a set of calculable, orderable forces – a technological *dispositif*. Science offers us only representations of things. It 'only ever encounters that which its manner of representation has previously admitted as a possible object for itself' (1977: 5). Everything becomes technologised. Heidegger's word for technology and its essence is *Gestell*. This has been rendered as 'positionality' by the translator of the Bremen lectures (2012), and as 'enframing' by the translator of 'The Question Concerning Technology' (1977). What Heidegger is concerned to show is the all-encompassing nature of technology, so that in every sphere of life, the natural, the practical and the social, we enter into a technologised relationship of enframing (*Gestell*), and this includes the notion of artificial intelligence. We need to understand artificial intelligence not as an extension of human powers and capabilities or even as a replacement for human activities, but as a way of focusing in and on the world: '(m)odern technology is not applied natural science, far more is modern natural science the application of the essence of technology'; nature is therefore 'the fundamental piece of inventory of the technological standing reserve – and nothing else' (1977: 5). For Heidegger, the call is to experience a more primal truth[192] as we try to move beyond and outside a technologised view of the world. Hypertextuality is a possible manifestation of this.

---

[192] It was in his search for this more primal truth that the controversy over his thinking then and now surfaced.

Hypertextuality

New media, in particular the internet, are acting to reconfigure the relationship between producers and consumers of content and, in particular, between teachers and learners. The role of the learner is, in some cases, changing from its traditional passive function to a more active and engaged role. The World Wide Web has given us the possibility of a more democratic relationship to the power of textual production so that it works on us and not through us, as learners.[193] This has been described as the hypertextual dissolution of centrality (cf. Landow, 1992); what this means is that new media allow the possibility of conversation rather than instruction so that no one ideology, agenda or viewpoint dominates any other. The hypertextual author, who is also a learner in a fundamental sense, combines the function of both reader and writer. They merge with each other and become intertwined. No longer does the reader or learner simply absorb the contents of a written text; she now has the potential to influence what she reads and, more importantly, how she reads it. Hypertext, which allows the possibility of having access to an almost infinite number of different texts produced by different authors, leads to an active and powerful reader/learner.[194]

Roland Barthes (1975) coined the terms 'readerly' (in French, *lisible*) and 'writerly' (in French, *scriptable*). These distinguish between two types of texts, and thus compel readers/learners to make sense of them in very different ways. In the first case, the readerly text is read in a conventional way, with the authority of the text residing in what is being read. The reader has very little scope to interpret the text in ways other than those intended by the author. Barthes contrasts this with a writerly text and, correspondingly, a writerly way of reading that text, where the reader, in her reading of that text, is able to create meanings from that text which do not necessarily conform to the intentions of the author (see chapter 1).

Prominent among the many hypertextual artificial intelligence learning systems that have been developed are: distance learning programmes, massive open online courses (MOOCs), hybrid learning models and blended pedagogic learning accessories. All aim to deliver learning in more efficient ways, with efficiency understood as:

---

[193] There are many variations of this, some of which are discussed in chapter 5.

[194] It also allows any and every type of knowledge to flourish, so that racist, misogynistic, homophobic, ill-considered, unfiltered knowledge enters into, and has effects on, the public domain.

accessibility, flexibility, hypertextuality, better control for learners in the pedagogic relationship and over the curriculum, more equal relations between teachers and learners, and more accurate identification and feedback processes leading to better forms of progression. Many of these advantages are exaggerated; however, it is still possible to suggest that learning processes are not just enhanced by technologies but fundamentally changed by them, so that new types of knowledge are being created, with subsequent wash-back effects[195] on identity formations and positionalities taken by these learners.

Instead of the pedagogic process acting merely to facilitate learning, it also acts in a variety of ways to transform the curriculum it is seeking to bring into being. Wash-back effects work on a range of objects and in different ways. So, for example, there are wash-back effects on the curriculum, on how we think we can evaluate the acquisition and retention of this knowledge that affects the curriculum, on the capacity of the individual and, more fundamentally, on the structures of knowledge, although these mechanisms are frequently conflated in the minds of educational stakeholders. Micro wash-back effects work directly on the person, whereas macro wash-back effects work directly on institutions and systems, which then subsequently have an impact on individuals within those institutions and learning systems. However, these systems are designed in particular ways that are in essence algorithmic and reductionist. This has consequences.

Claims and consequences

At the beginning of this chapter, I suggested that certain operations could be performed more efficiently by machines than by human beings. However, determining which operations these are and how they can be constituted has both epistemological and ethical dimensions. Technology, technique, technical-rationality thinking, artificial intelligence, technologies of power, technologies of truth, and technologisation have ethical dimensions and consequences. Deploying these terms in discursive configurations and in educational practices signifies an enframing of these actions. What I have suggested, and indeed argued for, is a view that

---

[195] By wash-back effects I mean that measuring, describing and evaluating human activities in the world also has the potentiality to change those behaviours and beliefs. Accounting and evaluation activities are never neutral, although strong advocates for them deny that is the effect or the intention. This is a manifestation of a power mechanism in action.

ethics always supervenes on epistemology (see chapter 5). Learning, the key concept in the field of education and in this book, likewise supervenes on epistemology and should be understood and, perhaps more importantly, practised as such.

I have been careful to suggest that the way in which technology is used in modern societies and in generative learning environments is as it is currently being used and not how it could be used. I also have some doubts about the much-heralded benefits of e-learning: for instance, flexibility, hypertextuality, better control for learners in the pedagogic relationship and over the curriculum, more equal relations between teachers and learners, and more accurate identification and feedback processes leading to better forms of progression. Our descriptions of reality and our means for accessing the world contribute to changing what we are accessing. In short, new ways of learning, through the internet and other technological means, cannot be neutral technologies, but are always content-rich. Knowledge, and consequently the way we access it, is subject to change. What I have been doing here is positioning knowledge acquisition and retention as pre-eminent dispositions of human beings and thus giving a privileged position to epistemology in the scheme of things. And what this means is that other human attributes and activities such as learning, ethics, or ways of behaving supervene on knowledge: the form that learning can assume depends on the epistemology that is adopted. The one determines the other, with this being both a logical and an empirical claim.

The essential question is: does this mean that technology, and in particular artificial intelligence, can ever transcend, or is capable of transcending, the boundaries or limits imposed on it by how it is constituted? At the moment, it can replicate certain types of learning only, and thus certain types of content in the world. And what this means is that it can produce particular types of knowledge and, subsequently, induce only certain types of behaviours, attributes and dispositions in the learner.

What, then, are these elements of consciousness that cannot as yet be replicated by artificial intelligence? Here are some suggestions: intentionality, non-deontological ways of being (after all a machine simply follows a set of complicated rules), reflexivity, meta-reflection and referential reflection, identity formation and, of course, acting in a virtuous way. Can a machine ever act in intentional, non-deontological, meta-reflective, identity-forming and virtuous ways? I think not, although I suppose one could imagine (just possibly) new material and substance inventions (made from chemicals and attached to artificial bodies) that replicate (or are superior to) human bodies, brains and of course minds, with the proviso that these machines would not be able to act intentionally and virtuously. After this discussion of the role of technology in learning, I now want to move on and examine a key part of the argument that I am making in this book – the need to understand the significance of the dispositional in learning – and to do this through a discussion of two key educational concepts, literacy and numeracy.

14
Literacy and numeracy

In this chapter I argue (provide compelling reasons) for accepting and endorsing a notion of dispositional realism. In *A Realist Theory of Science* (2008a: 212), Roy Bhaskar endorsed the anti-Humean argument that things have causal properties and thus causal powers:

> (a) thing acts, or at least tends to act, the way it is. It should be stressed that the difference between a thing which has the power or tends to behave in a certain way and the one which does not is not a difference between what they will do, since it is contingent upon the flux of conditions whether the power is ever manifested or tendency exercised. Rather, it is a difference in what they themselves are; i.e. in their intrinsic natures.

This refers to an important element of the claim or series of claims that I am making about learning in this book, which is that any coherent theory of learning needs to embrace a dispositional essentialism[196] (but not an identity essentialism),[197] and consequently an object, whether discursive, material, relational, configurational or person-oriented, has causal properties and thus dispositional powers. In accepting this, I am committing myself to an approach which suggests that objects have real powers by virtue of what they are, although, as we have seen, those powers are not always realised.[198] With regards to

---

[196] In using the term 'dispositional essentialism', I am referring to the capacity of objects to have properties, including causal powers. In starting this chapter with a long quotation from Bhaskar, I am using this textual device to provide evidence to support an argument that I am making in this chapter; however, I am framing the notion of evidence in its widest sense to mean, in addition to its conventional sense, reasons for making judgements about matters to do with learning – see chapter 3.

[197] I am not transposing the idea of dispositional essentialism to any form or type of human identity.

[198] I am drawing a distinction here between the potential powers of objects and their actual realisations, in that they have causal effects.

human beings, our fifth object-type, there are still a number of issues that need to be resolved before we can have confidence in this argument. The first is the claim that these dispositions are acquired (and not inherited) in the lifeworld. (How they are acquired is an issue that I will take up in the next chapter.) The second issue refers to the dynamic nature of objects, especially with regards to human beings: the changing object may be incompatible with a notion of a fixed disposition. In this and subsequent chapters I sketch out solutions to these problems, real or imagined.

Dispositions are the building blocks of a person, and indeed of any object in the world. For example, literacy and numeracy are properties of a person;[199] fragility and number are properties of, respectively, an artefact such as a glass vase and an abstraction such as a mathematical set. Dispositions, as inner states of objects, precede, condition and have some influence over actions, activities and events. A disposition is a habituation, a state of preparation or readiness and a tendency to act in a specific way. For Pierre Bourdieu (1986), the dispositions of a person have the power to allow him to take a specific position in a field. The habitus is the choice of the individual in taking up a position in that field according to his dispositions; but it cannot determine in any absolute sense what the person does. Dispositions of a person, artefact or abstraction then have this persistent quality; however, because they are time limited, they can be modified, that is, a person at the age of one may not have acquired the disposition of kindness but develops it at some point during his life, and all matter is subject to natural change.[200] Further to this, objects may relinquish their dispositions. An example of this is the glass vase referred to above being dropped. What remains no longer has the property of being fragile, since we can say that the object has exercised its fragility.

There are two types of conditions for the application of a disposition. The first of these refers to those conditions that enable or prevent the realisation of the intended disposition. An example of this is a match having a flammable disposition. A lack of oxygen in the environment prevents that match from lighting if struck; however, the match still retains its disposition of flammability. Another example is the human or at least male disposition of breeding. If there are no female human beings

---

[199] The issue of what a person might be is complicated, but it must include some notion of acquired properties that persist over time.

[200] Natural change is perhaps best expressed, in the fragments of writing that Heraclitus left us, as universal flux (cf. Bollack and Wismann, 1972).

to breed with then his breeding disposition cannot be realised, although he still retains his disposition of fertility.

The second type of condition for the application of a disposition comprises those enablements or constraints that respectively allow an object to be dispositionally active or prevent an object from exercising a dispositional capacity. For example, if a match is wet then it cannot be flammable; it does not have the disposition of flammability. If a man has a zero sperm count this stops that man from being fertile. In the absence of literary texts there can be no disposition of being literate. This distinction is of fundamental importance in that any theory of change, whether institutional, systemic or person-oriented, needs to take account of the nature of the relationship between an object and its properties, and whether these properties are intrinsic or attached. If an object changes its properties and consequently its powers to effect change in other objects and in the arrangement of objects in the world, it becomes a new object. However, if one or more but not all of its properties change, then we can say that we do not have a new object but only a modified one.[201]

A disposition, I am suggesting, is a functional property of an object. A property of a person is that he is, for example, literate or numerate; if he is, then that person can perform certain literate or numerate acts, although, first, those actions may not be as they were intended by the person, and second, they may not result in what the intention suggested would happen if the action had been performed. Dispositions have functional essences, and these are at the core of any social, discursive and physical object-ontology; indeed, the only way that dispositions can be construed is in their functional form. Being numerate or literate, then, involves the acquisition and expression of a complicated set of abilities understood as functions of an object-person. Furthermore, these abilities may be fully realised, partly realised or not realised at all.

I am referring here to the powers that objects have and their interactions with other objects. If I take the example of the glass vase with its property of fragility, then I can say that this property is realised only in relation to a set of conditions in the world, as I observed above. If that vase fell from a sufficient height onto a metal floor, which did not have flexibility as one of its properties, then it would break. I can confidently assert this. And conversely, if those conditions were not present and indeed other conditions were in place such as the length of the drop being insufficient to allow it to break on a feather-bedded floor, then the

---

[201] The distinction between a modified and new object is not definitive.

property of fragility would not be realised, although the object would still retain this property. Dispositions of human beings work in the same way. Human beings have powers to change personal, institutional and systemic arrangements, but they may not be realised because they operate in open systems.

Closed systems are characterised by two conditions: objects operate in consistent ways, and they do not change their essential nature. Neither of these conditions pertains to open systems. A closed system operates through deterministic rules, which govern its change processes. While this form of historical change leads to continually evolving systems and institutions, especially with regards to learning, the change that is produced is self-contained within the system itself. Feedback is thus generated within the system and has as its purpose the maintenance of equilibrium within that system. Closed and open systems can also be distinguished by the degree and type of determinism that each has, which is conditioned by the evolving network of other concepts of which it is a part.[202]

So, for example, in using concepts such as literacy and literacy acquisition, a network of other concepts is made available to the user. This framework of concepts might include: innateness, genetics, phenotypicality, reading, writing, listening, talking, the semantics of a text, constructivist whole language approaches, meaning construction, literary epistemic frameworks, naturalism, phonological awareness, word-identification skills and strategies, spelling–sound relationships, print-rich environments, visual and grapho-phonic cues and many more, and if we are to use this concept, then we have to give due consideration to this network of other concepts.

In addition, these networks have histories[203] and this is important for understanding key educational concepts such as literacy and numeracy. The point is that literacy and numeracy and a host of other concepts have different semantic contents at different moments in their histories. Thus, concepts are enframed in time; for example, hypertextual literacy has implications for how we read texts and is a very different activity from pre-digital literacy and those dispositions that are a part of it.

---

[202] Roy Bhaskar (2011) makes much of the distinction between open and closed systems and then gives this distinction a methodological twist.

[203] Concepts and conceptual arrangements have histories, and this is why Michel Foucault (1969) advocated a genealogical method of investigation.

Literacy

A distinction can be drawn between talking and writing, and not just the relatively trivial one that they have different physical forms. The transition from a non-literate society to a literate one was more than an extension of the available tools to access the world at the disposal of human beings, but in addition allowed a qualitative change as to how we live and how we are able to develop accounts of our lives. This change process had four elements. The first is that when we moved from a pre-literate to a literate society, we were able to internalise spoken language and bring it into consciousness so that it could become an object of reflection. Second, writing something down in however crude a form allows a record to be kept of what has been said. This means that in a written exchange, one or the other of the two parties can refer back to what he said, and this changes the nature of the exchange. In addition, writing provides a permanent record of our thoughts. Speech acts are immediately reversible. Third, written language tends to be more complex than speech and this allows it the possibility of entering into a more complex relationship with the world. Spoken language tends to be repetitious, incomplete, corrigible and full of interruptions. Writers receive no immediate feedback from their readers. Speech is a dynamic interaction between two or more people. And finally, written and spoken language use different modes to suggest timing, tone, volume, significance, emphasis and colour. Written material can be repeatedly analysed and revised, whereas spoken texts cannot be so amended, unless turned into written texts.

What is literacy? There are at least five different dispositional abilities or sets of organising principles that inhere in the concept. These can be broadly characterised as technical,[204] semantic,[205] referential,[206] ethical[207] and ideological.[208] A technical reading ability (of texts) entails the decoding and deciphering of words and relations between them. This ability has a limited semantic, referential and ideological content. A semantic ability, with an ability understood as a dispositional and

---

[204] Technical literary approaches have dominated policies for reading in countries around the world. This has meant that, for example, whole-book reading approaches have been neglected.

[205] Semantic approaches to literacy and reading prioritise meaning above all else.

[206] Concepts and conceptual arrangements have histories, and this is why Michel Foucault (1969) advocated a genealogical method of investigation.

[207] An ethical approach foregrounds the valued dimensions of literacy ontologically.

[208] The issues of ideology and ideological conceptions of literacy are complex. They relate to notions of truth and the real.

acquired capacity, refers to meaning construction whether intentionally, historically or conceptually framed. A referential capacity is an ability to understand the medium of the semantic content of the literary text; an example of this would be to distinguish between descriptive, narrative, expository and argumentative texts. An ethical approach to literacy would frame this ability as a set of normative behaviours, whether deontological, consequentialist or virtue-based. There are a number of different ways of reading a text. The first of these is monosemic. In using an intransitive historical method, the text gives up its meaning, and this is an unequivocal reading. A second approach is also monosemic, but here the intentions of the author are foregrounded. A third approach focuses on enframing the reading of the text, a position that I discussed at some length in chapter 1.

For Michel Foucault (1997), a literacy discourse consists of: discursive objects, for example, an illiterate person or an unintelligent subject; positionings within an array of orders and dispositions, such as a teacher of reading; conceptual relations between different fields, so, for example, literacy and economic productivity; and strategies that regulate and consolidate literary practices (both discursive and non-discursive) such as punitive inspection services and tests/examinations that structure (delimit what can be thought, practiced and reflected on) reading or literary practices. Discursive practices are the means by which, in Foucault's terms, regimes of truth come into being. Furthermore, a discursive configuration, such as the one I have briefly sketched out above, can never be a simple determinant of identity, behaviour or action. Everything I say here also applies to becoming a subject in the first place; and this has implications for being, thinking and acting. Foucault hinted at this when he coined a notion of desubjugation. Processes of desubjugation entail, first, the person resisting becoming a subject, in the sense that subjugation implies becoming something for someone else; and second, they entail active processes of criticising the limits of the discourse itself (and in the process, expanding the opportunity to think for, and conduct, oneself in the world, which is in opposition to what the discursive formation allows one to do).

A discursive arrangement,[209] then, may be seen as operating on three planes: a set of practices that delimit (and perhaps allow) certain types of thought, action and ethical conduct; a series of statements, which

---

[209] In using the term 'discursive arrangement', I am referring to the fourth part of my object-ontology: a discursive configuration.

act as carriers for the content of the discursive formation; and formations and arrangements that define categories, identify objects and relations between objects in the world, and delimit disciplines and fields of activity. Foucault in his later work (for example, *History of Sexuality*, volume 1, 1978b) extended this notion of discourse to show how over time governments use power strategies to effect the transformation of social, political, ecological and human relations with regards to the management of populations. For example, Foucault identified four forms of power implicit in a notion of governmentality:[210] sovereign power,[211] pastoral power,[212] disciplinary power[213] and biopower.[214]

Literacy discourses can therefore be analysed in relation to: their history – the changing nature of the concept over time; their cultural geography – the different ways in which the concept is used in different locations; the internal relations of the concept itself and those objects that are included or not chosen to be a part of the concept at any one moment or in any one location; the external relations in which the concept is embedded (concept-to-concept relations); valuations given to discursive and material objects in the world; and relations and connections with transcendental notions, such as truth, objectivity and the like (see chapter 2). The concept of literacy, then, has a number of forms, although we should be careful about giving these forms a specific time and place location. Numeracy is another important concept in the space of learning.

Numeracy

The concept of numeracy supervenes on mathematics – what mathematics and its relationship to the world is provides in the first instance the semantic content of the concept of numeracy.[215] Three important non-Platonic accounts of mathematics have been formulated: logicism,

---

[210] The Foucauldian concept of governmentality (1969) can be understood as the way in which governments produce citizens who are best suited to government beliefs and policies, and as those organised practices (thoughts, rationalities and techniques) through which subjects are governed.
[211] Sovereign power refers to power mechanisms that are supported by the state.
[212] Pastoral power is a form of power that guarantees the redemption of a person, accompanies him throughout his life, and invades that person's inner world.
[213] Disciplinary power has two meanings: the first is the exercise of power over another by virtue of his position or status, such as in master–slave relations. The second is the power that is exercised through disciplinary or domain regimes of knowledge.
[214] Biopower, for Foucault, is a practice of the modern state and its regulation of its subjects through 'an explosion of numerous and diverse techniques for achieving the subjugation of bodies and the control of populations' (Foucault, 1978b: 140).
[215] cf. Horsten (2019).

formalism and intuitionism. These were in effect responses to dominant (for long periods of time) Platonic views of mathematics. Within the Platonic conception, the subject matter of mathematics is abstractive qualities. Kurt Gödel (2003), a neo-Platonist, for example, argued that mathematical objects are objective insofar as their existence as entities does not depend on the actions and activities of human beings, including current members of the human population and past ones. They have timeless properties. One of the implications of this is that we enter into a relationship with these objective entities, which is analogous to the relationship between any other physical object and our minds; that is, we develop mathematical concepts. We do this, according to Gödel, through a form of mathematical intuition. Our mathematical intuition provides evidence for determining what these mathematical principles might be. Numeracy, then, would be the generalised capacity, operating at the level of the mind, to use these mathematical principles either in self-reflective ways or in actions or activities in the world.

Platonic views of mathematics were challenged in the twentieth century by logistic, intuitionist and formalist accounts. The first of these, logicism, is an attempt to reduce mathematics to logic.[216] The reason for attempting to do this is because it was thought that logical rules would be the objectifying bridge between mind and world, as they could then be understood as having both ontologically real properties and properties that allowed them to be construed as properties of the mind. This attempt at reducing mathematics to logical principles proved to be unsatisfactory for two reasons. First, it proved impossible to find equivalences between mathematical and logical operations in every single case, and logical principles failed to account for even basic mathematical operations. (There were other attempts, such as Frege's, 1980, but in the end these proved susceptible to logical inconsistencies.) Second, the move to express logical operations in mathematical form, and thus give them a role in conceptualising the important but difficult mind–world relationship, did not solve any of the epistemological problems associated with Platonic attempts at describing and explaining the world.

The second non-Platonist account of mathematics became known as intuitionism and, following a Kantian perspective, suggested that mathematics is in virtually every instance a construction or at least an activity of construction. For Kant, universal truths that play a part in the

---

[216] cf. Russell with Whitehead (1925–7).

concept of numeracy can be derived from particular representations, where these particular representations are construed as predicates in the mind. This raises issues with regards to the object that is being represented; what that representation is; how relations between objects in the world can be construed; and fundamentally what this intuitionist project actually entailed. It also places at risk the idea of forming and using a concept such as numeracy because the constructed nature of the activity seems to preclude mathematical knowledge being construed as an ontological and real universal of coherent thought[217] (see chapter 1).

The third non-Platonist account of mathematics is what became known as formalism. In this revision of Platonic ideas, it was suggested that natural numbers are foundational in mathematics. However, these are not constructions in the mind as the intuitionists understood them. Natural numbers are construed at the level of the mind as symbols, which are not thought of as abstract objects because they are simply embodiments of concrete objects. One of the problems with this conceptualisation of mathematics is that higher forms of the activity do not and cannot fit this pattern since they cannot be interpreted in a concrete manner or even transposed to an object level. On this account, the concept of numeracy comprises an ability to manipulate symbols both in providing authentic descriptions of the world and being able to use those symbols in concrete action settings.

Numeracy, then, which is the focus of this discussion, has to be[218] a disposition that is informed by a particular viewpoint about mathematics, about mathematical forms – whether Platonic, logistic, intuitionist or formalist – and how these forms relate to the world. Second, we can say that the semantic contents of the concept of numeracy are contested. Third, we might even want to say that the concept is polysemic, although this may be as a result of ignorance and misidentification rather than anything that is inherent in the concept itself.

Finally, the concept of numeracy can be understood as having six dimensions: technical, semantic, referential, normative, ideological and interpretive. A technical numeric ability would be a competence in completing a mathematical operation, without at the same time understanding in a satisfactory way the semantic content of this operation. A semantic numeric ability would be a competence in completing a mathematical operation and at the same time understanding

---

[217] cf. Strawson (1959).
[218] This is a logical necessity.

the purposes and functions of the various symbols being used. A referential numeric ability would be a competence, in addition to the technical and semantic functions of a mathematical activity, in understanding the medium of communication being used – for example, being able to distinguish between two common types of mathematical operations: unary and binary, where unary operations are understood as having only one value, and binary operations are understood as having two values. A normative dimension of numeracy would frame this ability as a set of behaviours, whether deontological, consequentialist or virtue-based, and would focus on the relations between mathematics and a person's ethical actions in the world. An ideological numeric ability would focus on the relations between the different dimensions of the disposition: technical, semantic, epistemic, normative and interpretive functions of mathematics. Finally, there is an interpretive dimension to this ability, and this refers to whether the mathematical text is monosemic or polysemic, and how it can be understood and used. These dimensions are not mutually exclusive. These two concepts (literacy and numeracy) also have pedagogic dimensions and it is to this matter that we now turn.

Conceptual learning

Conceptual learning or, as I have transposed it, dispositional learning, then, has a place in the language of learning. What this means is that concepts are understood as the properties of a person, as elements of knowledge and as having dispositional powers. Knowledge is transformed at the pedagogic site, through processes such as: simulation, representation, amplification, pedagogic control, progression, textual construction, temporality and feedback. What this means is that in the learning process, the learning object takes a new form as a result of changes to its properties.

The elements or dimensions of conceptual learning are seven-fold: technical, semantic, referential, normative, ideological, historical and interpretive. Theoretical and contextual considerations impact, then, on how elements of teaching and learning are realised. Acknowledging this allows the identification of a number of learning models: observation, coaching, goal-clarification, peer learning, trial and error, hypothesis-testing, reflection, meta-cognition and practice (see chapter 12). And each of these in turn is underpinned by a particular theory of learning (see chapter 11). What this means is that any model of learning employed is constructed in relation to a particular view of how we can know the world and what it is. Choosing between these models depends on the nature and constitution of the learning object; in other words, the former is logically dependent on the latter. In the next chapter I will attempt to apply this learning theory to the acquisition of concepts and, consequently, as I have argued above, to dispositions.

15
Dispositions – innateness and essentialism

In the last chapter, I examined two important educational dispositions: literacy (the concept) or being literate (the disposition), and numeracy (the concept) or being numerate (the disposition). As dispositions they have causal powers, even if these powers are not always realised. They are also concepts. This means that a concept is being understood in a particular way, and in a way of which Ludwig Wittgenstein would have approved, given his aversion to the idea of concepts as being representational images in the mind. In the *Philosophical Investigations* (1953), he suggested that concepts are not representations or images in the mind, but rather abilities or capabilities. According to the abilities view, it is wrong to maintain that concepts are particulars in the mind; rather, concepts are abilities that are distinctive to intelligible human beings. Concepts such as redness or being literate or being numerate or being careful in the world about our five types of object – discursive objects, material objects, relational objects, configurational objects and human beings – are abilities or dispositions of particular objects. This has implications for how we learn concepts, with some philosophers (such as Jerry Fodor, 1975) maintaining that we do not learn concepts, we reconstruct these concepts from previously held concepts that are in some sense innate.[219] Here is a reconstruction of Fodor's argument – perhaps best expressed in his *Concepts: Where cognitive science went wrong* (1998): concepts of both types (primitive and complex)[220] cannot be learnt by

---

[219] Innate theories of learning suffer from confused ideas about genetic determinacy and different potentialities.

[220] Fodor drew a distinction between primitive concepts, which are in some sense foundational, and complex concepts, which are made up of a number of primitive concepts.

testing hypotheses; there are no other ways by which a concept can be learnt; and therefore concepts cannot be learnt.

In this chapter I will attempt the difficult task of critically addressing, indeed refuting the possibility of, Fodor's (1975) paradox of learning. The reason for doing this is that if the paradox he has identified turns out to be truly constitutive of learning, then the only way out is to embrace a belief in innateness, with all of the problems that this creates. Indeed, on some accounts this would mean that there is no such thing as learning – an almost impossible idea to hold on to. The solution to Fodor's paradox of learning and thus to the reinstatement of learning as a coherent concept and viable practice is to show how the various ideas and connections between these ideas are misconceived; for example, that hypothesis-testing[221] is not the only way that concepts can be learnt or that concepts are not exclusively abstract entities in the mind. This would mean that there is indeed no paradox of learning.

My first task then is to give a faithful account of Fodor's paradox of learning. I want to consider an example of what on the surface seems to be a typical learnt behaviour: moral development. A child progresses from following rules that are defined for them by authoritative others to behaviours that are determined by social approval. The child is now motivated by a desire to win the approval or affection of these others. The child subscribes to wider concerns than close, usually familiar, ties and now operates through a belief in the worthwhileness of rules and laws to maintain social order.[222] This progression or movement from one state of being to another is an example of what we would normally think of as learning. The child having previously focused on seeking personal satisfaction and individual preferences now begins to realise that, first, this is not the only way of behaving and, second, externally devised rules in order to secure the social order as she understands it have some worth. This is a difference between egocentric desire satisfaction and social rule-following and both are underpinned by different sets of values.

In short, the child has acquired a new concept, or so it would seem. For Fodor (1975), it is this idea of conceptual growth that seems to be impossible. There are two possible ways of explaining this conceptual growth. The first is that the child has gained a new concept from the environment and from her efforts at working in and on the environment,

---

[221] Hypothesis-testing is a form of learning in which the learner develops an idea of how something in the world works and then proceeds to do something in the world with the express intention of confirming, disconfirming or partly confirming the original idea.
[222] cf. Kohlberg (1976).

and this then becomes an addition to or even a consolidation or extension of what was previously there, with this being understood as a form of conceptual development. The second explanation for this form of conceptual development is to suggest, as we will see from Fodor's account, that in fact this can be understood as the unfolding or realisation of something that was already there – or to put it in more general terms, all concept development is in fact dependent on previous concept acquisition and development.

The most plausible way to understand this conceptual development is to suggest that a child progresses in her learning by adding a new concept to an already existing concept. So, for example, the child having previously focused on seeking personal satisfaction and fulfilling individual desires now begins to realise that this is not the only way of behaving and that externally devised rules in order to secure the social order as she understands it have some worth. The new concept overrides the old one, which is that following an externally oriented set of rules is worthwhile. Two processes have taken place: first, there is now a recognition that there is another conceptual framework that could be followed; and second, there is a bestowal on this framework of a new sense of worthwhileness.

For Fodor, this cannot happen, both in the sense that any process being referred to here has not taken, and could not take, place, and in the sense that any conceptual framing of this process would be misguided. In order to acquire a new concept, the person must be able to identify for herself instances of this new state of affairs. However, the problem is that in order to be able to distinguish between cases of this new state of affairs and cases that are not exemplifications of this state of affairs, she must already have acquired the concept and thus the concept is not new. Any acquisition of a new concept requires the holder of that concept to be able to discriminate between instances of that concept in use, and this is not possible without some prior knowledge of, and capacity to use, that concept. Thus, all concept acquisition and use can be traced back to previous concept acquisition and use, and ultimately to the idea of concepts being innate. What this also implies is that human beings cannot learn new concepts; they can only allow, through social immersion, those concepts to come to some form of fruition or realisation. Learning presupposes the very concept or conceptual framework that is explained by the action of learning this new concept.[223]

---

[223] This theory assigns a limited role to learning, but it does not and cannot deny that some learning takes place. For Fodor, it is not a totally empty concept.

A way out of this dilemma is to suggest that concepts are acquired by people having experiences in the world. However, this cannot solve the problem, since any experiences that we may have are filtered through an organisational framework of one type or another, and this in turn requires the person to already have access to those meanings and conceptual framings that this organisational schema possesses; once again this requires a pre-developmental understanding of the concept, which is prior to the act of learning. We are forced back to Fodor's conclusion that concepts are innate.

An alternative way of thinking about this is to understand the idea of concept acquisition as driven by rules or principles, rather than by the person acquiring the new conceptual elements. This means that the person acquiring a new concept works out for herself the logical outcomes of applying these rules in the world. This requires a capacity to already know and be able to use rule-bound and logical processes (which may or may not be innate, but certainly pre-exist what we are calling acts of learning). However, it focuses on the logical processes rather than the substantive conceptual development under consideration. This cannot dissolve Fodor's paradox, since it could be argued that the substantive concept under consideration is implicit within the rules that are being followed to acquire the new concept. The problem is the same with each of these arguments: that in order to acquire a new concept, a person has to be able to identify instances of that new concept, and this requires some prior understanding of that concept (its history, its genealogy, its use, its relationship with other concepts) to do this. Thus, the weak case is that conceptual development is always prior to the act of learning a new concept and the stronger case is that this acquisition is innate. I want to suggest in the rest of this chapter that this is a mistaken viewpoint (certainly for the strong case and quite possibly for the weak case), and that it is mistaken because concepts and concept acquisition are dispositional in character and should be understood as abilities or capabilities, and thus do not conform to Jerry Fodor's conceptualisation of what a concept is. However, before I do this, I want to set out some examples of nativist theories of learning.

Nativist theories of learning

There are many examples of nativist theories of learning. Roy Bhaskar's theory of learning has the following elements. In foundational critical realism, what is said about learning relates to the development of beliefs.

With dialectical critical realism, learning is understood as involving all of the components of action, so there is learning at the level of values, learning at the level of wants, and learning at the level of being. In his *Philosophy of Meta-Reality* (2002), Bhaskar provided a model of learning, which he called 'the unfolding of the enfolded'.[224] This model of the unfolding of the enfolded understands learning not so much as learning something outside oneself, but as the unfolding of an implicit potential that each human being has. What happens in life is that human beings realise or fail to realise their potentials.

However, if not enough attention is paid to the external elements, then it is a one-sided model. The model of the unfolding of the enfolded has five elements: the cycle of creativity, the cycle of courting, the phase of formation, the phase of making and, finally, the cycle of reflection. This is not to deny the importance of the teacher, and it is not to deny the role of the catalyst. Knowledge is something the learner is trying to develop. Knowledge always pre-exists the learner, and knowledge and learning are central to any theory of being.

Another example of an innate theory of learning is Noam Chomsky's (1968) argument for language acquisition.[225] Underpinning his theory are three presuppositions. The first of these is that the way we as human beings acquire language is by realising (and in the process developing) a biologically determined programme for learning a language. This process is like the physical growth of the human being in normal human development. What this also means is that human beings start to speak at the same age and their progress follows a clear linear path, although there is likely to be some variation in how this is realised. The second of these is that this language programme comprises a set of rules, which we might want to call the grammar of the programme (although not in a Wittgensteinian sense – see chapter 1), and human beings have access to this set of rules and a special ability to decode this grammar, which is nativist or innate. What this means is that in most circumstances the child is able to learn the complexities of a language system in a short period of time. There may in some cases be environmental or physical factors that actively prevent its realisation, such as food deprivation or brain damage. The third underlying presupposition is that because children have different experiences during childhood and therefore there are environmental differences between children, there is bound to be some

---

[224] Roy Bhaskar's theory of learning is further discussed in the next chapter.
[225] Noam Chomsky's (1968) argument for innate language acquisition has certain regressive (in a political sense) tendencies.

variation in the speed and depth of language acquisition. This acknowledges the role of environmental factors in language acquisition, even if the knowledge that is being acquired is already there in the brain of the individual (although it has yet to be put to work and thus is non-functional).

The argument for this innate theory of knowledge acquisition is that first and foremost children in most circumstances are able to grasp their native language – a language, we should note, in which the child is fully immersed. Children learn to use complex language structures and even invent words that we do not use as adults but follow the grammar of the language we use. Chomsky argued that language is rule-bound and thus all human beings are equipped with a language acquisition device, which in all essential respects allows them to speak the language. In short, this is a mechanism that is in the brain (genetic) at birth. This language acquisition device comprises a universal grammar, which provides all human beings, regardless of the language they speak, with fixed grammatical elements that are common to all languages. For Chomsky, there are two elements. The first is substantive universals, which are features of the language such as phonemes or syntactic forms (for example, nouns or verbs). The second is general principles of grammar, although Chomsky was careful to point out that different languages have different types of grammar. This is what he called a language's core grammatical syntax. In addition, each language has peripheral elements, and it is these that allow one to argue that different languages have different grammatical structures. Without these formal universals, no child can learn a language and here at its starkest is an iteration of Fodor's learning paradox. Whether it is a concept or a language, there is a prior structure implanted in the human brain that facilitates the process of concept learning and use in the first instance and language learning and use in the second. Chomsky's work is highly controversial, in that it posits the idea that language structures exist in the mind before experience.[226] Another example of nativist thinking is how we use the concept of intelligence.

Intelligence

Learners are constructed pedagogically within a practice. An example of this process is the application of the notion of intelligence and, in

---

[226] Chomsky's theories of language acquisition should not be confused with his progressive arguments against the United States of America's neocolonial policies.

particular, the use of the idea of a fixed innate quality in human beings that can be measured and remains relatively stable throughout an individual's life.[227] This has come to be known as an intelligence quotient (IQ) and is measured by various forms of testing, for example, the 11+ test. The 11+ had a significant influence on the formation of the tripartite system of formal education in the UK in 1944 as it was used to classify children as appropriate for grammar schools (those who passed the 11+), technical schools (those who passed the 11+ but were considered to be better suited to receive a technical education) and secondary moderns (the vast majority who failed the 11+ and in the early days of the tripartite system left school without any formal qualifications). This system of education was largely replaced by a comprehensive system of schooling.

This illustrates one of the problems with an approach to the relationship between mind and reality that is technicist, scientistic and reductionist. What was considered to be a natural kind – innate qualities of intelligence in human beings – has been shown to have undeniably social or constructed dimensions to it. Powerful people had constructed a tool or apparatus for organising educational provision and given it credibility by suggesting that it was natural and thus had legitimacy. One manifestation of this discourse is the gifted and talented programmes that have been introduced into schools in the United Kingdom over the past 20 years. 'Gifted and talented' is a term used to describe children who have the potential to develop significantly beyond what is expected for their age. The suggestion is that some children have this potential and others do not. It is also closely allied to processes of individualisation and personalisation that are becoming commonplace in UK educational settings and has contributed to a sterility and impoverishment of learning approaches and outcomes in schools.

Central to the concept of the intelligence quotient is the tension between the relative emphasis given to genetically inherited characteristics and the influence of the environment. Many contemporary educationalists believe that children's early and continuing experiences at home and at school constitute the most significant influences on their intellectual achievements. However, early exponents of the argument that genetic inheritance determines intellectual potential saw intelligence, measured by tests, as the factor that could be isolated to produce a 'quotient' by which individuals could be classified.

---

[227] The belief in differentiated intelligences between people and groups of people has had profoundly deleterious effects on the body politic.

Regardless of environmental factors such as teaching and learning programmes or socioeconomic variables, it was argued, some people were born with low levels of intelligence. Schooling could bring them to a certain level of achievement, but there would always be a genetically imposed ceiling on their capabilities. An extreme version of this belief was that intelligence, like certain physical characteristics, followed a normal curve of distribution, so that within any given population there were a set number of intelligent people and a set number of less intelligent people. It was further argued that those individuals who were most generously endowed were obviously more fitted to govern and take decisions on behalf of those who were less fortunate.[228]

Rousseau's romantic expressivism

A fourth expression of innateness in learning is Jean-Jacques Rousseau's educational philosophy.[229] His notion of freedom or being free comprises an idea of innateness or natural capacity, where this is understood in essentialist terms, and as relating in a fundamental sense to the individual concerned, and as being subject to, in its full realisation, the contingencies of history and experience. His mature work, which focused on education, is called *Emile, or Treatise on Education* (in the original French: *Émile, ou de l'éducation*) (1979), and this has led, whether rightfully or not, to a notion of progressive education. *Émile*'s underlying principles seem to support a notion of child-centred education, which accords with a view of what progressive education is and what traditional education is not. A child's natural or innate capacities need to be allowed to come to fruition and this can be achieved through a process of self-discovery, as well as the avoidance of that child being dominated by others, especially teachers. So, both process and innate capacities are protected from the harmful effects of formal educational structures and life more generally. The young child is allowed to play by herself and with others, but only in and through learning environments that refrain from domination and subordination. At about the age of 12 or thereabouts, the child acquires abstract ideas. The third stage is early adolescence, which involved for Rousseau the regulation of a child's *amour-propre* (loving oneself), thus casting doubt on his notion that it is only through non-coercion that the

---

[228] These are eugenicist beliefs.
[229] Jean-Jacques Rousseau's writings on education have influenced some people's notion of what the idea of a progressive education might be (cf. Bertram, 2020).

child can successfully realise her potential. The teacher's task is to ensure that the child learns about *pitié* or compassion and that her *amour-propre* is developed along non-competitive lines. In this last phase, it is clear that certain values are inculcated into the child through particular pedagogic processes and that these have little to do with the fulfilment of certain innate tendencies or natural capacities in the child.

Rousseau reacted against the enlightenment notion of progress, since he argued that civilisation and even learning (certainly of a formal type) corrupt human nature, which he understood in a fixed and essentialist way. What in *Émile* he seemed to suggest was that we should celebrate the original, natural man (sic.), the noble savage who had never learnt to read or write, had no sense of private property and was free from the powerful institutions of the state. Rousseau implicitly or explicitly created a binary and debilitating opposition between nature and culture. Nature, the natural, the innate, is good and virtuous. Culture inevitably corrupts this, although the better social arrangements implied by Rousseau's political and social reforms are less corrupting than the status quo. Indeed, the problem is two-fold. The first of these is: how do we define the natural? Human beings have experiences in the world, some good, some bad, and the question then becomes: which of these are natural and which are unnatural? The second is that this sense of negative freedom that Rousseau encapsulates seems to suggest that it is only the absence of certain things that can guarantee the ideal state of upbringing for the child.

For Rousseau, there was a moral universe separate from human beings, a natural order of growing and learning, which for a variety of reasons could become distorted – leave a child to herself and this natural potential or being could be fulfilled. There is thus a natural ethic of being (for other enlightenment figures this was reason), so that a child had only to listen to her inner being and voice, filter out those siren voices that would ultimately lead to distortions and disfigurations of the natural and live the good life. Inner reflexivity then involves both the cultivation of these natural instincts and the resisting (with the help of others) of any distorting tendencies. This romantic expressivism, found in Rousseau but also in other European enlightenment figures, is an expression of innateness, and in different ways can be seen in Chomsky's language-acquisition device, Bhaskar's unfolding of the enfolded and Fodor's learning paradox. The implications for learning are profound: learning is understood as the expression and fulfilment of something that is already there, by virtue of being human.

Refutations

At this point in the argument I am making, I need to show how these arguments for nativism or innateness can be refuted. In chapter 1, I suggested that a number of concepts are used in the field of learning, such as: literacy, numeracy, meta-cognition, emotional intelligence, self-regulation, growth, progression, learning, intelligence and many more. I also suggested that it is possible to identify different types of concepts if we understand a concept-type in relation to how it can be used in a way of life. Some of these are: generalisations, abstractions, symbols in the mind, acquired dispositions, object categorisations, valued configurations, algorithmic formations and semantic conditionals.[230] This class of objects can be understood, as Wittgenstein (1953) did, as having family resemblances and not just logical or rationally formed relations or connections. There are three principal uses of the term 'concept': concepts as representations in the mind, concepts as abstract objects and concepts as abilities.

The first of these maintains that concepts are psychological entities; this view is underpinned by a representationalist theory of mind, with such a view of the mind–world relationship able to accommodate a notion of correspondence, reflection, sameness or manifestation. There is something in the world, outside of the structures of a mind, that can lead to an equivalent operation in that mind, and these operations can be thought of as beliefs, desires, concepts and the like. These are psychological states, which are sometimes divided into primitive or basic concepts and concepts that are dependent on them. Under this conceptualisation, concepts are taken to be foundational or basic, with thought – now understood as irremediably conceptual – grounded in these images in the mind. Fodor (1975) called this the *language of thought* hypothesis. This representational view of concepts is the default position in cognitive science. This is Fodor's view of what a concept is, and this has implications for how it can be learnt or acquired, if at all.

Here again is the argument Fodor made: concepts of both types (primitive and complex) cannot be learnt by testing hypotheses; there are no other ways by which a concept can be learnt, and therefore concepts cannot be learnt. The first problem with this apparently safe conclusion is that hypothesis-testing is not the only way we learn concepts. We also

---

[230] These different views about what a concept is can be encapsulated in the three principal views of concepts and conceptual developments discussed here.

learn concepts through processes such as observation, coaching, reflection, meta-cognition, problem-solving and practising. Many of these learning modes do not allow us to fall into the trap set by Fodor and, consequently, if we adopt a different view of what a concept is, such as that concepts are abilities, then other forms of learning can be deemed to be legitimate.

Hypothesis-testing implies that at every occasion in which hypotheses are formulated by the learner, they always contain elements of preformulated concepts. Concepts as dispositional acquisitions, I am suggesting in contrast, can be learnt ab initio, although subsequent forms of propositional, process and embodied forms of learning may require prior acquisition of specific dispositions. The second problem is that reflection and reflective processes would under Fodor's cognitivist account (see chapter 5) lose any sense of an inner process of serious thought about, or consideration of, a concept. Now, this perhaps is not a necessary element of a theory of learning,[231] but it creates a considerable problem if learning is understood as a conversation between the inner and the outer, as involving a capacity to operate outside of embodied, socially derived or genetic causal impulses, as accepting that reasons can be conceived as causes of human behaviour and as incorporating some or other notion of intentionality as a central element in any theory of the relationship between mind and world.

The second view of a concept is that concepts are abstract objects. Concepts, under this conceptualisation, are the meanings of words and word-complexes as opposed to objects and states of mind. Concepts as meanings mediate between thought and language *and* their referents. Gottlob Frege (1980) argued for a sense–reference distinction, although he did not use the term 'concept', but rather referred to the referents of a predicate. Again, he used the notion of thought as an equivalence of a proposition – thoughts are not psychological states but rather they are the meanings of states of mind. However, as Wittgenstein (1953) suggested (see chapter 1), there cannot logically be a private language of thought, only that for a statement to be meaningful (that is, for it to make sense and thus have a use-value), it must in principle and in reality be subjected to public criteria of justification to allow a judgement to be made about its truth-value. For Wittgenstein, the signs in language can work only where there is the possibility of public (comprising other people in specific time and place locales) affirmation or disaffirmation.

---

[231] A learning theory such as behaviourism deliberately eschews such processes, see chapter 11.

A difficulty with the idea of concepts as abstract objects is that they stand or seem to stand outside the causal process; that is, they cannot be accessed in the normal way in which we access objects in the world. As far as Frege was concerned, we grasp the sense of an expression, but this metaphor remains at the level of expression and has little ontological substance. And furthermore, it is unclear here how concepts can be learnt.

The third principal view of learning is that concepts are abilities, and this is the predominant way in which concepts have been understood in this book. This does not mean that some concepts cannot be understood and conceptualised as abstract objects; however, what this suggests is that primitive or basic concepts, such as learning, are neither representative images in the mind nor words and word-complexes in a language of thought. And this in effect renders Fodor's paradox of learning as inadequately conceptualised on two counts: first, that concepts are understood in too narrow a way so that learning inevitably becomes a peripheral activity; and second, that there is a variety of learning types that allow learning of concepts as abilities. In the next chapter I will address the issue of the connection or relation between different learning objectives, or, to put it in another way, progression in learning.

16
Progression and learning

Underpinning the notion of progression is a rationale for teaching some aspects of the knowledge domain before others and a belief that a curriculum can in fact be arranged in a reliable hierarchy. Examples of these frameworks are Jean Piaget's (1962)[232] schema comprising progression from concrete operational to formal operational thinking, and Lawrence Kohlberg's (1976)[233] stages of moral thought, where the individual progresses from pre-moral and conventional rule conformity levels to the acceptance of general rights and standards, and even to adopting individual principles of conduct. These hierarchies, it is claimed, are based on empirical investigation – this is how human beings actually progress. The other way of establishing knowledge hierarchies is through some form of logical ordering, where complexity comprises both a progressive development of more items of knowledge and the making of more complicated connections between these items of knowledge. Many school-based curricula around the world employ progression modes that are extensional in design, where this is understood as an increase in the amount, or range, of an activity, whether knowledge-based, skill-oriented or embodied.[234] This has the effect of limiting, and distorting, the notion of progression, both between items in a curriculum and in terms of the progress a learner makes within that curriculum.

---

[232] Jean Piaget's theory of cognitive development has been the subject of much criticism, principally that child development does not always follow a smooth and predictable path, for example, Donaldson (1978).

[233] Lawrence Kohlberg's theory of moral development has been the subject of much criticism, principally that a child's moral development does not always progress in the way suggested by the theory. For example, Gilligan (1990) offers a gendered perspective on moral development and a disputation of the stepped and developmental nature of such learning.

[234] If the only language you permit yourself to use is numbers, then the mode of progression you are likely to use will be extensional.

There are a number of other forms of progression that might allow us to give meaning to the concept. The first of these is prior condition. In the acquisition of particular knowledge, skill and dispositional elements, there are prerequisites in the learning process. Progression refers to the relations between operations within a domain. The learner in this case is not able to understand a particular operation unless he has also acquired knowledge of the previous one and is fully conversant with it – he can use it. What this means is that embedded logically in the second and higher concept is the operation referred to in the first and lower-level concept. This has to be in this conceptualisation of progression an integral part of the ability of the learner to grasp the concept. For example, counting and cardinality in mathematical thinking are prerequisites of operations, algebraic thinking and number and operations in base ten. Knowledge of counting and cardinality is a prior condition for learning to take place. These are logical relations, which are determined by the subject matter or domain content of the particular operation under consideration. This does not mean that they are natural or ahistorical, since they can be determined only by the current state of the domain, and domains ineluctably change their form and structure.[235]

A second type is intensification. Whereas extension refers to the amount or range of progression, intensification or complexity refers to the extent to which a sophisticated understanding has replaced a superficial understanding of a concept. In relation to the knowledge constructs, skills and embodiments implicit within a curriculum, there are four possible forms of complexity. These are behavioural complexity, symbolic complexity, affective complexity and perceptual complexity.[236] There is also a type of progression, abstracting, which involves moving from a concrete understanding of a phenomenon to a more abstract one. A pedagogic response to this type of progression is to revisit and reconstruct a set of ideas or operations at different levels of complexity at different stages in the learning programme (cf. Bruner, 1996).[237]

Another type of progression and thus learning is where the end result is already present at a first moment in time and is openly revealed

---

[235] The arguments for the inevitability of change are rehearsed in chapter 4.

[236] Behavioural complexity, symbolic complexity, affective complexity and perceptual complexity are different types of complexity because they refer to different human capacities and objects: behaviours, symbols, emotions and perceptions. As a result, they have different possible forms and trajectories.

[237] Jerome Bruner argued that there is a need to incorporate a spiral element into the curriculum, that is, a set of ideas or operations, once introduced, is revisited and reconstructed in a more formal or operational way, at different stages in the learning programme.

at a second moment in time. As we have already seen, in his *Philosophy of Meta-Reality* (2002), Roy Bhaskar provided a model of learning, which he called 'the unfolding of the enfolded'.[238] This model of the unfolding of the enfolded understands learning not so much as learning something that is external to the learner, but as the realisation of an implicit potential that human beings have.

A further type of progression is an increased capacity to articulate, explain or amplify an idea or construct; that is, the learner retains the ability to deploy the skill and, in addition, he can now articulate, explain or amplify what he is able to do and what he has done. In order to articulate an experience, there are a number of conditions: knowledge of the object, knowledge of the process and knowledge of how the object and the process can work.

And finally, progression can be understood as part of a process, and this refers to the way in which the learner interacts with the learning object. Progression and thus learning are understood as movements from a dispositional state to a progressively higher or better dispositional state. An example of this would be moving from a dependent state, as in another person or institution, to an independent state, where the person does not now rely upon any other person or institution. He has achieved some independence in his learning.

This suggests that curricula as they are presently conceived around the world are deficient if they employ extensional forms of progression exclusively at the expense of a range of other types. These forms of progression are not of the same order because they refer to different aspects of the process of learning. They are linked by their capacity to affect different parts of the learning process and, in particular, where a person moves from one state of being to another. For example, extensional forms of progression focus on the objects of learning, whereas procedural forms of progression focus on the learner and the way in which he can and does respond to these objects. I need to provide some examples of progressive schema.

Scribbling

A first example of a progressive schema is scribbling. With young children, scribbling can be categorised in fixed developmental phases, milestones or stages:

---

[238] Roy Bhaskar's model of learning is explained in more detail in chapter 15. It is seriously deficient.

Stage 1: (broadly 1–2 years old) random or uncontrolled scribbling, featuring large movements from the shoulder, fist-held tools, a whole body scrubbing motion and an emphasis on sensory experience. There is little or no concern for what marks are made.

Stage 2: (2–3 years old) controlled scribbling; attributed to better muscle control and pencil grip. Children make repeated marks on the page – open circles, diagonal, curved, horizontal or vertical lines.

Stage 3: (3+ years) moving towards controlled lines and patterns that are viewed as emerging or early signs of developmental writing, the naming of scribbling, or what has been called 'fortuitous realism'. (Lowenfeld, 1949)

A child progresses through these stages of learning.[239]

Moral development

Another example of progression is Lawrence Kohlberg's schema of moral development,[240] which I referred to in the last chapter. This is based on thinking processes inferred from particular types of behaviours: how a person decided to respond to a particular moral dilemma. Kohlberg argued that these decisions could be arranged sequentially into six stages. Level one, which he called the pre-conventional level, comprises two stages. At this level morality is externally sourced. Individuals follow rules that are defined for them by others. The individual operates through ethical precepts that encourage the idea that they can get away with certain things or that they should always seek personal satisfaction. There are two stages at level one. The first of these is where punishment and the avoidance of it is the dominant motivational behaviour. The second is where the individual focuses on receiving rewards or satisfying personal needs.

Level two is the conventional level. Following social rules is still considered to be important; but the concerns of the individual are now

---

[239] Viktor Lowenfeld's influential model of scribbling could have been constructed in a different way, given the available evidence then. It has now become the accepted way to understand scribbling and thus has become normalised and accepted practice.

[240] Regardless of the correctness of his theory, then, it is now true, or at least aspires to be true.

focused on relationships with other people and even social relations in general. Again, at this second level there are two asynchronic stages. In the first of these, behaviour is determined by social approval. The individual is motivated by a desire to win the approval or affection of others. The second of these manifestations is where the individual subscribes to wider concerns than close, usually familiar ties, and now operates through a belief in the worthwhileness of rules and laws to maintain social order.

For Kohlberg there is a third level, the post-conventional or principled level. At this level, the individual starts to act from a set of principles that he has developed. Morality is defined as a set of abstract principles that apply to all human beings in all times and in all places, and thus has a universal quality about it. Again, there are two stages. The first is a social contractual orientation, where laws and rules are not considered to be absolutely right but the best we have and are sanctioned by contracts freely entered into by individuals. The second stage is for Kohlberg the highest state of being (and this is a requirement of any stratified system). Here the individual operates through freely chosen ethical principles of conscience, which may override principles relating to laws or socially defined rules. Frequent empirical investigations have shown that in relation to progression this is how human beings develop. In other words, they move from lower levels to higher levels in accord with this theoretical schema of progression. And further to this, some understanding of and practice at the lower levels is a prerequisite of moving satisfactorily to the higher levels. However, these are not just logical or empirical accounts of what happens; they are also preferential statements by Kohlberg, writing as he did more than 50 years ago, although they may have become actual normative progressions since.[241]

Formal assessment

Another example of progression is the 2014 Research Excellence Framework (REF). A similar exercise is being conducted in 2021. These are the most recent iterations in a series of national assessments (formerly known as Research Assessment Exercises [RAEs]) of the quality of research in British universities going back to 1986. The Higher Education

---

[241] cf. McLeod (2013) – it is the linear nature of the progression mode that has bothered a great many people.

Funding Council for England (HEFCE) and its equivalent bodies in Wales (Higher Education Funding Council for Wales [HEFCW]), Scotland (Scottish Funding Council [SFC]) and Northern Ireland (Department of Education [DoE]) are responsible for organising the REF and accountable to the government for doing so. As a result, HEFCE and the other three bodies allocate research monies to UK universities using a formula that is decided after the exercise has been completed (in some of these exercises, 2* outputs were funded generously, whereas in others they received only a cursory reward). In 2014, universities were required to submit four outputs per member of staff (with some exceptions) (65% of the aggregated score), a series of impact case studies (20% of the aggregated score) and an account of their institutional research environment (15% of the aggregated score) to 36 discipline-based subpanels.

In 2014, 155 institutions submitted the research outputs of 52,077 research staff members for scrutiny and assessment. In total, the 36 subpanels were required to read 191,232 individual research outputs and grade them on a scale that ranged through 4* (quality that is world-leading in terms of originality, significance and rigour), 3* (quality that is internationally excellent in terms of originality, significance and rigour, but which falls short of the highest standards of excellence), 2* (quality that is recognised internationally in terms of originality, significance and rigour), 1* (quality that is recognised nationally in terms of originality, significance and rigour) to unclassified (quality that falls below the standard of nationally recognised work). Some panel members have admitted they were advised to spend roughly 20 minutes on each piece, which might be a 250-page book, a 10,000-word article in a learned journal or a 15,000-word chapter in a book. Time constraints meant that only a superficial reading of the pieces could be made, and it is therefore possible to conclude from this that the longer and more substantial the piece of work, the less reliable was the judgement being made of it. One consequence of this was the mistaken assumption made by research directors in universities that researchers should submit refereed articles rather than books or book chapters, an output model that members of natural science bodies felt more comfortable with than those working in the humanities or in some parts of the social science community. The judgements made by panel members were meant to be criteria-referenced, although subsequent accounts of the deliberations that were made after the initial assessments were completed have confirmed that adjustments were made to these initial assessments to bring the 36 subpanels into line with each other, thus providing contradictory evidence to the claims made by university research directors that their internal assessment exercises were in line with, or accurate predictions of, actual results.

At this point it is enough to suggest some problems with this model. First, excellence was being defined in terms of geographical scope and thus a neat and largely meaningless hierarchy was being set up that did not reflect the depth and meaning-in-use of the concept of excellence. (Self-evidently, meanings-in-use definitions of words or concepts change in relation to different conditions and consequently have histories.) Bizarrely, the guidance for the 2014 REF denied that this form of words is about geographical scope, although the explanation for the use of these words does not add much to how they could and should be interpreted. The second point is that the three subcategories used (originality, significance and rigour) were understood differently by different disciplines or even (and this is more important given the nature of the divisions used by HEFCE, that is, the 36 subpanels) within those disciplines themselves. Evidence that allows a judgement to be made about a piece of work is domain-specific, and this includes those criteria that an exercise such as the REF uses to make these judgements (whether they are actually used is a different issue, but this is certainly the intention). The third point is that in effect the readers or assessors were being asked to grade each piece of work on a five-point scale without paying much attention to any criteria relating to excellence and, consequently, their judgements were based on the idea that this piece of work is better than this piece, which is better than this other piece, and so on. The reasons then for making these judgements were implicit and therefore, presumably, a variety of notions (some of which are directly in contradiction with each other) of what makes one piece better than another was being used.[242] At a meta-level, history can be understood in progressivist terms.

An idealist sense of history

Georg Hegel is the philosopher who was most concerned to articulate a notion of progression. Here, in an idealist sense, history is said to encompass a view that one set of arrangements in the history of a people

---

[242] This was the subject of a British Educational Research Association (BERA) blog (Scott, 2017b). Despite the many criticisms made of the REF, it still persists. The reason for this is that it is not meant to be helpful or formative, but it is meant to corral and control academics and restrict the types of knowledge that can be developed.

is better or an improvement on a previous set of arrangements, and this may even result in a perfectly rational set of arrangements coming to fruition, in which we can say that nothing could be improved on. The objects and relations between objects in the world are now so conceived and actualised that any different set of arrangements would constitute a diminished (in terms of some notion of ideational completeness) set of arrangements. What this amounts to is the identification of a hierarchy of goods or a stratified arrangement of human affairs, which can be shown to be better at higher levels than at lower levels.

The philosophical problems are four-fold: first, there are problems with identifying what these progressive stages might be; second, there are problems with identifying the relations between these different stages; third, there is a problem with identifying an end point (for example, the end of history as Francis Fukuyama suggested),[243] and fourth, and perhaps most importantly, there are problems with conflating current ways of understanding historical events and happenings with ahistorical and universal ways of understanding these matters. With regards to the shape and trajectory of human history and the way it progresses, the only definitive clues that we have are that an object has changed (or will inevitably change) and that this something has become better (or has the potentiality to change in a better way). What this amounts to is making a claim that there is a large organising theme (for example, Hegel's theory of events as the unfolding of human history), meaning (monosemic inevitability) or direction (cyclical, teleological or progressive) in history; and that this is not just a retrospective judgement but one that has implications for the future or will determine what happens in the future. This, then, is different from a goal that a human being or set of human beings has, which may or may not be fulfilled depending on the circumstances that prevail at the time and the work that is put in. It thus treats history as non-arbitrary but as having some underlying purpose.

These underlying purposes were more easily expressed in terms of some notion of a metaphysical being and becoming one with it. For example, Saint Augustine constructed a theology of the self in the *Confessions* (*Confessiones* in Latin) (2017) and a theology of history in the *City of God against the Pagans* (*De civitate Dei contra paganos*) (2003). Progression in history begins with the Creation, moves through this to the

---

[243] This neo-Hegelian theory about the end of history and the triumph of liberal democracies and capitalist modes of ownership and distribution looks at the present time to be fallacious.

dysfunctionality of person-made states – with the implication that generically humankind is as yet incomplete in some way or another – to the realisation of perfection (understood in rational terms) in the Kingdom of God. Likewise, the self as part of this project can progress towards fulfilment or completion only in God. This is a belief in the universality of divine revelation. This does not mean that it is inevitable, only that this is the sole way in which real and authentic notions of progression can be sustained. There is a divinely ordered plan for the universe, and history is understood as theodicy or as eschatology.

Enlightenment thinkers moved away from eschatological interpretations of history and introduced a new idea to the concept of progress: a better or more perfectly organised arrangement for civilisation (examples of this form of writing can be found in Condorcet, 2012; and in Montesquieu, 1892). This required some assumptions or claims to be made about human beings, such as, that human nature is constant over time and place, and thus it is possible to identify the different stages that all human civilisations go through. It finds perhaps its most important expression in Hegel's philosophy of history, which was in turn inverted in Marx's materialistic theory of the development of economic modes of production (cf. Marx, 2009). Other macro-theories of progression such as Spengler (2013) understood human history as passing through specific stages of youth, maturity and senescence, and that, given what human nature is, this is inevitable.

An important criticism of all of these theories of progression is that they assume the existence of an ineluctable process whereas in reality none exists or can exist. Notions of stages or levels or improvements or progressions are simply fanciful notions of what human beings aspire to, but there is no inevitability about them happening or nothing in previous arrangements or conceptions of human life that lead inevitably to certain states of being. There is no super-agent lying behind historical events.

Hegel's philosophy of history is another super-agential theory, but in this case the super-agent is the realisation of human freedom: '(t)he question at issue is therefore the ultimate end of mankind, the end which the spirit sets itself in the world' (1977: 63). Hegel understood human history as a narrative of progressive manifestations of human freedom,[244] from the limited freedoms enshrined in the Ancient Greek polis to the individualisation of the Protestant Reformation, to Napoleon in the first

---

[244] Freedom is a much more complicated concept than most people who use it, especially politicians, realise.

establishment of a rational bureaucratic state, and then to our rights enshrined in modern expressions of the nation state, such as the Bill of Rights in the United States of America. These are expressions of progress in history, with the latter events being better or more rational than the former ones.

Hegel's method is dialectical, although he hardly ever used the term in his writings. What this method consisted of was a way of relating specific events, happenings and objects in nature to an absolute idea, in which a claim (thesis) is necessarily or contingently opposed by its apparent opposite (antithesis), which in turn can only be reconciled at a higher level of truth (and thus this incorporates a notion of progression) by a third claim (a synthesis). Roy Bhaskar understood the dialectic in a different way. He provided a formal description of the dialectic as a 'process of conceptual or social ... conflict, interconnection and change' (2008b: 32). The dialectic results in a real process of human flourishing because it allows the removal of obstacles that can change the conditions of existence. Such obstacles are conceived of as absences that must in turn be absented in a real, contingent dialectical process of emancipatory critique: '(o)ntological dialectics is concerned with reality, epistemological dialectics is concerned with what is known about reality, and relational dialectics metacritically situates our knowledge in relation to what is known' (2008b: 3). Bhaskar understood humanity as having a core human nature (which fundamentally is subject to change), and this manifests itself in different ways under different conditions.

Learning has to incorporate a notion of progression; that is, movement from one state of being to another, with the latter being understood as better in some way or another. This introduces an ethical dimension to the concept of progression, and thus ineluctably an epistemological dimension. We can rise to or reach higher kinds of knowledge only through a supersession of what we perceive to be a lower kind. Another important learning concept is reflection and I discuss this idea in the next chapter.

17
Pedagogy as reflection and imagination

A concept, such as pedagogy, is both a material and discursive object and consequently has all the characteristics that we have come to associate with these types of object. In the real world, boundaries are drawn between objects. As a discursive object, the concept of pedagogy has certain properties, such as being polysemic, semantically contested, networked, interactive, powerful and dynamic. In addition, as an object it has causal powers, both as a conceptual object and also because it is in the world, or at least in a world.[245] It is also central to any theory of learning for which we might want to argue – as the argument I am making throughout is that both formal and informal learning environments are pedagogically formed.

There are many different views of what pedagogy might be and how broad it is as a concept, with three principal theories in existence.[246] The first is a model of pedagogy that can be built up around the idea that knowledge is transposed from and to many different locations, and that it emanates from outside the learner. The second is a model of pedagogy that understands pedagogy as a carrier of something such as identity, social positioning, concept acquisition and much more. Basil Bernstein (2002) argued that pedagogy was the means by which the accumulated knowledge of a society could be produced, distributed and allocated, then transposed into an institutional form, and finally changed into a set of criterial standards. (Wittgenstein would have argued that these were already there, although implicit.) In Bernstein's terms, this pedagogisation

---

[245] Pedagogy, then, can be understood as a concept in the traditional propositional sense, and in addition as a practice.

[246] Alternative views of what pedagogy is invariably technicise the notion.

comprised three fields of activity: an area of production and distribution, a field of recontextualisation and a field of reproduction.[247] A third approach, then, is the one argued for in this book, which is that pedagogy is a mechanism (using this word without its mechanical and deterministic elements) and has properties, including causal powers, that operate in the churn of other objects (discursive, material, relational and perhaps more importantly human).

A concept such as pedagogy has a history. In ancient Greek society, a distinction was made between the activities of teachers or pedagogues (*paidagögus*) and subject teachers (*didáskalos*). In order to understand a concept, in this case pedagogy, it is necessary to examine in the first instance the history of differences and distinctions that have been made to and within it.[248] Here is one iteration: a pedagogue is a moral guide and custodian of a child-learner (this is complicated by the fact that many of these pedagogues were trusted slaves, who assumed an authority role in relation to their charges), and in addition a pedagogue is not a subject teacher. This revision and modification of the master–slave role is captured in remarks attributed to Socrates by Plato (1997: 692). In a conversation between Socrates and a young boy called Lysis, Socrates asked Lysis whether there is anyone who controls him. Lysis replied, 'Yes, he is my tutor here.' Socrates then asked whether he is a slave. Lysis responded, 'Why certainly, he belongs to us.' Socrates concluded the exchange by saying, 'What a strange thing … a free person controlled by a slave.'[249] The subject teacher, who was not a pedagogue, was known as a schoolmaster. A pedagogue, and consequently a pedagogic activity, thus became divorced from the idea of a subject teacher and from a notion of didactics or learning a subject or subjects.

Immanuel Kant, writing in the latter part of the eighteenth century and early part of the nineteenth century, in his work *On Pedagogy* distinguished between the nurturing of the child and formal instruction, the point being that pedagogy was at this time understood as more than just instruction. Kant made a further distinction between the two insofar as he suggested that instruction is a training for school, and guidance is a training for life. The distinction between education and training had not yet taken on its modern meaning. The instructional element in pedagogy

---

[247] Without a full understanding of what knowledge is, Bernstein trivialises the conception of the transformative process. In addition, he treats culture and cultural formations as rationally coherent and logically consistent.

[248] See chapter 6, 'Difference'.

[249] *Lysis* is one of Plato's dialogues. It discusses the nature of *philia*, or friendship, even though the word originally referred to a more intimate bond.

had earlier been introduced, at least in an unformed way, with the publication of John Comenius' book, *The Great Didactic* (*Didactica Magna*) (2012).[250] This development of didactics suggested that the point of life was to develop as a rational, self-regulated and devout human being. The book concludes with some trivial, although this is not intentional, remarks about: the need to respect a learner's stage of development, what knowledge is, the idea that teaching should be at the level of specifics and that generalisations should be built from these, the injunction that teaching should not cover too many themes or issues at the same time,[251] and the further injunction that teaching should proceed in a slow and methodical fashion. Its triviality provides of course no evidence of its importance or influence, and Comenius' book is now thought of as the foundation document for a notion of didactics. One of Kant's successors, Johann Friedrich Herbart, introduced into the concept of pedagogy a further distinction between education (*educatio* in the original Latin) and teaching (*instructio* in the original Latin).[252] To some extent this mirrored or at least reinforced the distinction that I referred to earlier between pedagogic activity (*paidagögus*) and didactics (*didáskalos*) common in Ancient Greek society; however, the effect was to bring into the clustered concept of pedagogy the notion of didactics, to interiorise what was for some an external activity. For Herbart, education was about the shaping of character, teaching was about the acquiring of knowledge. Herbart in addition wanted to subordinate the concept of teaching to education.

Another way of framing the concept is through determining what counts as a pedagogic activity. This sense of inclusion and exclusion is an ever-present concern, with the stress on instrumentality and examinability as criteria for certain types of knowledge being included in a curriculum and others being excluded. Indeed, the concept of pedagogy is now understood as exclusively didactic, with this borrowed idea more in line with how pedagogy is used as a concept in Europe. Didactics now has a more instrumental function.

An alternative notion of pedagogy is what has become known as social pedagogy,[253] which has its roots in Continental Europe and Scandinavia; and it also takes us back to Ancient Greek notions of

---

[250] *The Great Didactic (Didactica Magna)* was first published in Czech in 1648, Latin in 1657 and English in 1896.
[251] This mimics Andreas Schleicher's (2015) unsuccessful attempt at determining protocols for learning from a comparative survey.
[252] cf. Blyth (1981).
[253] Some of the features of social pedagogy are discussed in Smith (2009).

pedagogy, expressed through the figure of the pedagogue. The principle behind this new or revived form of pedagogy is the flourishing child, or at least a focus not on the narrow instrumentalism of learning but learning as an integral part of being and becoming a human being. So, the emphasis is not just on a child learning a particular aspect of living – for instance, how to read a particular type of text – but on the consequences of being able to do this in and for the child's own life and the lives of other peoples. The scope of pedagogic activity has been widened to include notions of reflection, meta-cognition and self-awareness. The first of these elements is reflection.

Reflection

Reflective learning as a concept has been understood in a variety of ways. However, in order to make any sense of these notions, I want to make a number of claims about learning. The first is that in accessing the world, which is a precondition for saying anything at all about learning, there has to be an acknowledgement that we are dealing with: i) a person with the capacity to access the environment, who is distinct in some form or another from another person; ii) a learning object, that is, something that is to be learnt, that is in all respects at a certain moment in time distinct from the person with the capacity to learn; iii) a means whereby the learning object can be accessed by the person, in short, a learning strategy (an interiorisation process); and iv) a subsequent, and thus after-the-event, process where the person reconnects with the environment by using powers that have resulted from this initial learning event (an exteriorisation process). The focus of a reflective activity relates to the third of these claims.

What seems here to be a straightforward process of interiorisation and then exteriorisation is replete with difficulties. The first difficulty is being able to conceptualise the idea of a person or self-conscious being, material object or living thing as a central motivating force. One of the characteristics attached to a person is a sense of identity; however, put in this way, this presupposes that there is something else besides this sense of identity to which the latter attaches itself. Another difficulty is the notion of personhood, so we can say that a person or self has some characteristics, without which she would not qualify to be a person. For example, does a foetus qualify as a person? Does a person in a vegetative state qualify as a person? Does this mean that for a person to qualify as a person she has to have certain properties of the mind? (I am taking for granted that she has to have certain bodily properties; that is, she has to be physically conscious in some sense of that word-complex.) Then there is a sense of personal identity over time. What this precludes is the person being only a piece of furniture in the mind, a receptacle for thoughts, sensations, reflexes and the like. And the reason for this is that what persists through time is literally the changing object of the mind, which may be given a form and a substance in different ways at different time moments. It is not empty, and it is temporally situated.

A number of answers to the question of what a person is have been proposed. For example, human beings are biological organisms, with the consequence that any notion of free will that we may entertain is merely an illusion. This dissolves the binary divide between the brain and the mind and suggests that physicalism – the idea that all of our activities in the mind are subject to molecular causative processes – is correct. Human beings are material objects. They progress or move between different time moments in specific ways.[254]

In contrast, human beings throughout the ages have been understood as immaterial substances or as having souls in a religious sense, which are distinct from material bodies, although our language structures are not yet developed enough to give a complete account of these immaterial substances. Human beings have also been described by David Hume (2000), among others, as being 'bundles of perceptions' – there is no organising vessel, only sets of internalities, externalities and relations between them. This characterisation of the learning-self is derived from Hume's associationism rather than any material causality that is implied by the way the world might work.

Margaret Archer's (2007) notion of a mind has as its centrepiece a model of individual reflexivity that includes a notion of inner speech, where parts of the mind talk to or communicate with other parts of the mind. This internal conversation has three conditioning structures. The first is that it is a genuinely interior phenomenon, which implies that a human being has a private life – this is not to be confused with a private language because, first, speech or language may not be the medium used and, second, if it is, then it is a public language. The second conditioning structure is that this sense of subjectivity has a first-person ontology – it relates directly to a particular person. And third, it possesses causal powers, in that material and discursive consequences could follow directly from the particular internal conversation.

---

[254] I discussed these notions of physicalism in chapter 9.

This is a notion of reflection, or even reflexivity, which is a way of saying that a human object can be disposed to reflect back on itself. Archer (2007) identified four types of reflexive action. The first of these is what she called *communicative reflexivity*. Here the life of the mind is characterised by an internal conversation that is a part of the whole process of learning. The second type of reflexive action is what she called *autonomous reflexivity*, and here the processes of the internal conversation are foreshortened and may be automatic and involuntary, insofar as they lead to actions. The self-referential conversations have taken place in the past; the externalisation process is given emphasis. Then there are *meta-reflexive processes*, in which the principal focus is the internal conversation; interiorisation and exteriorisation processes are neglected. The purpose is for one part of the mind to interrogate other parts or contents of the mind – to be, in other words, critically reflexive. This is an internal process, although there may be consequences in relation to future actions. Finally, Archer suggested that there may also be *fractured reflexive processes*, in which the interrogation by one part of the mind of another part does not proceed smoothly and coherently, leading to distress and disorientation.

Reflection is a seminal form of learning. It has been variously described as critical reflection, reflective practice, reflective thinking and reflexivity. Whereas some see these terms as interchangeable and as having similar meanings, others have sought to differentiate between different types and levels of reflective activity. Critical reflection is seen as a precursor to transformative learning[255] by supporting the development of meta-cognition through the use of critical reflective practices. It is widely recognised as a key component in the learning processes of individuals and organisations. There is a wide variation in the techniques and approaches used in the practice of critical reflection. There is, however, general agreement that the process of critical reflection needs to be facilitated, with approaches ranging from informal discussions to highly structured interventions. The second element is meta-cognition.

Meta-cognitive learning

Meta-cognitive learning[256] refers to learners' awareness of their own knowledge and their ability to understand, control and manipulate their

---

[255] Transformative learning fails to give any real semantic content to the notion.
[256] cf. Butler (2015).

own cognitive processes. There are three types of meta-cognitive processes that have been identified. The first is meta-memorisation. This refers to the learner's awareness of her own memory systems and her ability to deploy strategies for using her memories effectively. The second is meta-comprehension. This refers to the learner's ability to monitor the degree to which she understands the information being communicated to her, to recognise her failures to comprehend, and to employ repair strategies.

The third of these is self-regulation. This refers to the learner's ability to make adjustments to her own learning processes. The concept of self-regulation overlaps with meta-memorisation and meta-comprehension; its focus is on the capacity of the learners themselves to monitor their own learning (without external stimuli or persuasion) and to act independently. These regulatory processes may be highly automated, making it difficult for the learner to articulate them. Self-regulated learning approaches stress the importance of three regulatory processes: regulation of the self; regulation of the learning process; and regulation of information processing mechanisms. The efficacy of the self-regulation process depends on the aggregated effect of cognitive, meta-cognitive and motivational elements. The third element is self-awareness.

Self-awareness

Self-awareness demands some form of reflection. Being conscious makes sense only in relation to the presence of a relevant meta-state of mind and it is this that constitutes a reflective ability. Reflection in this sense, then, is both a relationship between different activities in the mind and a determinant of the capacity of the self to engage in these activities. Phenomenologists explicitly deny that self-consciousness, indeed the reflective process, is to be understood in terms of a judgement being made about its conformity to a higher-order evaluative marker. Rather, it is to be understood as an intrinsic feature of the experience itself. The phenomenologist insists on the existence of some form of pre-reflective self-consciousness. What this implies is that any account of learning, and in particular learning that involves an examination of internal activities in the mind, does not and cannot predicate a self that acts separately and in a controlling manner over the stream of consciousness. This self-awareness or reflective capacity is not an added extra, a different part of the experience. It is implicit in the experience itself and excludes other types of reflection on existing thoughts.

Temporality, or our temporal existence, allows us to return to and investigate our past experiences, but only at the expense of intruding on the process of living or having those experiences. Our knowledge of our experiences is therefore literally out of step with the ontological reality of our lived experiences. Any knowledge we have about learning and learning processes never fits in an absolute sense with what is actually happening. However, we should and do still engage in self-referential and self-critical acts. We do this by reflectively directing our thoughts back on themselves, and by practical acts of self-determination, self-willing and self-formation, in the process modifying those capacities and what they are about. In addition, what is being reflected on is transformed by the act of reflection. The object of learning is neither perfectly mirrored as a result of the reflective activity nor is it constitutively the same as it was before.

Furthermore, the act of reflective self-awareness is an embodied act, which acts to position the individual in relation to the world. This suggests a sense of embodied agency in learning and in other actions in the world. Judgements that I make about myself, criteria that I appropriate in the making of these judgements, ethical positions that I take up and adopt in the course of my life, are all constrained and enabled by social expectations, language structures, conceptual framings and cultural values. These three notions of reflection, meta-cognition and self-awareness are essential elements of a pedagogy of imaginative possibility.

Imaginative possibilities

Some examples of learning objects are: learning how to behave in a classroom; learning that two plus two equals four; learning what a concept such as succession might mean; learning how one should behave in settings outside school; learning how to read; learning about the spatiality of objects in the world; learning what grammar is; learning to be kind; learning how to take part in a conversation; learning a language; learning a new language; learning how to catch a ball; learning how to trap a football; learning what trapping a football might mean; learning how to build a house; learning how to be literate and numerate and becoming literate and numerate; learning how to express a wish; learning what a father is and what love is; learning what being a part of a form of life might be like and many more. All of these learning objects have dispositional elements – so, for example, you do not just learn how to count up to six, you understand the activity of counting upwards as enframed in a complicated network of concepts and what things are.

Stanley Cavell (1979: 177) described this enframing in the following way:

> In learning language, you do not merely learn the pronunciation of sounds, and their grammatical orders, but the 'forms of life' which make those sounds the words they are, do what they do – e.g. name, call, point, express a wish or affection, indicate a choice or an aversion, etc. And Wittgenstein sees the relationships among *these* forms as 'grammatical' also.

For Wittgenstein, grammar is a semantic idea; in trying to understand the grammar of a collection of pedagogic processes and learning objects, we are always looking at what is meant by them and their arrangements. Grammar is not understood in terms of its linguistic reference, but rather in terms of how it can show meaning – what concerned Wittgenstein was the semantic possibilities of the grammar of a pedagogic process or learning object.

A child learns by using her imagination and being allowed to use her imagination. The reason for this is to develop and extend a child's ability to determine the possibilities of objects (Wittgenstein's phenomenal possibilities).[257] Throughout this book I have been constructing an argument that concept learning is about developing the imaginative possibilities of how a concept can be used in a way of life. This mirrors Wittgenstein's notion of learning as being about dispositional concepts and acquiring these dispositional concepts as they are used in the world and as they fit within a framework or network of other dispositional concepts in the world, through determining the possibilities of use and being that inhere in that object (concept or otherwise), even if only temporally. A pedagogy of imaginative possibility can be construed as a play-pedagogy.

---

[257] To reiterate: '(w)e feel as if we had to *see right into* phenomena: yet our investigation is directed not towards *phenomena*, but rather as one might say, towards the "*possibilities*" of phenomena. What this means is that we call to mind the *kinds of statement* that we make about phenomena' (Wittgenstein, 1953: §90, his italics).

A play-pedagogy

The principles that ground a notion of play-pedagogy have been set out in the various chapters of the book that you have read so far, if your reading proceeded chapter by chapter in a sequential order. These principles are: i) a play-pedagogy is a compound word-object that gets its semantic content from meanings that are given to both words and then used in combination; ii) word-objects (compound or otherwise) can be understood only in relation to how they are used in the world or a world; iii) using criteria, or acknowledging that there are always criteria being used in judgements that are made, points to the purpose or function of these criteria – the use of any criteria signifies a set of enablements and constraints as to how a word-compound or a concept such as play-pedagogy can be used; iv) a play-pedagogy is a compound concept that in its use allows us to say something about two human activities or practices: playing and learning; v) a concept such as play-pedagogy is better understood as an active, engaged and committed activity in the world, rather than as a proposition, skill or embodiment; vi) play-pedagogy as a concept has a binding relationship to knowledge and this can be expressed as a means for learning particular objects that are in the world, but that can be learnt only in a particular way; vii) the activity or learning task has a logical relationship with the learning model being employed; viii) ethical and taxonomic valuations that inhere in the concept and in the practice of play-pedagogy are central to the meanings we give to this compound concept; ix) knowledge of the concept and how it is used in the world is transformed at the pedagogic site, so it is possible to suggest that properties such as: the simulation of the learning object, the representational mode of the object, its degree and type of amplification, control in the pedagogic relationship, progression or its relations with other learning objects, the type of pedagogic text, relations with other people in the learning process, the organisation of time (temporal relations) and types of feedback mechanism are fundamental components of this pedagogic transformation (see chapter 12); x) what this means is that in the learning process, the learning object, in this case play-pedagogy, takes a new form as a result of changes to its properties; and xi) the concept of play-pedagogy has attached to it properties that relate to the grammar of the pedagogic process within which the learner is embedded.

The concept and practice of play is grounded in the proposition that looking at things as if they could be otherwise is a worthwhile activity.

Play is about transformational possibilities; that is, it both creates the conditions for being imaginative, and it allows the practice of imagination to function. This transformational process refers to ideas, materials, media and actions, creating in the process novel ways of thinking about these activities. Maxine Greene[258] suggested that play allows the shifting of perspectives and different ways of seeing. There are three possibilities here: introducing into the learning setting alternative ways of seeing and thinking of which the learner was not aware; reworking the meanings that the learner has given to objects, object-relations and object-configurations in the mind; and filling in the gaps by making something more coherent than it is at present.

Lev Vygotsky's (1978) emphasis on play as a pedagogy has been one of the most significant omissions in discussions of his work. Play allows the child – although it could be any learner exercising her imagination – to create her own rules of behaviour and to become the central organiser of those rules. Play allows the child to attach meanings to objects, both in relation to those semantic networks that any play activity operates within and in relation to her sense of self. Play, for Vygotsky, allows the child to fulfil desires that otherwise are denied to her by adults and teachers: '(p)lay is such that the explanation for it must always be that it is imaginary, illusory realisation of unrealizable desires' (Vygotsky, 1978: 6). As a consequence, play allows children to initiate and act out desires that are outside of their normal daily routines and experiences. Play is the externalisation of acts of imagination into actions in the world. When children play with toys, for example, what they are being allowed to do is violate the rules and especially the norms in their lifeworld, albeit a limited lifeworld, and thus this leads in a learning sense to the expansion of the possibilities of use of an object: play is 'a novel form of behaviour in which the child is liberated from situational constraints through his (sic) activity in an imaginary situation' (Vygotsky, 1978: 11).

Understanding the relationship between imagination and memory is salient here. A standard account of memory is that it has three elements: *non-declarative memory*, where the person cannot access the content of the activity under consideration, such as learning to walk, but can still perform the activity; *semantic declarative memory*, which consists of propositions about the world and does not include references to the contents of that person's mind; and *episodic declarative memory*, which

---

[258] Maxine Greene (2000: 5) wrote as follows: '(s)ocial imagination is the capacity to invent visions of what should be in our deficit society, in the streets where we live and in our schools. Social imagination not only suggests but also requires that one take action to repair or renew.'

makes direct reference to the person and can be divided into past, present-past and future happenings. There are some significant differences between the concepts of imagination and memory. David Hume (2000: 13), in *A Treatise of Human Nature*, distinguished between them in terms of strength of impression: 'the ideas of the memory are much more lively and strong than those of the imagination'. Aristotle, in *De Anima* (*On the Soul*; 1987),[259] suggested that a causal connection between memories and what happened in the past was present in memory but not present in imaginings. Memory can also be understood in a different way from how it is understood by many cognitive scientists, as a process of constructing and reconstructing the contents of the mind in response to changing circumstances, both in the mind and in the world generally. Imaginings do not and cannot have this function. A distinction can also be drawn between supposition and imagination. Supposition involves only those functions that we associate with cognition, whereas imagination involves a range of functions and activities, including cognition.[260]

There is also the sense that can be given to imagination of understanding and connecting with other people's minds and circumstances. This argument has been made by Maxine Greene (2000) in its strongest form: in order to behave well towards other people and to empathise with them and their circumstances, we must have a strong sense of imagination because in imagining we step outside of our own beliefs, understandings, reflections and memories in a transgressive sense, and thus implicitly accept that there is another person or persons not like us. This both affirms to us the existence of other people and other minds and allows us to behave in ways that are not purely solipsistic.

Another sense that can be given to the term imagination is that it allows one to develop alternative meanings of a concept or word-complex. This is after all what I have been doing throughout this book: following Wittgenstein's injunction that in trying to understand a phenomenon, one has to work out the possibilities of use that inhere in that phenomenon. We, of course, have to do more than this, such as also trying to understand

---

[259] *De Anima* can be translated as 'On the Soul'.

[260] Pretending and imagining are sometimes thought of as homologous concepts. An obvious distinction between the two is that one is a state of the mind and the other is a behaviour in the world. Some psychopathologies such as autism and delusionary disorder have been described as disorders of the imagination; what is meant by this is that the autistic person or the delusional person is lacking an imaginative capacity. They cannot imagine what it is like to be another person or a different person, and thus their beliefs, self-reflections and actions are wholly self-oriented. There is a great deal of controversy attached to these notional states and thus also to their association with a lack of imagination.

how it fits into a network of other concepts, propositions, embodiments and processes. Imaginative processes are not inductive, deductive, retroductive or abductive; they operate in the space of possibility.

The key for us here is to work out what the connection might be between an act of imagination and a specific act of learning. In learning, we are engaging in a number of processes, such as responding to a learning stimulus, internalising something from an environment, reflecting in different types of ways on that learning object, assimilating that learning object into the array of other objects in the mind, and then externalising and establishing a new relationship with the environment, even though this might have changed as a result of the actions of other human beings. At the reflective level, there may be room for imagining what the learning object is not – an imaginative recreation of the possibilities that inhere in the object. For example, counterfactuals in history are an imaginative way of determining the possible explanations of an object-configuration in time. Modal arguments work on the assumption that some functions of an object may be fallible, including knowledge in general, and it is this fallibility and corrigibility that can act as a guide to what is really possible in a broad sense. Thought experiments, such as Galileo's injunction to contrast the falling of a composite of a heavy and a light object against the falling of a heavy object on its own, is another example.[261]

Following the principle that a pedagogy or learning process is logically dependent on the meanings that inhere in the learning object, play as a practice would seem to fit this best. And this is because play has characteristics that better align with the exercise and development of an imaginative capacity in the learner. Playing then, is not a rest from learning – a way of renewing the energies and capacities of the learner before she embarks on harder and more demanding tasks – but an essential pedagogic process for learning certain types of object in the world and, perhaps more significantly, for learning, and laying the foundations for learning, other types of object as well. What I have been arguing for here also applies to two other important knowledge concepts – curriculum and assessment – and I focus on these in the next chapter.

---

[261] cf. Enrique Zeleny (2011), 'Galileo's Thought Experiment on Inertia'.

18
Curriculum and assessment

I have already pointed to and therefore implicitly endorsed a notion of error (see chapter 1), or at least the possibility of operating with and through a flawed theoretical perspective. In this chapter I examine a particular theory of curriculum knowledge (cf. Young and Muller, 2007; 2010; Young, 2005). Despite its imperfections, it has been enormously influential. I want to suggest that it is incorrect, or at least imperfect, and can be doubted – that is, doubted in a philosophical sense.[262] The question, then, that immediately comes to mind is: what are the grounds for saying this, both in relation to this theory and generally? If one wants to critically examine a theory in the world (let us call this theory T_1), then one has to do two things: first, set out a more complete or adequate theory (let us call this T_2) and provide compelling reasons as to why T_2 is complete or fundamentally sound; and second, show that the original theory that is being critically analysed (T_1) fails to satisfy the standards or criteria implicit in T_2. Two inferences can be made from this: the first is that all knowledge is flawed or incomplete or inadequate to some degree, and for good reasons, and thus the judgement being made here is one of the relative inadequacy of T_1 in relation to a set of criteria in which there is an acknowledgement that it can never be perfectly adequate or sufficient. And the second type of inference that can be made is that it operates against criteria that have some universal and transcendental properties (see chapter 2). These two arguments are not compatible.

The first type of judgement needs to be enframed within a notion of epistemic[263] fallibility. Fundamentally, a judgement about knowledge has

---

[262] Doubt is a concept and should be understood, in line with the argument that I am making in this book, as doubting in an active and dispositional sense.

[263] I am using the word 'epistemic' in two ways: as relating to knowledge or epistemology and as relating to one of the justifications for knowledge: what is outside the mind but has an influence on its contents.

a background to it, and in part this reflects the degree to which that knowledge is considered to be fallible. A number of different types of fallibilism have been suggested. The first sense that can be given to this notion is where the person believes that because he is positioned in relation to the external world, then his perspective is limited and thus the knowledge he produces is compromised and incorrigible. A second type of fallibilism comprises the possibility of making mistakes that in theory could be corrected and this is therefore a corrigible version of fallibilism. A third type is a form of epistemic scepticism, in that the individual holds that no true knowledge is possible because there are no convincing arguments to refute the possibility of being radically deceived. Again, this type is incorrigible because, if it is accepted, there could be no possibility of correction. A fourth type reflects Karl Popper's (2002) hypothesis that knowledge is produced through processes of conjecture and refutation, but this can never attain to a perfect form of knowledge, since the changing and emergent nature of reality means that knowledge always lags behind its referent. Again, this is an incorrigible version of fallibilism because there is no possibility of ever keeping abreast with the way the world is currently structured. Epistemological fallibilism may also cast doubt as to whether the various forms of logical relations between items are sufficiently robust to allow the production of knowledge. The application of epistemic criteria in judgement is therefore determined by the degree and type of fallibility underpinning the epistemology used by the investigator in making his knowledge claim.

In relation to the second type of judgement, it may be possible to develop criteria for making judgements that allow us to say that T_2 is a better description or gives a better account of the world, or a specific part of it, than T_1. As I noted in chapter 2, a minimum set of conditions for a belief to be thought of as rational or intelligible is as follows: there are reasons for supporting a belief and these reasons can be construed in evidential form; these reasons are relevant to this belief insofar as they are necessary and sufficient for holding it and using it in the world; there are no contrary reasons publicly available or imagined for not holding that belief; this set of reasons is internally coherent; and there are a series of logical connectives, conditionals and inferential methods available for use, so that there is a reliable method that can be used for connecting evidence, reasons and beliefs. On these grounds, then, we can be confident in our judgement that T_2 is preferable to T_1.

There are other grounds as well, which consist of our four tests for making a judgement about a theory (see chapter 3). The first is epistemic, where one theory is better than another because the relationship between knowledge of the world and how the world is structured is better aligned. The second element or process is where a theory or description of the world is superior to another because within it there are fewer contradictions and logical anomalies. A third approach focuses on the capacity of the theory or model to be more rational and intelligible than its rivals; and a fourth approach suggests that a theory is to be preferred to another because it is more practically adequate or has stronger links to extant frameworks of meaning. These four processes, once they have been reconciled, allow us to make judgements about theories, models and descriptions of the world.

In one of his later works, *On Certainty*, Wittgenstein (1969: §58) suggested that knowledge of anything implies the logical possibility of doubt:

> If 'I know etc.' is conceived as a grammatical proposition, of course the 'I' cannot be important. And it properly means 'There is no such thing as a doubt in this case' or 'The expression "I do not know" makes no sense in this case'. And of course, it follows from this that 'I know' makes no sense either.

Wittgenstein in both the *Investigations* (1953) and in *On Certainty* rejected the Cartesian idea that true knowledge consists of the absence of doubt. The example he gave in the *Investigations* is about pain, where he argued that because he could not seriously doubt that he was in pain, it made no sense to say that he knew he was in pain. For him, making a judgement is a cognitive achievement, and this includes the possibility of failure. This notion of cognitive achievement is central to the particular idea of a concept – what a concept is – that is being used in this book.[264]

Non-arbitrary knowledge

The more complete or adequate theory (T_2) in turn needs to be justified, or at least a compelling set of reasons needs to be provided to show that it is superior in some way or another to an alternative theory (a T_1). An expression of this superiority is to call the more complete or adequate theory non-arbitrary knowledge and to call the inferior versions arbitrary,

---

[264] A notion of cognitive achievement is central to how we can understand what a concept is and how it can be acquired.

insofar as these versions of knowledge do not and cannot be justified in any reasonable way. There are thus a number of features of knowledge that might qualify the knowledge set to be non-arbitrary; for example, its ontogenesis, its disciplinarity, its sociality, its testability, its purposive or intentional nature, and its capacity to transcend the uniqueness of particular standpoints. There are other features, such as its rationality, its representative capacity and its integrity, but these have been addressed in previous chapters (see chapters 1, 2 and 3). The question that needs to be answered is: do any of these characteristics allow us to argue that knowledge can be non-arbitrary?

The first of these is ontogenesis. Knowledge emerges from previous knowledge, and therefore has historical roots. The non-arbitrary element is its heritage, and this suggests that ideas develop; it is this genesis that constitutes non-arbitrariness. However, if an assumption is made that knowledge – whether within the disciplines or outside of them – comes about because a person or a group of people produce a new version of knowledge, and this is rooted in previous iterations of that knowledge domain, then ontogenesis is a weak rationale for knowledge. The reason for this is that both arbitrary and non-arbitrary knowledge could have this characteristic. However, if we extend this argument so that knowledge becomes, as a result of its genesis, better at explaining the real world (the epistemic construal), or providing a greater degree of epistemic integration (the coherentist argument), or offering an improved resource for society (the pragmatic justification), then the ontogenetic argument is strengthened.

A second feature of knowledge, which might provide us with a reason or set of reasons for identifying a non-arbitrary dimension, is disciplinarity. I have already referred to various disciplinary knowledge classifications; for example, Bernstein's (2000) typology comprising a distinction between vertical and horizontal knowledges. There may be external reasons for the development of these disciplinary forms of knowledge as well as internal reasons. For example, the development of computer technology produced a new discipline devoted to the production of a specialised language, protocol for behaving, set of evaluative criteria and a division of labour within the discipline, including a differentiated knowledge base for that division of labour. Changes in disciplinary knowledge therefore may be derived from internal and external sources; and external factors may act to strengthen the non-arbitrary dimension of the knowledge domain under consideration, insofar as this contributes to the epistemic construal becoming more adequate.

As a consequence of these internal and external changes, evolving disciplinary forms of knowledge change their mode of operation. This refers to their spatial components, their applications, their relations to the practicum and their emanations. For example, Gibbons et al. (1994) distinguished between Mode 1 and Mode 2 knowledge. Mode 1 knowledge is linear, causal and cumulative, originates in the university, is applied to the practice setting, is disciplinary-sourced, and reductionist. Mode 2 knowledge, in contrast, is trans-disciplinary, practicum-sourced, heterarchical, transient and produced in situ. Mode 2 knowledge is developed and used outside of the disciplinary setting. Furthermore, it has been suggested that Mode 2 knowledge has replaced Mode 1 knowledge as the dominant form of knowledge in society.[265]

Even if social relations of power have featured in the genesis of a discipline, it may still be possible to distinguish between moments in the development of the discipline initiated by historically situated social relations of power, and moments initiated by drivers that are independent of these social relations of power. This would allow one to suggest that these moments are non-arbitrary. This does not mean that the production and development of this knowledge domain was independent of those working in the discipline, but only that their work contributed to a knowledge domain that could in principle be judged to be superior to another domain on grounds other than social relations of power. However, what this argument then requires is a justification for knowledge that does not refer to these social relations of power.

A third feature is its sociality. Even if a distinction is made between internal and external relations with regards to the genesis of knowledge, this cannot mean that the former operates outside of the social and the latter incorporates all that we mean by the social, which includes any references to relative or arbitrary knowledge. The point is that even if one accepts that the production of knowledge is not tied inexorably to the development of particular vested interests, including cognitive interests, this does not mean that we can rule out cognitive values that are independent of local power struggles. These are universal values. It might also mean that there are no cognitive values that are relative to particular places and times or specific discourse communities (in other words, these values are local or relative); or that there are no means for determining that one theory is better than another theory (that is, these means are

---

[265] Mode 1 and Mode 2 types of knowledge, and the distinctions between them, have been enormously influential; however, it is hard to see how they can be sustained as forms of true knowledge.

universally justified); or even that there is no infrastructure for the production of knowledge that transcends time and place (this would provide a universal means of legitimation). Each of these four alternatives needs to be justified in turn, and then compared in order to determine which is the strongest argument. And that argument needs to embrace the idea of the social production of knowledge, and not rule out transcendental and therefore universal criteria for determining that one theory is better than another theory, which is the basis for any knowledge claim.

Michael Young (2005) took the view that disciplinary knowledge is not arbitrary, is social, but cannot be equated with the results of power struggles between people engaged in arguments about what is or is not true knowledge – arguments that engage academics throughout their working lives. This refers to the idea that there are power struggles about knowledge, which one of the protagonists wins in the end, and that this results in the legitimation of one version and the delegitimation of the other. However, this does not mean that ineluctably the stronger or the more coherent or the more correct version is the one that is adopted. If this were so, then this would render those struggles about knowledge irrelevant, because there would then be an inevitability to the adoption of the more correct idea, and as I have suggested previously, incorrect ideas may be accepted in society, even if they have the potential over time to become more truthful, because of the looping nature of the relationship between description and object.

A fourth feature is its testability or its capacity to be tested for its truth-value in a variety of settings, such as practical, laboratory, research and workshop environments. This is a variant on a disciplinary justification: if knowledge is tested in various ways, this therefore reduces its arbitrariness, and consequently knowledge can be thought of as non-arbitrary because it conforms to the rules developed in the disciplines or domains for knowledge development, which means that knowledge is tested against a set of discipline- or domain-specific criteria. If we want to argue that the only rationale for knowledge development is that it conforms to a set of rules developed in this way, then we are reverting to an internal justification for knowledge development.[266] What this position emphatically rejects is any reference point to an external reality outside our internal beliefs. This takes us further from an initial rejection of a correspondence or mirroring relationship between language and reality

---

[266] This is Richard Rorty's (1979: 185) position, since he argues that 'nothing counts as justification unless by reference to what we already accept, and that there is no way to get outside our beliefs and our language so as to find some test other than coherence'.

to a position where reference can be internal only, and an external world cannot even be contemplated.

A fifth feature is its intentionality, and an argument is constructed to the effect that knowledge is arbitrary if it does not have a convincing purpose. This feature is consequentialist, because it is concerned with the consequences or effects of using this knowledge in the world. There may be a number of reasons why intentions are not translated into practices. For example, there may be unintended consequences involved. The problem with this viewpoint is that knowledge may be produced for reasons other than utility, such as explanation or intrinsic worth. Insofar as each of these meets a human need (such as the satisfaction of curiosity, or providing order in the world), a purpose is fulfilled or at least there is an intention behind the activity. However, a distinction can be made between these essentially intrinsic and extrinsic processes, which emphasise external purposes such as revaluations and rearrangements of allocative and authoritative resources in society. Intrinsic purposes may result in extrinsic gains; however, this is not their intention.

A sixth feature of knowledge is its capacity to transcend the uniqueness of particular standpoints, with a standpoint or position understood in an epistemological, ethical or geo-historical sense. There are two arguments being articulated here. The first of these is that non-arbitrary or universal knowledge has generalisable properties so that it applies to objects with family characteristics and therefore transcends or goes beyond the particular. The second argument focuses on the notion of transferability insofar as an object has properties, which allows it to be relevant to a number of similar settings. The object is plural. The problem with this is that it assumes a particular ontology, which is that the world consists of individual and family items that are in a definite relationship to each other and, further to this, arbitrariness is equated with uniqueness. This is a difficult argument to sustain. However, the second argument suggests that if the world is constructed in this and not in another way, then it makes sense to say that knowledge is not arbitrary because it is a truthful representation of the world.

Two types of arguments are being used above. The first is that knowledge claims are legitimated on the basis of external relations of power, and the second is that knowledge claims are legitimated by principles intrinsic to knowledge itself. These intrinsic principles are: a greater rationality, that is, the giving of more or better reasons for actions; fewer deficiencies leading to a greater comprehensiveness or adequacy; an enhanced ability to bridge the divide between the epistemic and ontic realms; and higher levels of abstraction or theorisation. Knowledge, then, it is argued, is non-arbitrary because it conforms to one, or more than one, of these internal principles. And knowledge is arbitrary if it does not conform to one or more of these principles. I suggested in chapter 12 that knowledge and learning are homologous concepts and that this has implications for an understanding of the curriculum. This is the next part of the general argument that I need to make.

A curriculum perspective

Michael Young and Johan Muller's (2007; 2010; 2015) curriculum argument is underpinned by two precepts; the first is that a curriculum should comprise objective knowledge and that a notion of objectivity is a precondition for any inquiry or practical application of knowledge in a curriculum. The second precept is that this knowledge emerges from and cannot be reduced to the contexts of its production and acquisition – it thus has some transcendental characteristics. This means that real knowledge and consequently powerful knowledge is emergent, non-reducible and socially differentiated. The claims, then, that Young and Muller (2010) made are as follows: i) there is and should be a clear demarcation between curriculum and pedagogy; ii) the boundaries between knowledge domains and between school knowledge and everyday knowledge are not arbitrary and need to be maintained; iii) the guardians of these distinctions are teachers and other experts, especially those concerned with learning; iv) pedagogy has an ineluctably hierarchical nature; v) there are epistemological constraints on the scope of policies for widening participation and promoting social inclusion; vi) generic skills are deemed to be of less importance than subject-specific knowledge; vii) a distinction should be made and maintained between this subject knowledge, derived as it is from the disciplines, and information; and viii) boundaries in general have to be strengthened and maintained. Among the expressions of this boundary weakening are: the integration of school subjects; the stipulation of curricular content in generic, usually skill or outcome terms; the promotion of formative over summative assessment; the introduction of unified national qualification frameworks; and the promotion of facilitative rather than directive teaching. As we have already seen, these stipulations are derived from a fallacious Durkheimian epistemological perspective (1939)[267] (see chapter 2).

---

[267] Durkheim's (1939) epistemological perspective is positivist and empiricist (see chapter 2).

Young and Muller's curriculum argument, then, is flawed on a number of grounds, principally that their conception of learning is erroneous. At the beginning of this chapter, I suggested that if one wants to critically examine a theory in the world (let us call this theory T_1), then one has to do two things: first, set out a more complete or adequate theory (let us call this T_2) and provide compelling reasons as to why T_2 is complete or fundamentally sound; and second, show that the original theory that is being critically assessed (T_1) fails to meet the standards or criteria implicit in T_2. Young and Muller's curriculum argument can serve in this instance as a T_1, and thus can be compared with the curriculum theory that I have argued for in this book, T_2. This theory (T_2) begins with an explication of learning as a concept.

The concept of learning is potentially polysemic and can be understood only in relation to how it is used in the world. A key determination of the meaning of this concept is whether and in what way it relates to a meta-theory, which invokes a relation between mind and world, and which has transcendental elements. In line with Wittgenstein (1953), I suggested that concepts cannot be fully determined with regards to their meaning in definitional and essentialising ways, but only in terms of how they are used in a way of life. I then suggested that a distinction could be made between knowledge of the world and meta-knowledge, which directly refers to knowledge of this world and not to the world itself. And further to this, that all knowledge, including knowledge of learning, uses or is enframed in criteria, whether these criteria are implicit or explicit.

Learning as a process has a set of pedagogic relations; that is, it incorporates a relationship between a learner and a learning object. A theory of learning pivots on the idea that there is an entity called, for the sake of convenience, a human being, and this entity has a relationship (both inward and outward) with an environment. As a concept, learning is fundamentally related to knowledge, and therefore if we are thinking about learning and the practices of learning, we also need to make reference to what is to be, and how it is, learnt. Typically, what we are aiming at in such considerations is some form of knowledge. Knowledge is fundamental to the three types of learning that I have identified: cognitive (relating to propositions), skill-based (relating to processes) and embodied (relating to bodily accomplishments). Prior to each of these is a set of dispositions, without which cognitive, skill-based and embodied learning would be unsustainable. Acting in the world requires the use of, and is underpinned by, conceptual frameworks of one type or another. Propositional knowledge or making a claim that this or that is the case is, in common with the other two forms of knowledge, a process of doing and thus of knowing how to do something or other. And this results in all of these types of knowledge having the same general form, which allows them, in this form, to be understood as learning actions or acts of learning. In order to make a claim of knowing, we are not, as is commonly thought, providing a description of an experience (that is, constructing propositional knowledge), but making a claim about it in what has been described as 'a space of reasons'; what follows from this is that we can and should understand and use concepts specifically in relation to current and future-oriented networks of meanings.

There are five types of object in the world, each of which has different characteristics: discursive objects, material objects, relational objects, structural-institutional-systemic objects – this type includes both discursive configurations and material configurations – and people, including the self, which is always experienced differently from the way other people are experienced.[268] Each has different characteristics and, because objects have a dynamic structure, in rare circumstances they may change their status as objects; indeed, what constitutes an object-type is also dynamic. In an object-ontology, objects, including human beings, have acquired dispositions. This theory of learning needs to be positioned within a concept of curriculum. A curriculum indicates what is intended to happen in a programme of learning and the circumstances in which these activities can take place. The activities referred to here are learning activities; a curriculum is a collection of exercises and tasks that culminates in learning of one type or another.

This is underpinned by a number of axioms. The first is that there is a logical connection between the learning object and its pedagogic form and thus its learning mode. Theoretical and contextual considerations impact, then, on how elements of teaching and learning are realised. Acknowledging this allows the identification of a number of learning models: observation, coaching, goal-clarification, peer-learning, trial and error, hypothesis-testing, reflection, meta-cognition and practice (see chapter 12). Choosing between these models depends on the nature and constitution of the learning object; in other words, the former is logically dependent on the latter. A second axiom is that boundaries and categories used at the discipline or domain level, temporary as they are, cannot be translated, without serious distortion, into organisational principles for

---

[268] These five types of object, and the distinctions between them, are fundamental aspects of knowledge and being.

the development of a school curriculum. And a third axiom is that curriculum work is enframed in epistemological, ontological and relational arrangements. Young and Muller's theory of curriculum is replete with difficulties, aporias and unresolved dilemmas. This does not of course mean that it has not been enormously influential, since the power of simple messages (for example, their idea of powerful knowledge) is undeniable. This has implications for any theory of curriculum and assessment that we might want to develop.

The curriculum and assessment field

Classifying and categorising the field schematically is fraught with difficulty, and this is because a history, exposition, delineation or explanation of an idea is essentially a contested activity. Whether a person adopts a conventional view of narration or chronicling with its trans-historical subject and immersion in originary knowledge modes, or seeks to genealogise such a narrative or chronicle by subverting the naturalness of the categories and delineations in common sense discourses, it is still important that he confronts his own position as historian, genealogist, expositor, academic or critic. In other words, the person still has to take account of the originary status of his viewpoint about knowledge, his epistemic position.

A curriculum points to what is intended to happen in a programme of learning and the circumstances in which these activities can take place. There are five possible curriculum frameworks (there may be more, but they have not yet been codified or much used in the world): the systemic-technological, the critical-reconceptualist, the cognitive-constructionist, the interpretive and the instrumentalist. To these should be added neoliberal curriculum frameworks, focusing on competences, and extra-national single-surface comparative and assessment-driven implementation mechanisms.

Neoliberal curriculum frameworks are in the ascendancy. Governments around the world and coordinators and curriculum developers of systems of education such as Young and Muller (2007; 2010; 2015), with a few notable exceptions, have reached an agreement about the nature of the school curriculum, learning approaches and assessment practices. This consensus now operates at all levels of education systems, and can be expressed in terms of a number of propositions: traditional knowledge forms and strong insulations between them need to be preserved; each of these knowledge forms can be expressed in terms of lower- and higher-level domains, and the latter have to be taught before the former and sequenced correctly; knowledge can be understood in behaviourist and objectivist terms (see chapter 11); certain groups of children are better able to access the curriculum than other children, and, as a result, a differentiated curriculum is required to meet the needs of all school learners; the teacher's role is to impart this body of knowledge in the most effective way, and thus his brief cannot concern itself with the ends to which education is directed, but only the means for its efficient delivery; and the school's role is to deliver a public service that meets the targets set for it by governments and education systems.

The key to understanding these various curriculum models and frameworks is how each of them conceptualises the notion of assessment. Particular assessment practices reflect decisions that have been made and will be made in the future about who and what is assessed, for what reason and in what way. Assessment serves a wide variety of purposes, ranging from the most commonplace of exchanges in a restaurant, for example, to school reports and high-stakes examinations, from individual job interviews to national monitoring. What unites all of these is the sense in which assessment first and foremost is a proxy for determining the quality of something or someone. It therefore operates as a mechanism for placing that person or object in a particular hierarchy of values: this person is better than this other person with regards to a particular range of skills and this school is better than this other school because its students have graduated with better examination results. This spectrum of communication ranges from the most informal of exchanges to the extremely formal, the common factor being the use of assessment data of one kind or another as a publicly acceptable code for quality. Closely associated with this is the issue of legitimacy. The results of any particular assessment device have to be trusted by the public if the consequences are to be acceptable. Sadly, assessment issues are generally treated as technical matters, as focusing on improving the methodologies used to assess people rather than on the purposes or consequences of using such approaches, or as essential elements of a specific pedagogic approach.

What this means in effect is that on occasions clear contradictions and tensions between common assessment practices emerge. An example of this is the incompatibility between an increasingly test-driven educational and curricular culture and an explicit commitment to lifelong learning processes. Another example might be the tension between summative and formative purposes in an assessment. This learning agenda, exemplified in the notion of formative assessment, is at odds with the use of punitive high-stakes testing, which has as its principal purpose raising standards, although the notion of a standard is in itself a contentious issue.

An extremely important aspect of assessment is its increasing internationalisation, exemplified by large-scale cross-national assessment studies, such as the Programme for International Student Assessment (PISA). It is possible to argue that there is now a world trade in educational policies, especially in relation to assessment issues. This 'policy borrowing', the take-up of apparently good ideas developed in one country by another, has further strengthened the grip of conventional assessment assumptions. Despite the significant evidence concerning flaws in international comparisons of student achievement (see chapter 4), the power of the simple messages that can be and are derived from them about relative national success in a world of increasing global competition has acted to reinforce the prevailing domination of established forms of educational assessment. The collection of data has become in itself a major instrument of social control, whether this is at the level of the individual, the institution or indeed whole operational systems such as that of education. And thus, we need to understand learning (making a knowledge claim in relation to a network of concepts and making the subsequent commitments that this entails) in historical, archaeological and genealogical ways.

19
A history, archaeology and genealogy of learning

In this chapter I want to focus on learning, as a concept and as a practice, and its historical, archaeological and genealogical connections and relations. In the first instance, I need to consider how these three types of event-methodologies, which refer to events in the past and in the present-past, can be distinguished from each other. Historical, archaeological and genealogical methodologies are framed by time, although this core category is construed differently in each of them. A further shared element is that they produce configurations of discursive objects, such as learning discourses relating to, for example, disengaged reasoning, curricularisation, scientism, atomisation, innatism, bureaucratisation, naturalism and representationalism. These discursive object-configurations are understood in different ways historically, archaeo-logically and genealogically. The key, then, to understanding what they are lies with the types of relations that exist between objects in their formation and reformation.

Archaeology is the term used by Michel Foucault in his earlier writings (1970, for example) to describe his approach to history and writing history.[269] This approach focuses on the discursive trace-objects and object-arrangements (the order of things) left from the past, which enable us to write a history in the present-past. He contrasted this with a genealogical approach.[270] Although there is some confusion in his

---

[269] Michel Foucault focused above all else on writing a history of the present. In his later writings, this became a critical history of the present, or, as I am calling it, the present-past. He described his archaeological method as a history of thought, and not a history of ideas, and he did this because he wanted to uncover the discursive traces of distinct historical periods, each with its own types of truthful statements and orders of discourse (internal and external).

[270] Michel Foucault understood the genealogical method as being qualitatively different from the archaeological method, although there are traces of each in the other. The archaeological method

later work about the differences between the two modes of historical theorising, this approach is designed to critically interrogate belief formations by attempting to explain the scope, extent, breadth and totality of discourses that are in existence. Both of these approaches are historical in a conventional sense, in that an event, a discursive or material happening, or a configuration relating to either of these, has occurred prior to other object-events, objects and configurations of objects. There is a temporal order between these objects.

Foucault revived the notion of genealogy as it had been used in the past, and in particular developed the idea from the one used by Friedrich Nietzsche in his *On the Genealogy of Morality* (1998).[271] Foucault's principal concern in his *The Order of Things* (1970) is to offer an account of how knowledge through the ages has changed, and the implications this has for practices such as psychiatry and clinical medicine, and for disciplines such as economics, biology and philology. Throughout this book, I have pointed to historical, archaeological and genealogical ways of thinking, which operate at particular time moments in history. We might want to call them *Weltanschauungen*,[272] or universal-views, held by a community in place and time – discursive configurations that are in history. Having said that, it is important not to overvalue and thus exaggerate the efficacy of the properties of these historical configurations, and especially the property of absolute reach or ambit.

Representationalism

An example of Foucault's use of the archaeological method in *The Order of Things* (1970) is his explanation of the notion of representation, although this account also has genealogical elements. This is an

---

focused on structural order, difference and discontinuities between the past and the present-past. The genealogical method tried to show descent and emergence, and the continuities between the past and the present-past. The differences between the two are not clear-cut. The point about a genealogy of knowledge as opposed to an archaeology of knowledge is to include within it elements of power and its many variations in the construction of knowledge and understanding.

[271] Michel Foucault acknowledged his debt to Nietzsche and especially to Nietzsche's *On the Genealogy of Morality* (1998). The commonality in their works lies in the subject matter of their concerns: the disunity of the subject, powerful practices, continuities and discontinuities in history, and experimentation.

[272] The need to use a German word, *Weltanschauung*, here is because there is nothing in English that fully covers all of the various meanings that attach themselves to it.

archaeological account of an object in the world – in this case, a discursive object and a discursive object-configuration. There is a historical element in his description of the discursive object, and this therefore implies that the one gives way to the other. However, the process of transformation from one discursive configuration to another cannot be characterised as occurring at a particular time point, as it is sometimes portrayed in popular histories.

The transformative process of a discursive object such as representation has three distinct stages or levels. In the pre-classical age,[273] the concept of representation was understood as the employment of ideas to represent the object to which it referred. Knowledge was thought of as resemblance – the idea in the mind resembled the object it was seeking to represent. This pre-classical age gave way in time to what has been described as the classical age,[274] a body of thought and thinking that was qualitatively different from what there was before. Again, we must be careful not to subscribe to a belief that this was how everyone in the world understood the relationship between mind and world. This *Weltanschauung* is a discursive object-configuration, which had its being in the mind, and had implications for how people lived.

In time, a new discursive formation developed, but not as a part of a preset pattern or ineluctable process. Whereas the pre-classical age understood the relationship as one of resemblance between things or objects, now representation was understood as a bridging mechanism between mind and world, and as an abstract structure that underpinned our knowledge of what was in the world and to which it made reference. René Descartes (1988), for example, suggested that we can have direct access to the abstract qualities of our thoughts, and we can also alter those thoughts in order to produce different representations of these objects. The classical view had to confront the difficulty of determining what an adequate representation of an object might be. This cannot be achieved by arguing that we can know the object by separating it out from its representation in the mind because this would preconfigure what we are attempting to describe. The only way to answer the question of what an adequate representation might be is through an external notion, such

---

[273] The pre-classical age is ill-defined in the work of Foucault, but certainly embraces the European Renaissance and much more besides. This problem of historical definition points to the need to reaffirm the idea that archaeological and genealogical time points are not and cannot be definitively set.
[274] Again, the classical age can be only loosely identified. It would, however, include the European Enlightenment and more than this.

as, in Descartes' case, that it gives a 'clear and distinct perception',[275] or in Hume's case, that it is a simple impression.[276] The classical theory of representation, then, is that of abstract qualities in the mind, with these being representations of what is out there in the world. Furthermore, because these abstract qualities were not thought of as being causally efficacious, they were not able to influence what was there in the world, and thus language and languaging could not have a fundamental role in the development of the mind and the development of the world.

The classical era, in its turn, gave way to what Foucault described as modern philosophy,[277] and the story takes us up to and beyond Kant's rejection of classical representation, although we should be careful not to position his critique as a specific historical event. Kant wanted to reject altogether the idea of representation as an appropriate descriptor of the mind–world relationship and replace it with something other than representation. He suggested that some thoughts or abstractions were themselves the product of processes that belonged to a specific epistemic order of the mind, which he called transcendental subjectivity.[278] This is an example of the idealistic tendencies for which he has been and continues to be criticised.[279] Kant opened up the possibility that all knowledge was essentially historical, and consequently could be applied only to particular and specific communities of knowers. This thought and injunction thus paved the way for the emergence of Nietzschean and indeed Foucauldian postmodernist and post-structuralist idealistic views of the world and especially those that referred to the key relationship that concerns us here: the relationship between mind and world.

In *The Order of Things* (1970), Foucault understood this post-classical or modernist notion of representation through two important processes: the reinstatement at a conceptual level of the importance of language and the rebirth of man (sic) (and its swift repudiation). In the classical age, human beings were thought of as the site of knowledge

---

[275] Clear and distinct perceptions for Descartes (1988) are such because they are perceptions that prove to be self-evident. In other words, they cannot be doubted, although here doubting is being understood in a Cartesian (this is to be expected) and not in a Wittgensteinian sense.

[276] Hume's (2000) notion of simple impressions has a very similar meaning.

[277] Foucault argued that the fundamental turning point in history for the modern period occurred with the publication of Kant's *Critique of Pure Reason* in 1781, although this seems to be somewhat early in the history of thought.

[278] Kant's notion of transcendental subjectivity (2007) has two dimensions. In the first case, there is what Kant referred to as the empirical self, and in the second case there is the transcendental self. This is an attempt by Kant to suggest a theory of subjectivity that is not impersonal, scientist and atomistic. It is rooted in his idealist perspective, with subjectivity being another idea of the absolute.

[279] cf. Strawson (1959).

because they have in their minds those ideas that represent what is in and of the world. Foucault (1978b, for example), writing as a modernist, went on to disabuse us of this notion of a transcendental human being. This was because of, what he called, the 'finitude of man' (sic), and the 'analytic of finitude'[280] (1978b) that is attached to it. In the modernist era, some philosophers tried to compensate for this by grounding human beings in natural processes, substances or viewpoints. In its Romantic iteration, which Charles Taylor (1998) talks about so compellingly,[281] we have an attempt at naturalising human beings, to in effect explain and justify knowledge in terms of natural processes and as being in conformity with what already existed in nature.

What Foucault was doing here was archaeology and not genealogy, although his discussion of representation and the various forms that it takes certainly has genealogical elements. This preferred methodology is now understood as the identification of epistemological and ontological elements in political, social, economic, ethical and taxonomic orders of reality. The key principle behind the archaeological method as he used it in the *History of Madness* (first published in France in 1961 as *Folie et déraison: Histoire de la folie à l'âge classique*) and the *Birth of the Clinic* (first published in France in 1963 as *Naissance de la clinique: Une archéologie du regard médical*) is that systems of thought and knowledge in general are rule-governed and define the boundaries of thought within a specific domain or period: what can be said and thought so that one can

---

[280] Foucault's notion of the finitude of man is very like Heidegger's (1962) version. Here is Foucault in his own words: 'In one sense, man is governed by labour, life, and language: his concrete existence finds its determinations in them; it is possible to have access to him only through his words, his organism, the objects he makes – as though it is they who possess the truth in the first place (and they alone perhaps); and he, as soon as he thinks, merely unveils himself to his own eyes in the form of a being who is already, in a necessarily subjacent density, in an irreducible anteriority, a living being, an instrument of production, a vehicle for words which exist before him. All these contents that his knowledge reveals to him as exterior to himself, and older than his own birth, anticipate him, overhang him with all their solidity, and traverse him as though he were merely an object of nature, a face doomed to be erased in the course of history. Man's finitude is heralded – and imperiously so – in the positivity of knowledge; we know that man is finite, as we know the anatomy of the brain, the mechanics of production costs, or the system of Indo-European conjugation; or rather, like a watermark running through all these solid, positive, and full forms, we perceive the finitude and limits they impose, we sense, as though on their blank reverse sides, all that they make impossible.' (Foucault, 1970: 341–2).

[281] In my copy of the book *Sources of the Self: The making of the modern identity* by Charles Taylor, there is on the flyleaf a handwritten note from my daughter: 'Dearest Dad, Happy 50th Birthday, Lots of Love, Sarah'. Since I was 68 at the time of writing this book, I can identify the year my daughter gave me Taylor's book – 2002. I have to say that since then I have read and reread it many times and gleaned from it a great deal of what little I know about philosophy. This book seems to me to be one of the most profound and enlightening works of philosophy that has been written. It has proved over and over again to be a source of inspiration.

engage in an intelligible conversation. He used the genealogical method for the first time in *Surveiller et punir* (1975). Whether we call it archaeological or genealogical, the use of the method has implications for the history of a discursive configuration such as learning and, in particular, the idea of representation.

Symbol-processing accounts of learning

One of the consequences of understanding the mind as a vehicle for representing the world is that the learning process becomes a means of making a correct and given representation of it. A distinction can be drawn between symbol-processing views of learning and sociocultural or constructivist views of learning (see chapter 11).[282] The first of these theories, the computational or symbol-processing view, conceptualises learning as a three-fold process of sorting, storing and retrieving coded information that has been received from an external source, which mirrors the way a computer processes data (see chapter 13). The mind is a tabula rasa, and learning comes from experience and perception. Information or data is inputted into the mind, and this consists of predigested facts about the world, which represent in a clear and unambiguous way how the world works. The theory of mind that this represents conceptualises each act of learning in input and output terms, and this assimilative process means that, as a result of the learning process, adjustments are made to the store of facts and theories that the person already holds, in the light of new information that the learner receives. This is a mechanistic, indeed technologised (see chapter 13), event-process, and the notion of interpretation is subsequently reduced to the assimilation of new information and the reformulation of the mindset of the learner. Learning is understood as a passive reflection of the world, with particular learning episodes being understood as more or less efficiently realised.

Symbol processing approaches have their origins in the philosophical theory of empiricism, proponents of which understood the world as given and then received by individual minds. Adopting this theoretical framework means that language is separated out from reality and the individual is separated out from society.[283] The first of these, the language-reality split, suggests that facts can be collected about the world, which

---

[282] cf. Bruner (1996).
[283] cf. Bredo (1999).

are atheoretic and separate from the belief systems of the collector. These facts are understood as true statements about the world. Furthermore, the theory of learning that emanates from it points to the need to discover what they are, and then develop appropriate models to explain them. The claim being made here is that language is a transparent medium and has the capacity to faithfully represent what is external to it. There is, however, a more appropriate solution to the problem of the relationship between mind and reality, which is that representations of reality are not given in a prior sense because of the nature of reality, or because the mind is constructed in a certain way, but as a result of individual human beings actively constructing and reconstructing that reality in conjunction with other human beings – some contemporary, some long since dead.

There is a second dualism that critics of symbol-processing approaches have suggested is problematic. This is the separation of the individual from society. If a learner is given a task to complete, she has to figure out for herself what the problem is and how it can be solved. The task is framed by a set of social assumptions made by the teacher. The problem with the symbol-processing view is that an assumption is made that both learner and teacher understand the task, and the way it can be solved, in the same way. However, this is an assumption that should not be made, and one of the consequences of making it is that the learner who then fails to solve the problem is considered to be inadequate in a specific way, rather than someone who has reconfigured or interpreted the problem in a way that is incongruent with that of the teacher or observer. (Here we have the birth or at least the rebirth of one of the most important concepts in the learning network, that of innatism.[284]) The individual/civic distinction, which is central to a symbol-processing view of cognition, separates out individual operations in the mind from the construction of knowledge by communities of people, and this leaves it incomplete as a theory of learning. Even then, it still has archaeological elements.

Bureaucratisation

A different account of learning has bureaucratic elements. Max Weber's (1964) notion of rational activity has three constituents: increasing knowledge, enhanced impersonality and improved control. Rational

---

[284] Innatism is one of the most powerful concepts in the history of ideas and it is used as a device for creating divisions between people, categories, concepts, societies, objects, object-configurations and much more.

action presupposes knowledge insofar as it requires an understanding of those economic, political and social circumstances that form the backdrop of our actions, because to act rationally is in part to be able to reflect on them in relation to the probable consequences of any actions that might be contemplated. Rationalisation is here understood by Weber not as the post-hoc reinterpreting of a previous historical event but as the way in which we develop our ability to provide an accurate account of the world, which for Weber meant a rational account of the world. The second element in his thinking was impersonality, where modern societies demand a sense of objectification, such as in reducing the complicated lives of individuals to sets of numbers and placing them within suitable categories.[285] For Weber, one of the seeds of this impersonality was the protestant vocational ethic, which was predicated on a monotheistic theology that reduced human beings to elements of God's goodness. The third element is control. Rationalisation involved increasing control of human beings in the lifeworld, prompted in part by scientific and technological mechanisms, both material and discursive (see chapter 13). This meant that human beings were increasingly subject to legal, technical, political and social enablements and constraints, and, perhaps more importantly, forms of discipline and control that were reflections of the puritan ethic that so pervaded the society in which Weber lived. Weber called this an 'inner-worldly asceticism' and it has many of the meanings that Foucault found to be attached to the control of the body in his work on sexuality (cf. Foucault's *History of Sexuality*, volume 1, 1978b).

A particular manifestation of the bureaucratic ethic lies with the discursive learning formation, *new public management*, and this has had significant effects on the governance of UK higher education institutions and, no doubt, elsewhere. The major goals of this discourse are to improve the effectiveness and efficiency of the public sector, enhance the responsiveness of public agencies to their clients and customers, reduce public expenditure and improve managerial accountability. In addition, it has resulted in the creation of a new cadre of managers. These new managers consume resources that could have been spent elsewhere, although the argument is made that they produce efficiencies. Such

---

[285] cf. Kim, 'Max Weber' (2019). Even simple mathematical computations such as a mean average, or a median average, or a model average, have reductionist tendencies. The mean is defined as adding up all the numbers you have collected and then dividing this by the number of numbers that you have. The median is the middle value in a list of numbers. The mode is the value that occurs most often. In all three computations, some meaning that is there in a list of cases is lost.

efficiencies are achieved in a number of ways: by making staff (academic and administrative, although this distinction has archaeological dimensions) work harder and in more productive ways; by constructing and using a particular type of knowledge, broadly conceived as technicist and bureaucratic; and by injecting into the system as much competition as possible (this involves a reconstitution of the notion of academic identity, so that loyalty is towards the institution rather than to the discipline). New hierarchies are established so that old hierarchies constructed around a notion of academic capacities (expertise in the core activities of academic life, such as researching, writing and teaching) are replaced with hierarchies that are underpinned by bureaucratic forms of knowledge. The way signs are interpreted, and judgements made, is reconstituted by the bureaucratic model of organisation – this is the bureaucratic discourse acting in a causally efficacious way. Furthermore, these acts of interpretation and judgement are reduced to binary choices, and this affects how we can understand the object and how we can interact with it. Professional loyalties are marginalised, and rewards and sanctions are tailored to fit this model, so that knowledge construction within the academy assumes a new form, which relates to both the behaviour of the academic within the institution and her academic work.

Max Weber (1964: 219) argued that bureaucracies are 'the most rational known means of carrying out imperative control over human beings' and that a bureaucratic administration achieves its purpose by 'domination through knowledge'. He suggested that a bureaucracy has six features. The first is that the area of life which forms the bureaucracy should be delimited and governed exclusively by rules. This entails a clear division of labour (a hierarchical division of labour prevents duplication of roles, allows people to specialise and enables them to develop expertise in that area) and standard operating procedures. Second, a hierarchy of roles has to be set up with clear responsibilities and statuses, designations of power and authority, and chains of command. Power flows in a downward direction. Third, any actions performed by members of the bureaucracy need to be written down and preserved so that a permanent record can be kept, to allow accountability mechanisms to operate in the most effective way. Fourth, expert training for its members is a prerequisite so that the knowledge the bureaucrats possess is formed and reformed in accord with technological, organisational and market imperatives. The final two precepts are that members of the bureaucracy should devote their full attention to their work, and, more importantly, that they should become accustomed to learning, following and enforcing rules, which can be unequivocally interpreted. The overall effect is to increase efficiency and predictability. Finally, these rules and regulations and the administrative procedures that accompany them are designed to limit personal favouritism and promote fairness and equity for the benefit of the organisation as a whole. The bureaucratic discourse is extremely powerful and has had powerful effects.

A theory of bureaucratic learning suggests that knowledge can be broken down into its smallest parts, with only those elements of it that can be incorporated into a bureaucratic view retained. The rest are discarded. This process therefore values, through elimination, those dispositional, propositional, skill-based and embodied forms of knowledge, learning and being that fit into a bureaucratic ethic and ethos. This mode of learning is rule-based insofar as the detheorised objects of learning, the pedagogic methods employed and, fundamentally, the assessment and evaluation practices that accompany bureaucratic learning, are given prior to, and priority in, any acts of learning that might take place, and reflect a particular arrangement of knowledge and learning practices that are hierarchical, identity-forming and reductionist.[286] Naturalism is another discursive configuration.

Naturalism

There was a family of views in the late eighteenth century that understood the natural as an inner source of motivation and action. It is possible to place these under the collective term of expressive romanticism – although we should be careful about placing all of its many iterations under one single banner or label. Each of these iterations has some elements in common; they have, in Wittgensteinian terms, family relations.[287] In contrast to the classical emphasis on form, tradition and harmony, some romanticists argued for the expression of feeling and imagination in the construction of knowledge. There are two consequences of this. The first is expressive in a fundamental sense, so that we can talk about the nurturing of an inner voice; this echoes the development of the inner Catholic voice, which I suggested in chapter 8 might be regarded as an important Catholic pedagogy. The second is entering into a particular relation to nature, one of conservation, respect and care for it. In this sense, nature means more than just the environment but also extends its

---

[286] Bureaucratic modes of management have some very unpleasant consequences.
[287] Wittgenstein's notion of family resemblances comes from the two books that, I think, best encapsulate his mature thinking: *Philosophical Investigations* (1953) and *On Certainty* (1969).

meaning into what is considered natural. Thus, some sexual practices were considered to be abhorrent because they did not conform to what is natural or given (see chapter 6). We can then talk about a naturalistic ethic in which our behaviours, intentions and thoughts are aligned with a natural norm. This is also a form of legitimation in that human beings now had a clear way of distinguishing between those activities that are natural and those that are abnormal, and consequently those activities that they should own and those activities that they should disown.

Jean-Jacques Rousseau,[288] as we saw in chapter 15, subscribed to a form of naturalism with regards to learning, with the natural process of the development of the child being commended and the unnatural or cultural view of education being an imposition, an unjustified and almost certainly injurious intervention, with damaging consequences for the life of the child. For Rousseau, our access to the natural is first and foremost inward and internal. It is also the harbinger of a notion of fulfilling our potential, an idea that was transposed in various forms into a harsh and unyielding expression of innate differences between people. This process reached its apotheosis in the revival of eugenics in the last part of the nineteenth century and the early part of the twentieth century,[289] and also of course in the Holocaust in Europe in the middle of the last century. These racist theories persist to this day.

Another example refers to the boundaries we develop between concepts. There are many ways of describing and redescribing the world and thus of dividing it up into objects, object-relations and object-configurations. And what this implies is that there are no criteria in and of the world that would allow us to say that one of these is superior to the rest. Natural differences between kinds constitute the boundaries between real entities; here I am referring to relations between different manifestations of an object, object-relation or object-configuration over time. Instead of talking about similarities and differences, perhaps we should be talking about the genesis and development of these differences and similarities. This implies that the similarities and

---

[288] In chapter 15, I suggest that there are some fundamental difficulties with the educational philosophy of Jean-Jacques Rousseau.

[289] Eugenics was a perfectly respectable doctrine in late Victorian and early Edwardian society, with Francis Galton from the university where I work (University College London) one of its most prominent advocates. James Watson, one of the discoverers of the DNA sequence, more recently argued along eugenicist lines. Another eugenicist working from University College London was Karl Pearson, whose claim to fame was the development of a number of statistical methods, such as the chi-squared test. There are some important and complicated connections and relations between the development of eugenicist beliefs and these analytical methods.

differences that we formulate at the epistemological level are not only descriptions of kinds, but in addition are a part of a causal sequence and thus potentially have causal effects.

And what this means is that, first, all of these kinds are constructed human activities in history; second, these kinds of object are brought into being by human beings living with each other in physical, social, discursive or epistemic communities; and third, if those kinds can be formed, then they can also be reformed. Processes of classifying and reclassifying change the nature of objects, object-relations and object-configurations. All references to the world involve the identification, manipulation, transformation and reconstruction of the categories, and we cannot avoid this. The scientific method, with its claims for the possibility of positional objectivity, that concepts can be reduced to measurable constructs, and that we should adopt a representational ontology, is negligent of these.

Romantic expressivism has a number of variations. What could be considered to be a learning object in formal educational settings was given an authority previously denied to it, in that some learning objects were considered to be natural and some were not. Because the romantic era essentially embraced an inwardness, a sense of inner reflection, a view of the person as a natural source of being, that needed to be opened, discovered and explored as a learning medium, this became the norm. This learning process assumed a relationship with nature that was wholly essential and good, and this view of learning marginalised the idea of learning as engaging in a reshaping of those objects in a life project. In order to live properly, human beings are enjoined to enter into productive relationships with nature, if only they can find the right way of doing this. To adopt a correct moral and practical stance towards nature is to develop an inner voice, and this becomes the essential tenet of learning.

A fourth learning element is that this directs us away from cognitive forms of learning and towards the cultivation of dispositions and sentiments. Even if sentiments are understood as a particular type of disposition, or even that all dispositions have sentiments at their heart, this still allows us to separate the two – to in effect divorce the one from the other in later time moments and in different *Weltanschauungs* or communities of practice. A fifth consequence is that the learner during the process of reconnecting with the environment, which was the source of the original learning act, is also enjoined to express (or articulate as with propositional forms of knowledge) that inner process of learning in the world. In the expressive act there is a sense of self-formation, both with regards to this inner being, which Christians refer to as the soul, but also to a shaping of the life project, and a capacity to be able to do this.

Curriculum and learning

I now want to focus on an important archaeological process – the curricularisation of knowledge for learning – and suggest that this should not be understood as an event occurring at a particular time point, but as an event-process in time. In the first instance, I want to give brief accounts of two important historical events: the curriculum in the early grammar schools; and the medieval university curriculum in England.

The grammar schools were different in function from the song schools, with the latter being almost exclusively concerned with performances of Christian rituals in the cathedrals[290] and the former more concerned to provide a general education for the professions, as well as members of the clergy. Saint Augustine's idea of a curriculum, being derived as it was from the Roman and Hellenistic schools of rhetoric (this word having a distinctive classical meaning and being different from its contemporary common usage), comprised the study of grammar, rhetoric, logic, arithmetic, geometry, music and astronomy, with these considered to be a preparation for the professions of theology, law and medicine. In practice, these early grammar schools focused on Latin grammar and literature, as they saw their primary function as being to prepare initiates for the priesthood.

A second example of a curriculum event is the medieval university curriculum. In medieval England, the university curriculum comprised a six-year Master of Arts programme of study, which consisted of a combined Bachelor and Master's degree. The curriculum, such as it was, comprised arithmetic, geometry, astronomy, music theory, grammar, logic and rhetoric. The trivium consisted of the latter three subjects and the quadrivium of the former four subjects. At a later period, the curriculum came to include three Aristotelian philosophies: physics, metaphysics and moral philosophy. The language of delivery was Latin, and the preferred pedagogy or method of learning was scholasticism, with its strong emphasis on dialectical reasoning, inferential analysis and the resolution of contradictions, usually in common texts. Having successfully completed a Master of Arts degree, some students went on

---

[290] This is a history and not a genealogy.

to complete studies in law, medicine or theology, leading to a doctorate. These accounts of the development of the school curriculum and the medieval university curriculum are histories, with little reference being made to archaeological and genealogical elements.

A number of features of these curricula stand out. The first is the limited range of subjects covered, if we understand limited as referring to all of the possible human activities and all of the possible ways of understanding those human activities. The second is the reference to previous subject categorisations, in this case, Aristotelian categories. The third is that there was for a long period of time a common means of delivery and a common language to deliver it. This had the effect of developing a stronger boundary between scientific or first-principle knowledge and everyday knowledge (see chapter 8). It conferred a special status on the knowledge produced and used in schools and universities. The fourth insight that we can glean from these two curriculum accounts is that the divisions between the different knowledge silos are understood in highly abstract terms and not by reference to particular ways of living; so, for example, grammar is understood as the connections and relations between word-objects, word-complexes, sentence constructions and so on, as the written text (in Latin) decreed, and within this process and others can be seen the origins of absolutism or correctness in language, in this instance. In the twentieth and twentieth-first centuries, we can see the beginnings of a new notion of curriculum, which is underpinned by a new epistemological settlement. Its characteristics are: a much more clearly defined set of subject areas; an atomisation of knowledge in which each knowledge area is broken down into its most basic elements; justifications for knowledge practices that are discipline-specific (see Young, 2005; Bernstein, 2000); the choosing of knowledge items for the formal curriculum on the grounds that they can be tested or evaluated in formal procedures such as examinations; clear boundaries established between curricula and pedagogy; the development of learning practices that pivot on notions of fixed capacity and potentiality; and the acceptance of linear progressions and pathways through the knowledge canon. This form of curricularisation rapidly became the norm, and it was underpinned by a form of disengaged reasoning.[291]

---

[291] Forms of disengaged reason are now dominant in meanings and practices that operate in the field of learning. They are hegemonic, with the most obvious example being the Research Excellence Framework (REF), which is laying waste to excellent research, writing and philosophy, driven on by management zealots who feel that this is the way we have to go and there is no alternative. There is an alternative, which involves refining our sensibilities and deepening our understandings of our relations with the world.

Disengaged reasoning and curricularisation

It is possible to sketch out an archaeology of these two important processes as having three staging posts: an original theistic grounding of the notion of reason; a naturalism of disengaged reasoning, which took the form of scientism;[292] and, as we have seen, a family of views that take their inspiration from a romantic expressivism, or even, and at a later point in time, one of the many modernist viewpoints, some of which are still with us. One form that this sense of disengaged reasoning took was a particular view of epistemology. When in the nineteenth century the social sciences were beginning to be developed, they did so under the shadow of the physical sciences. Therefore, as immature sciences, they sought to mirror the epistemic and methodological approaches adopted by the natural sciences (see chapter 2). And what this meant was that a rational and correct behaviour or judgement was construed as free of any form of valuation. This is a type of disengaged reasoning, and it was complicit in a new notion of curricularisation.

This new notion of curricularisation in the form of behavioural objectives comprised an atomisation of knowledge. This was an argument for precision, objectivity, prediction and the use of the scientific method to establish once and for all what should be taught in schools and indeed how educational knowledge should be ordered. Arguments for behavioural objectives were repeatedly made, and these comprised a notion of objective analysis whereby designated skills were broken down into their constituent elements. These skills were derived from the activities of experts in a variety of fields essential to the wellbeing of society, and curricular aims and objectives were derived from an objective examination of such activities. Furthermore, these skills and their component subskills were expressed as specific teaching objectives, which were so arranged that the curriculum was designed around them. This work is behaviourist in that learning is understood as the acquiring of these skills and the evaluation of sets of behaviours in order to determine whether these skills had been successfully acquired by the learner (see chapter 11). This is the origin of the behavioural objectives movement that influenced curriculum-making in the 1970s and 1980s, and which continues to shape global, national and local curricula round the world.

---

[292] 'Scientism' is a term used by Jurgen Habermas (1981) and others to denote a mode of thinking that equates science with truth.

What is noteworthy is the underpinning belief in science as the model for the essential practical activity of determining what should be included in a curriculum and how it should be delivered. Atomism, pre-specification and control are therefore foregrounded, with the curriculum conceptualised in terms of behavioural objectives and an input–output model of schooling. A behavioural objectives model has to be operationalised and, since the process involves the specification of observable performances and not inner states of being of the learner, behavioural indicators can serve only as approximations of these inner states. Words that refer to those inner states are acceptable as general statements of intent, but then have to be broken down into behaviours. The logic of this argument is that if words and phrases used in constructing objectives are clarified properly, they can be translated into actions for the learner, so that the verification of those behaviours is not open to misinterpretation. While it may seem that this follows directly from the need to clarify these objectives, in reality this introduces a new idea. The learner's behaviour that is being evaluated can qualify as a proper objective only if it is capable of being evaluated in an unequivocal way. This would seem to preclude the evaluation of a number of behaviours and therefore a number of inner states of the individual because any use of them is always open to interpretation as logically they can be framed only in this way. Some worthwhile educational activities are designed to be open to a number of interpretations, and thus, within the strict boundaries of a behavioural objectives model, these would have to be excluded. It is clear here that the model fits certain types of activities better than others and, consequently, to include all worthwhile activities necessarily involves a distortion or packaging of some of them to fit the model. Examples of these might include the more expressive objectives of the curriculum.

There is a further problem with the atomised model of knowledge and learning that is being proposed. A subject or discipline is broken down into its constituent parts, which are then expressed in terms of behavioural objectives. In such a specification of the knowledge process, no account is taken of any unintended effects. Since the purpose is effectively achieved if the learner can perform the clearly and explicitly stated action, the means to achieve this become irrelevant. Consequently, there is both an issue about unintended effects and an issue about the ethical consequences of arguing that any means are appropriate if the desired end is to be achieved. Means, furthermore in this scenario, are treated as ethically neutral, because they are thought of as actions for reaching a particular endpoint. Means are judged by criteria such as efficiency and effectiveness. With this clear separation of means and ends, governments around the world have developed curricula within a behavioural objectives model, and at the same time have intervened in the specification of the means as well. Thus, the logic of behavioural objectives has been commandeered to produce a performative model in which teachers are held accountable both for the production of good ends and the efficient following of means (teaching approaches) specified by outside bodies.[293]

In this chapter I have artificially separated out a number of key processes from a narrative about learning. These key processes are disengaged reasoning, curricularisation, scientism, atomisation, innatism, bureaucratisation, naturalism and representationalism. There are other processes and discursive configurations that there is not the time and space to discuss here, many of them given pride of place in Charles Taylor's monumental archaeology of identity formations, *Sources of the Self: The making of the modern identity* (Taylor, 1998). It is also worth noting that Taylor sets out his work in a fairly straightforward historical manner, although of course his subject matter is not strictly historical events but important discursive and material formations in the history of the world. I have been referring throughout this chapter to the issue of time. In the next chapter I want to suggest that time and temporality are essential building blocks in the theory of objects and object-relations that I have developed in this book.

---

[293] cf. Dunne (1988).

20
Time and learning

It is said that the Hopi people do not have a concept of time or have never developed an ability to conceptualise and use time (see Whorf, 1956).[294] This is hard to believe since they plant crops that mature at later periods of time than when they planted them – intention and purpose are time-oriented. Despite there being no trace of a concept relating to past, present and future events in the language they use (Hopilavayi, a Uto-Aztecan variety), this does not mean that they do not have a sense of time passing, since there might be a disjuncture between the language in use and the thought processes, beliefs and networks of meaning that are a part of how they go on in life. However, without some notion of time, the concept of memory – that is, remembering an event that happened in the past and is no longer happening – becomes a problem. This also reminds us that time is a concept and thus should be understood as a conceptual activity in the world.

Learning itself, if it is understood as an activity, has a temporal element to it. If we understand it as a process – event A produces or leads to event B, which in turn leads to event C – then we are identifying three time points, where each of these time points is arranged sequentially. The philosopher Henri Bergson (1999) suggested that the present is not in time but should be understood as *presencing*, where what this means is that any talk of the present and indeed any *presencing* activity is an intrusive act in the ceaseless flow of time.[295] In addition, self-reflection or

---

[294] Malotki (1983) refuted Whorf's claim that the Hopi did not have in their language any sense of time. He identified many examples of Hopi words and more importantly grammatical forms that refer to temporal relations. Malotki also argued that the Hopi language has tense constructions that distinguish between future and non-future tenses. This debate, and indeed dispute, shows how arguments can be conducted at one level, in this case the language level, and ignore other levels, such as the semantic one.

[295] Heidegger (1962) borrowed from Bergson the notion of presencing, though his claim was that he used it in an entirely original way.

taking part in an internal conversation or in an examination of the self (especially in a religious sense) all refer to past occurrences – they are never acts of reflection about present occurrences. The whole present is never available for self-examination. This notion of reflection and examination has important consequences for learning, pedagogic relations and going on in life (as we have seen in chapter 9).

For Martin Heidegger (1962), human beings are future-oriented[296] at every time point. He was concerned to repudiate a conventional notion of time, in which time is understood as a uniform, linear and given series of what he called 'now points' – the future is not yet in the present or not yet now, the past is no longer now, and the present is thought of as the confluence of past to future events at each and every time moment. For Heidegger, this is a weak sense of time and it implies that the present is always foregrounded. He was also concerned to avoid metaphysical notions of time. Heidegger wanted to enframe time within a notion of human beings ineluctably moving towards their end, which he called being-towards-death. The human being does not and cannot live in the present but always projects themselves towards their end.[297] This projection into the future entails a carrying forward of the person's having-been-ness;[298] however, this does not mean that the person is inexorably a prisoner of his past. He can liberate or free himself from his past by choosing what he does. The present then can be captured in what Heidegger described as a moment of vision,[299] leading to an authentic sense of being (or *Dasein*). Time can be grasped only as a unity of its three dimensions: past, present and future. However, time is finite; it ends in death. Time also has a use-function.

Categorisations of time and the temporal order

There are perhaps three categorisations of time in use. The first of these is fixed time, and this is best exemplified by scientific measurements such as atomic time. There are two different measures of this. The first is what is

---

[296] *Zukünftig* in the original German. The reason for providing the original German word is because translation (in this case from German to English) is never straightforward.
[297] *Zukommen* in the original German. The reason for providing the original German word is because translation (in this case from German to English) is never straightforward.
[298] *Gewesenheit* in the original German. The reason for providing the original German word is because translation (in this case from German to English) is never straightforward.
[299] *Augenblick* in the original German. The reason for providing the original German word is because translation (in this case from German to English) is never straightforward.

called international atomic time, which is a timescale based on 400 very precisely calibrated atomic clocks and comprises divisions between time such as 60 seconds constituting one minute or 60 minutes constituting one hour. These divisions are essentially arbitrary in that there is nothing in nature that corresponds to a second, but what a second is corresponds to agreements reached in history and retained in some form or another. The second measure of fixed time is what is known as universal or astronomical time, and here the standard used to differentiate one day from the next is the rotation of the earth and the actual length of a day on earth. A day represents a 24-hour rotation of the earth on its axis and a year represents 365.25 days, or the equivalent of one rotation of the earth round the sun. Again, we should note that within this broad metric, the subdivisions of time, such as minutes and seconds, are arbitrarily chosen. It allows the timetabling and structuring of learning, especially in formal settings.

The second categorisation of time is what has been called biological time. In this mode, chronological age – and not it should be noted experiential or familiar time – is given precedence. An example in a formal learning setting such as a school is where children of the same age cohort are taught together and expectations of what they can do are framed in terms of being ahead, or perhaps more significantly (for them) being behind, those levels of knowledge, skill, dispositional or embodied acquisitions designated for this age group. The organising principle is time, and much flows from it, such as the comparative principle, which allows children to be compared to each other.

The third category of time is social time. Many of our temporal classifications are the results of decisions made in the past and the present about how we should organise learning, and each of these decisions, when formally ratified, builds on other decisions made in the past. Furthermore, the contexts, including the historical contexts of these collective decisions, may include different notions of relations between human activity and time. Particular attitudes towards time may have pedagogic implications, so that schools may choose to privilege what Anthony Giddens (1986: 35) has called 'durable co-present interactions', as in classes of children in different schools being taught about the same topic at the same time; this can be compared with fragmented temporal interactions, such as various forms of internet-based learning. These two examples of the influence of time on pedagogic arrangements point to the way in which different conceptualisations of time influence, and to some extent determine, the conduct of learning, and therefore how or what is acquired by learners. These conceptualisations of time can be construed as philosophies.

Philosophies of time

A particular philosophical perspective on time is fatalism.[300] This can be understood as an assertion that regardless of whether there is a human intervention or not, any event or happening in the future is unavoidable. It will happen. A number of objections have been made to this idea. There is no evidence (and this includes reasons) for the proposition since it is wholly future-oriented; that is, there are no signs in the present or the present-past to indicate or allow one to speculate that the future is already mapped out and consequently that there is nothing one can do about this. There is a way of determining whether fatalism is true or not, but this investigation would have to be conducted over a period of time and suffers from the flaw that there is no way of determining that the fatalist assumption at a first time point is an accurate prediction and does not in any way contribute to the state of affairs observed at a second time point. When we talk about an event happening in the future, the truth-value of this proposition is also future-oriented. We can tell only whether it is true or false by observing and being present at that future event. Propositions have truth-values at particular times rather than truth-values simpliciter or atemporal truth-values.

I have suggested how and in what way the present works in relation to the past (and this is why I am calling it the present-past) and equally how and in what way the present works in relation to the future. Every material or discursive event has a history, and this may be concealed. Further to this, when we make a decision in the present, we are inevitably thinking about what the consequences are of this decision being enacted in the future. This is different from understanding the past and the future as necessarily embedded in the present.

A dimension of time is necessarily attached to any change process – could there be a timeless process of change or a period of time when nothing changes? If the latter is possible, then it is also possible that a million years have passed (in what has been called objective time) since you started reading this sentence. This does not make a lot of sense as it assumes that objective time can pass without there being any change at all, and this assertion separates out time and change, so that they operate independently. We have moved here from a linguistic or conceptual argument or description of what is happening in the world to a belief that this is how the world actually works. What the opposing argument implies

---

[300] cf. Markosian (2016), 'Time'.

is that since we cannot separate out time from internal change in objects in the world and from changes to objects caused by interactions between objects in the world, we therefore have to understand time as a necessary element or property of all objects in the world and of all relations and interactions between these objects.

This argument has implications for the topology of the timeline since if we subscribe to the notion that time is a property of an object in the world or a dimension of object-relations, then the shape that the topological line can assume is dependent on the nature of these objects and object-relations. If, on the other hand, there is no necessary relation in a Platonic sense between time and objects in the world, time exists independently from the motion of these objects and relations. And this means that we can never know what the shape of the topological line is: is it linear and singular, or multi-streamed, or beginningless or endless, or branching, or a closed loop, or discontinuous? I have been focusing in this book on learning objects and their relations, and thus the topography of time has direct implications for curriculum progression, school timetables, examination syllabuses, disciplinary knowledge and learning trajectories.

There are multiplicities of time: lived, experienced, generated, allocated or used as an exchange. Time allows repetitive cycles of activities in formal institutions of learning and is usually expressed quantitatively. As a result, it can be separated into slots or blocks or sections and allocated for subject learning. This means that comparison, a key educational concept, is frequently construed in quantitative terms – this is not inevitable and has implications for how learning environments, formal or informal, are constructed in the present.

Our own obsessions with ordering time can in part be traced back to the ascetic daily rounds of Benedictine monastic life. It was in the monasteries of the West that the desire for order and power first manifested itself after the breakdown of the Roman Empire. Within the walls of the monastery there was sanctuary; under the rule of the Benedictine Order, surprise, doubt and irregularity were put to one side. Time, then, can also have this tendency to regularise the activities and actions of human beings, especially in their learning form.

A restricted temporality comprises the simultaneous coexistence of future, present and past events. This implies that since they coexist, human activity cannot alter the future-present. The universe is closed and not open and not susceptible to directional change. An example of this is where science postulates time laws governing the present, so that future-present-past events are preordained before they are caused.[301] A restricted form of temporality is not compatible with embodied agency because this involves the potentiality for transformative change. The universe is not yet made, which means that some form of separation between past, present and future events is necessary. This entails a modification and refinement of the idea that all present events and happenings have been formed in the past and in the future. When we say that a present event or happening is past-orientated, what we mean is that the conditions for decision-making and the instantiation of those decisions are antecedently formed, and when we say that future acts or happenings are always future-orientated, we are suggesting, and no more than this, that our limited understanding of what might happen in the future constitutes a dimension, albeit an important one, of our decision-making and being in the present.

Temporal framings

Time is also influential in social theorising and thus in all of our relations with the world. We can contrast a naive realist position with a belief in radical relativism. Here, observations that we make about the world are never conceived of as theory-neutral, but are always mediated through temporal structures, time-paradigms and chronological worldviews. Furthermore, these are not just epistemological frameworks but normative beliefs about how researchers would like the world to be. The implication of this is that no one framework is superior to another and that we simply have to live with such value disagreements. The way in which we settle disputes is practical, by the exercise of power, whereby those with greater control of allocative (material features of the environment and the means of material production and reproduction) and authoritative (the organisation of time-space, the body and life chances in society) resources (Giddens, 1986) impose their view on the world. This results in various forms of idealism that imply a radical conjoining of thought and reality. Indeed, it challenges the distinction between statements and referents, and implies that statements refer only to other statements and not to any underlying reality. This can be

---

[301] This is why it is difficult to apply evolutionary theories to the full gamut of human activity in history, although evolutionary psychologists suggest that human behaviour in most of its manifestations is the result of psychological adaptations that evolved to solve problems encountered in past events and happenings.

contrasted with the doctrine of naive objectivism referred to above, which signifies another conflation of thought and reality, but this time of a different order. Whereas naive objectivism collapses a description of the world into its referent, radical relativism does the same but in reverse order, collapsing reality into text.

For social and learning theorists, there is always a problem with the relationship between the agency of the individual and those relatively enduring structures within which they are positioned. Agency is a self-constructed form of action; the person constructs and reconstructs himself in the course of his life and through other people's accounts of him. It is forever in a state of flux. In addition, it is possible to suggest that those structural relations within which we are embedded are in history and therefore also subject to change. However, the most fundamental insight of the hermeneuticist[302] is that these structural relations can be known in the first instance only through their reconstruction by a person or persons.

A naive realist position would suggest that structural influences can be understood without reference to the way in which they are conceptualised by individuals. An alternative position suggests that those structures and mechanisms that underpin social life are competently reflected in actors' descriptions of the world and their worlds. In other words, social actors can give adequate accounts of their skilled performances under the right conditions, and these reflect how society works. A third position seeks to reconcile the first two positions. Agency and structure operate as a duality. Actors continually draw upon sets of rules and resources, which, once substantiated, allow social life to continue as they become normalised. Human beings make the world in the context of previous attempts by them and other people (this creates structural properties), and at the same time transform those structures and change those conditions that influence subsequent reconstructions of the world. Furthermore, while agency is responsible for structural transformation, it is also being simultaneously transformed itself. Structures therefore have only substance, and then only fleetingly, in the skilled performances of actors within society and over time.

Giddens' (1986) 'tendential voluntarism' has been criticised by Margaret Archer (2007), among others, because it suggests too close a relationship between agency and structure. For Archer, social structures and systems have a relative independence from the activities and beliefs of social agents. Archer offered a solution to this dilemma, which she

---

[302] Anthony Giddens is an example.

called analytical dualism. Even as she recognised the interdependence of structure and agency, she strongly argued for them operating on different timescales. At any particular time moment, antecedently operating structures constrain and as importantly enable agents; the interactions between them have consequences, both intended and unintended, which lead to structural elaboration, where much changes, or to stasis, where nothing changes. All of this is conducted over time. Social processes are an endless array of sequences of morphogenesis or morphostasis – their elements are temporally ordered. Some of these are brief, some take a long time. This allows accounts of how structural and agential phenomena interlink over time to be developed.

John Stuart Mill's four principles of difference that I referred to in chapter 4 – agreement, difference, residue and concomitant variation (the third one that I referred to earlier is a combined method involving the first two principles) – formed the basis for three types of investigative models, which established the foundations of a temporal theory of causation. The first of these is the deductive-nomological model, also known as Hempel's (1965) model, or the Hempel-Oppenheim model (1948), and this is an extension of the original logical positivist model. Here, premises, general law statements and statements of antecedent conditions (the explanans) allow a conclusion to be drawn, which is a statement describing the event (the explanandum). Temporality is thus built into this model. The second is the inductive-statistical model in which probabilistic or statistical generalisations are made, rather than general law-like statements resulting in probabilistic statements of antecedent conditions. This is the dominant model in the field of education around the world. Hempel's model was reworked by Karl Popper (2002), so that instead of confirming a conjecture or theory, its truth-value depends on whether or not it can be potentially falsified. These three models attempt to both explain what is happening in the world and predict what might happen in the future. It is the element of prediction that locates these theories in the temporal dimension. The emphasis on constant event patterns that allow the possibility of predicting future events – this pattern is not just present-orientated but extends into the future – is a consequence of understanding causation in this Humean[303] way and of understanding cause-and-effect relations as constant conjunctions rather than the interplay of deep-lying mechanisms in open systems (see chapter 4).

---

[303] cf. David Hume's *A Treatise of Human Nature* (2000).

A further point about time is relevant to the architecture of objects and object-divisions that I have argued for in this book. I have asserted previously, and perhaps in a somewhat unreflective manner, that there are five types of object in the world: discursive, material, relational, configurational and persons. It might be argued that there is no clear distinction between, or no good reason for separating out, discursive/material objects and configurations of objects because even discursive/material objects are dynamic and configurational – they have a variety of characteristics at particular moments of time. What distinguishes the two, however, is their temporality – a configurational object (as an object-type) endures over a longer period of time – and their generality – an object is singular, a configuration is plural.

Learning temporalities

I have suggested in this chapter that time and temporal relations can be understood in a variety of ways, which has implications for how we conceptualise learning. This means that those many linguistic and conceptual manifestations of time – order, organisation, synchronisation, change between fixed points, rates of change, repetition, regulation, duration, sequencing, irreversible direction, passage, the rate at which events occur, timing, parameter and measure – can be and frequently are enframed in different ways. For example, the temporal dimension of order can be understood as a Foucauldian technology of power and truth or as a rational way of arranging human affairs. In the former case, power through time is understood as diffuse, embodied, enacted, discursive and constitutive of agency.

An important dimension of learning is time and temporal relations. This works through activities such as: progressions and trajectories of the learner; knowledge formations; progression and emergence of learning objects and relations between them; logical prerequisites of learning objects and relations; institutional temporal relations such as timetables, lesson durations, school days and learning holidays; examination and test progressions; age-related competences and more. Indeed, it could be said that time and temporal flows are essential to understanding the concept, process, institutionalising and practice of learning. In addition, it is possible to argue that the way we conceptualise learning is deeply embedded in temporal enframings. Our investigations of learning are structured, paced, timed and sequenced. Time becomes an ever-present idea in any thinking we might want to do about what learning is and could be. In the next chapter I discuss its companionate concept, that of space.

21
Spatial relations

Many philosophers have argued that time and space are not ultimately real; they only appear to be so. What is real, and this is of course a contentious issue, is not subject to temporal and spatial conditions. For example, Plato (1997) suggested that ultimate reality resides in the forms, which are neither time-bound nor spatially dimensioned.[304] Christian philosophers such as Saint Augustine of Hippo sought to affirm the existence of an everlasting and ever-present God.[305] This God was the source of all space and time relations. Immanuel Kant (2007) argued that human beings experience the world as located in space and situated in time, but that this was in the mind and not outside it. For him, these experiences were intuitions and inferences concerning space and time. Thus, it is only in a weak sense that he asserted the objective reality of these two important categories. Space and time are bound up with their particular manifestations and for him only the particular could be real.[306]

Classrooms, learning environments and educational institutions have different spatial geometries, which support certain types of interaction and communication. Prominent among the many spatially oriented learning systems that have been developed are: distance learning programmes; massive open online courses (MOOCs); hybrid learning models; and blended pedagogic learning accessories. As I suggested in

---

[304] In the *Timaeus*, Plato (1997) understood time and space as eternal forms. Time, he identified as the period of motion of the heavenly bodies, and space as that in which things come to be.

[305] In his *Confessions* (2017: 201), Augustine of Hippo suggested that: '(y)ou are not the mind itself. For you are the Lord God of the mind. All these things are liable to change, but you remain immutable above all things.'

[306] Immanuel Kant (2007: 39) wrote as follows: '(s)pace is a necessary *a priori* representation that underlies all outer intuitions. One can never forge a representation of the absence of space, though one can quite well think that no things are to be met within it. It must therefore be regarded as the condition of the possibility of appearances, and not as a determination dependent upon them, and it is an *a priori* representation that necessarily underlies outer appearances.'

chapter 13, all of them aim to deliver learning in more efficient ways, with efficiency understood as: accessibility; flexibility; hypertextuality; better control for learners in the pedagogic relationship and over the curriculum; more equal relations between teachers and learners; and more accurate identification and feedback processes leading to better forms of progression. Many of these advantages are exaggerated; however, it is still possible to suggest that learning processes are not just enhanced by technologies, but fundamentally changed by them, so that new types of knowledge are being created, with subsequent wash-back effects on identity formations and learning positions taken by these learners.

With regards to learning environments, spatial orientations include notions of: open; distance; distributed and flexible learning; student-centredness; border-crossings; communities of practice; the spatial ordering of people; a spiral curriculum; spatial identity positionings; and comparative learning methodologies. Michel Foucault (1986) referred to the current world as the era of space in the sense that we are now in and formed by simultaneous, juxtapositioned, near and far, side-by-side and dispersed sets of relations.[307] Such relations have significant consequences for the formation of learning environments, and we need to understand their spatiality.

Spatiality

In this book I have argued throughout for the existence of five types of object: discursive objects, material objects, relational objects, configurational objects and persons. Objects have emergent properties that interact with each other and, as a result, new properties are created or emerge from old combinations of objects. This means that the relation between the structure of objects and the agency (agencies) of the person (or people) is the key framing device at the ontological level. Spatial relations, then, are one dimension of how we organise objects in the world.

On 23 June 2016, Britain voted to leave the European Union and thus establish a new political geography.[308] Brexit has been characterised as an issue of sovereignty, although this is better understood as a displacement rationale. This is because Brexit, in whatever form, will

---

[307] cf. Foucault (1997).
[308] At the time of writing, the United Kingdom had not yet left the European Union.

not be a reclamation of sovereignty. Rather, it is about new arrangements of power in the world and specifically about how that power can be distributed and thus exercised. Being inside or outside the European Union, then, may not be the most significant issue; rather, it is about the UK's capacity to resist globalising pressures, in relation to their intensity, the velocity of these global flows and the impact they are likely to have – all of which have spatial elements. However, it would be a mistake to think that globalisation, a spatial phenomenon, acts as the sole driver of policy and practice within an individual country, and therefore it would be a further mistake to understand the process of globalisation as deterministic, linear, inevitable and all-embracing, and to argue that global influences are always more powerful than national interests and agendas.

Globalising processes, insofar as they have real effects, work in two ways: first, national governments operate within global markets and therefore fashion their policies to fit this agenda or to exploit it; and second, national governments are subject to pressure from forces outside their jurisdiction, which influence their policies and practices. Further to this, the success of any intervention (by another body operating outside the boundaries of the State), or at least the path it takes, is not just determined by the system into which it is being introduced but also by the type of intervention that is being made. Interventions are time sequenced, so they are likely to have different effects at different moments in the history of a nation.

This takes place against a background of an apparently growing commitment to improving and, in part, standardising social institutions and practices, seen as important in the light of dominant market-based theories, and against a backdrop of neoliberal ideas. The most widely predicted response to the global financial crisis of 2008 was a return to a more measured Keynesian approach, and yet capitalism, markets and neoliberal economics still seem to be in the ascendancy, and this has direct consequences for nations around the world.

Globalisation works in a number of ways; for example, it can be understood as a cultural phenomenon. So instead of distinct national forms and identities, there is a cross-fertilisation of ideas, a creation of hybrid cultural forms, a homogenisation of culture, and a standardisation of cultural products. This may lead to a sense of cultural sameness or conformism. Globalisation also points to the establishment of globalised markets and global consumer identities.

Globalisation can refer to the nation state and the ways in which its powers have declined; an example of this is the way in which global capital has now broken free from national boundaries. This means that local legal codes, currencies, habits and customs now serve as constraints on the free movement of capital across national boundaries. Another manifestation of globalisation is the expanding nature of capitalisation.[309] This can take a number of forms. For example, it is spatial as capital seeks to fill the potential social, geographical and physical spaces available to it. Capitalisation may also expand through the invention of new types of commodity, and it may act to intensify or deepen and develop its influence in the world.

Globalisation may also refer to the way in which the labour process is constituted and reconstituted, and, in particular, to how all of the activities involved in work are commodified; and as a result are given a value so that a profit can be made in relation to any surplus that can be created. Traditional modes of working, notions of public service, and sets of professional ethics give way to the need to make a profit, as systems, institutions and people reconfigure themselves and in turn are reconfigured by global forces.

These new forms of globalisation coalesce around notions of the commercialisation, privatisation and capitalisation of social goods. Commercialisation describes the ways in which institutions, their products, their protocols and their epistemologies become marketable properties. Privatisation involves the takeover (either directly or indirectly) of schools, hospitals, universities and the like for the purposes of generating profits. Capitalisation entails labour taking on a new form, so that profits can be made from any surplus value. It also involves the erosion of public service values. It changes the nature of labour (its motivation, its purposes, and its organisation and management) in social institutions.

What globalisation implies is that the world now comprises multiple and developing spatial relations: a complex system of finance, production and trade; a positioning of corporations around the world; and these flows of capital and goods. These may lead to certain pathologies, or at least potential pathologies, such as excessive financialisation, debt-dependence, exploitations of people and, perhaps more fundamentally, environments, and distortions of the three orders of reality: the natural, the practical and the social, and our spatial relationships within them.[310]

---

[309] Capitalisation – what it is, how it works and how it could work – is the key issue in world politics at the moment.

[310] Margaret Archer writes as follows: '(c)onstituted as we are, and the world being the way it is, human beings interact with three different orders of reality: the natural, the practical and the social.

These pathologies are better counteracted at the supranational rather than the national level, and, with regards, for example, to issues concerning environmental sustainability, at the global level. Conceptualising a notion of globalisation also has implications for how we should understand policy learning models and their spatial dimensions.

Policy learning models

Change within a system can have spatial dimensions. An education system is an example of our fourth type of object – a spatial configuration. Knowledge-transfer between nations identifies a set of successful practices, which are then transferred to another national setting, in which a problem or need has been identified. Previously, such models were thought of exclusively as processes of borrowing policy from other countries or jurisdictions, and then turning these policies into practices, which were subsequently implemented. However, this is a flawed model if we are to understand change as inherent in a system and learning as a necessary part of the process. It would be wrong for us to see this kind of activity exclusively as borrowing rather than as a deeper form of learning, just because of the origin of the policy under consideration. Bearing that in mind, it is helpful to explore a number of different models to see how far they represent examples of this kind of deeper learning through engagement with alternative external models.

The first of these alternative models focuses on reconciling the external policy model, borrowed from countries or jurisdictions where it seemed to be operating in a successful or effective way, with local conditions in which these policies are to be implemented.[311] This consists of providing a working model of the practice to be transferred, understanding how context impacted on that model – both contextual elements of the donor country or jurisdiction as well as contextual elements from the recipient country or jurisdiction – stripping out these contextual elements from the model being implemented and then replacing them with those contextual elements that were found to be of significance in the recipient country. This model suffers from a common fault in knowledge transfer processes, which is that it is assumed context

---

We have to sustain organic relationships, work relationships and social relationships, if we are to survive and thrive. Therefore, we cannot afford to be indifferent about the concerns that are embedded in each of these three orders.' (Archer, 2002: 132).
[311] An example is Phillips and Schweisfurth (2008).

can be stripped out of these theoretical models without in some way distorting or impoverishing the models themselves, and that in like fashion recontextualising these models so that they are fit for the new environment does not consequently lead to a distortion of the original models. In short, it would be better to start from scratch and develop a model of a productive practice that is wholly appropriate to the recipient setting.

However, this model can be usefully amended. It still retains a notion of transfer and replacement of one context with another. And it still retains the element of transformation prior to implementation. It is more precise about the activities at the different stages of the process. The first step is where the investigator provides a description of the focus of the investigation. She then identifies a mechanism within the country from which the policy is being borrowed. A third step is understanding how this mechanism works – epistemologically, socially, politically and geo-historically – in the original country; in other words, identifying those features in this country that allow the mechanism to work as it was intended or at least as it has been adapted to a new set of circumstances (over time but still within this same country). A fourth step is identifying another country that seems to be a suitable recipient for this mechanism because it seems to have some similarities to the donor's context. A fifth step is identifying those similarities and differences that exist between the two countries. A sixth step is making a judgement about the degree of similarity and difference between the two settings and subsequently about the amount and type of change required for the mechanism to work in the country for which the policy transfer is intended; this also requires a judgement to be made about whether the mechanism is working or not. This involves predicting how one mechanism, which seems to work in one particular setting, should work in another that is characterised by a different set of structures. And finally, having identified the consequences of transferring the mechanism to the new country, the policy transfer is allowed to take place.

A third model is a policy-learning model, and it therefore has built into it the characteristics of a learning process. An accepted, but not uncontested, view of learning is to theorise it as a process, with a range of characteristics. It has a set of pedagogic relations; that is, it incorporates a relationship between a learner and a catalyst. A change process is required, either internal to the learner or external to the community of which this learner is a member. In any learning episode, there are temporal and spatial arrangements, and these can be understood in two ways: that learning is internally structured, and that learning episodes are externally located in time and space. This has the advantage of resembling more organic forms of learning and is likely to be more durable over time.

Globalisation and policy transfers, then, operate at a macro-level. Micro-level properties and processes also have spatial elements, such as: the shape, positioning and function of school buildings; classroom arrangements such as the positioning of the teacher's desk, the arrangement of children within the classroom, the storage of books and other resources; the spatial dimensions of reading a text such as the proximity, direction, layout and organisation of objects in the text; the spatiality of a timetable; the element of the curriculum that focuses on space, such as geography; the way in which knowledge is spatially formed, both in discursive communities and around the world, with direct implications for the curriculum; and the embodied nature of learning. All of these and more point to the importance of space in learning discourses and in the construction of knowledge. In the last chapter, I want to return to two important epistemological issues: what knowledge is and how we can know anything at all.

22
A conclusion – learning as a disposition

I have used a variety of textual devices in this book (referentiality, linearity, fragility, corrigibility, enframing and coherentism) and I want to draw attention to some of them here. The first of these is the insertion of a large number of references – an unusually large number – to other chapters in the book. This is designed to show that every concept being used here has a referential structure, in that every conceptual (and thus semantic) activity is framed and then reframed in relation to the possibilities that inhere in the concept and in a network of other concepts. This demands a complicated reading of this text, although no more difficult than reading an encyclopaedia, dictionary or work of reference. The point of this is to suggest or show that one important part of the argument I am making is that meaning, or the semantic dimension, is both dynamic and embedded within a network of other concepts, with their own semantic possibilities.

A second device that I have used here is more traditional. This refers to the linear structure of the text, in which a series of premises are introduced and justified, connections and relations are established between them, and conclusions are then drawn. In contrast, Ludwig Wittgenstein organised his material in the two books with which I have been principally concerned – the *Philosophical Investigations* and *On Certainty* – in units of remarks. In the first paragraph of the Preface to the *Investigations*, he suggested that: 'I have written down all these thoughts as remarks, short paragraphs, sometimes in longer chains about the same subject, sometimes jumping, in a sudden change, from one area to another' (1953: Preface). He qualified this in the second paragraph, after first suggesting that he had tried to write philosophy in a conventional manner, in the following way:

... my thoughts soon grew feeble if I tried to force them along a single track against their natural inclination. – And this was, of course, connected with the very nature of the investigation. For it compels us to travel criss-cross in every direction over a wide field of thought. – The philosophical remarks in this book are, as it were, a number of sketches of landscapes, which were made in the course of these long and meandering journeys. (Wittgenstein, 1953: Preface)

This hypertextual mode has a non-linear structure. The textuality that it implies mirrors the structure of the substantive argument that is being made and is not solely the result of Wittgenstein's natural modesty. My textuality in this book, then, is of a more conventional type. I have set out an argument, and the elements that make up this argument, and nothing more; that is, I have been making a case for a particular viewpoint about knowledge and learning, and what they refer to.

A third device concerns the fragility of the writing, and what I mean by this is the sense in which I as the author have had to struggle throughout with finding the right words, set of words, sentence constructions, paragraph arrangements and so forth, which can approximately bridge the gap (an ever-present and always-changing gap) between the text that I have produced and what it refers to outside of the confines of the text itself. If we abandon the idea of categorical and timeless definitions of words that represent in some magical way what is out there in the world, then the attempt at writing the world into being is always a struggle and always insufficient. The point I am making is that this is not a confession of inadequacy, but an acknowledgement that our words, word-sets, sentences and paragraphs are never adequate or sufficient and cannot be so given the task that is being attempted – although most writers addressing issues to do with learning are unaware of this.

A fourth device that I have used here is to discuss at all times and in as many ways as I can the issue of corrigibility. Am I correct in what I say? Am I producing truthful knowledge? Is this the best I can do? If one wants to criticise a position taken by someone else, or if one wants to make a claim that this other position is insufficiently evidenced or superficially formulated or conceptually inadequate or logically deficient, then one can do this only by comparing it with a position that is evidenced or in depth or conceptually adequate or logically sufficient. In short, one needs criteria about truthful knowledge in order to make a judgement about a position or approach. If one wants to correct an idea, then one has to have some foundation from which to do it.

A fifth textual and methodological device is that in every word, word-complex, sentence, paragraph and chapter in this book, I have made a series of assumptions about the world and my knowledge of it, some of which are explicit, some of which are not. These preconceptions can be broadly summarised as: a realist theory of ontology and thus of epistemology (what this cannot imply is that everyone is a realist); an ontic and epistemic theory of valuations; that we can know the world but only with the greatest of difficulty; and that these key ontological objects – knowledge and the world – should be analysed as separate entities. This textual device is one I use throughout the book and is of some significance.

A final textual and methodological device that I have used extensively in this book is to set a series of general arguments against other arguments developed by other people. I referred to this in the preface to the book. The point is that this is what most philosophers and thinkers actually do, even if they do not always make it explicit. This leaves open the possibility that one could write an archaeology of learning without such referencing and, indeed, there must have been a time in which every thought was new or at least not related to what other people said.

What you have just been reading is a text and a particular type of text. As a text, I have argued throughout that it is a signifying practice, and as a signifying practice it has to question its own textuality and indeed the discursive contents to which it is committing. This argument also places in suspension the notion of certainty that Wittgenstein in his later period of writing was so concerned about. Before I discuss this, I want to set out two key learning discourses that have been influential in the field or space of learning.

Learning discourses

The theory of learning that I have outlined in this book has to be set against current and other discourses – discursive configurations – of learning. A discourse is a set of propositions about the world joined together by a set of connectives and relations that offer an account of an object or objects in the world. This formulation of discourse (as concepts-in-use) will become clearer in the accounts of discursive formations that I offer below. It refers to a person, although this does not signify an essentialist or fundamentalist form that the human being takes or can take, and is in part focused on the nature, role and position that the individual can assume (but is not necessarily assumed for him) in relation to a discursive construction. Below I critically analyse two influential discursive constructions in the field of learning: school effectiveness and field construction.

One of the most influential framings of learning over the past 30 years in the United Kingdom is the school effectiveness/school improvement discourse. School effectiveness research has its origins in a general dissatisfaction with the deterministic and pessimistic view of schooling which suggested that schools, teachers and education generally have little effect on the different ways in which students perform in schools and subsequently. Other background factors are more influential, and there is little that schools can do to counteract their effects. The discourse is deliberately designed in opposition to this. Thus, the suggestion is that schools and other educational institutions can make a difference to the life chances and lifeworlds of individuals, and that these educational factors can be measured.[312]

Indeed, the claim is now made that it is possible to plot the different ways in which those background causal factors can impact on the learning experiences of children. However, despite advances in statistical techniques, mathematical modelling is able to deal only with those background influences by processing them in particular ways. The problem lies with how the *variable*, as a conceptual framing device, is understood and used. We have here a process of knowledge reduction, insofar as the variable works as a representational device and this leads to an illegitimate conclusion that this in fact is how reality is constituted (see chapter 4). An example of this is the effects of one-family parenthood on children's development, which is assumed to be the same for all children of one-parent families. Although it is now possible to plot changes in family status over time, what it is not possible to do is model

---

[312] This discourse has also influenced research into higher education. Here are the first three of ten principles of effective pedagogy that emanated from the work of the Teaching, Learning and Research Programme in the United Kingdom (TLRP, 2010): 'PRINCIPLE 1: Effective pedagogy equips learners for life in its broadest sense. Learning should aim to help individuals and groups to develop the intellectual, personal and social resources that will enable them to participate as active citizens, contribute to economic development and flourish as individuals in a diverse and changing society. This means adopting a broad conception of worthwhile learning outcomes and taking seriously issues of equity and social justice for all. PRINCIPLE 2: Effective pedagogy engages with valued forms of knowledge. Pedagogy should engage learners with the big ideas, key processes, modes of discourse, ways of thinking and practising, attitudes and relationships, which are the most valued learning processes and outcomes in particular contexts. They need to understand what constitutes quality, standards and expertise in different settings. PRINCIPLE 3: Effective pedagogy recognises the importance of prior experience and learning. Pedagogy should take account of what the learner knows already in order for them, and those who support their learning, to plan their next steps. This includes building on prior learning but also taking account of the personal and cultural experiences of different groups of learners.

mathematically the different ways in which family status impacts on individual children at different points in their lives, because there are conceptual elements involved in these relationships. The relationship has to be expressed in a linear fashion to meet the methodological demands of such modelling. Furthermore, the methodology being employed suggests that values are not an important dimension of understanding what happens in schools and other educational institutions. Ideas such as gender, social class, teaching style and management are all value-rich concepts; that is, they do not function purely as descriptive terms, but operate to impose a particular way of ordering on the world. They are ideological constructions, even if they do not compel the recipient, and need to be understood as such.

School effectiveness/school improvement researchers disregard the contextual, the historical and the social; the preoccupation with what works ignores the question of whose interests shape the nature and process of the work. There is no recognition of the problematic nature of curriculum or of the possibility that schooling may be organised in the interests of, for example, dominant ethnic groups, males or the ruling classes. Indeed, the socially situated nature of the discourse, which at the same time seeks to conceal its sociality, is deficient with regards to how knowledge of self and others is constructed by society and through educational processes. Discourses can be fractured, full of contradictions and internally incoherent, but still hold together. This is because their internal relations are not only logical, but also refer inferentially and retroductively to other social, political and epistemological discourses and practices in the world.

Discourses can frame political agendas. Norman Fairclough (2000), for example, suggested that the new UK Labour Government between 1997 and 2010 developed an educational agenda that was underpinned by a combination of a social integrationist discourse, with the focus on shifting people from welfare to work, and a moral underclass discourse. He argued that there are three possible ways of framing notions of equality as a political discourse. The first is a redistributionist discourse, which focuses on reducing poverty by redistributing wealth. A second discourse is socially integrationist in form, and here exclusion is primarily caused by unemployment and other social problems, with the solution being to reduce these high levels of unemployment and get people into work. And the third discourse, a moral underclass discourse, is perhaps more significant, insofar as deficiencies are identified as existing in the culture and experiences of those who are excluded, with the solution to this being cultural change and the imposition of education programmes to facilitate inclusion. This last is therefore very much a deficit model, which focuses on the right ways of behaving in society, rather than on specific outcomes from particular socioeconomic arrangements. The new Labour governments of the late twentieth and early twenty-first centuries were also attracted by communitarian thinking, which attempted to link three themes: economic efficiency, social cohesion and morality.

UK Conservative and Coalition Government policy after 2010 was more concerned with issues surrounding the erosion of responsibility in society, caused, as their political representatives repeatedly stressed, by an overwhelming paternalistic state. The prime ministers during this time, David Cameron and Theresa May, argued for a collective culture of responsibility and an ethos of self-betterment. The state in this vision has two principal roles – the efficient delivery of public services and early life interventions – achieved through paternalistic nudges to the populace, described by others as guided choice strategies. If this does not work, then the state is forced to mobilise its repressive resources to ensure the good order of society, and these punitive measures can take the form of either the withdrawal of goods usually provided by the state or restrictions on people's freedom.

Another discursive construction is the field. Field formation in the first place is a discursive activity. Values are central to the activity of research; that is, both the values of the researcher and the values of those being researched. These values, or conceptual frameworks, are located within historical contexts or traditions of knowledge (see chapter 5). The production of knowledge, therefore, has a close relationship with the way in which society is organised. However, to conceptualise knowledge and power as inseparable is to erect too rigid a straitjacket on the relationship between social arrangements and knowledge (both about them and other matters). This argument can be extended to the realm of curricula or to the way in which knowledge is produced and reproduced in educational institutions by examining one element of the process: the way knowledge is organised (its boundary definitions). The argument that I am making here is that how we divide up knowledge has an effect on the way we can and do understand the world.

Each discursive field has a history, is composed of individuals with different projects who form and re-form them at different moments and in different ways. (I am using this term to describe a specific demarcation or boundary point between domains of knowledge.) There are, therefore, micro-political struggles within the history of each field. But, more importantly, at the level of the academy, those struggles involve the establishment of various organs of dissemination and of criteria by which the knowledge-producing activity is judged. In the first place, a new field needs to produce: books and articles in academic journals; new journals that reflect the epistemological assumptions of the field; positions of office in universities; access to the popular media; the development of a cadre of taught and research students; research funding for projects; and the establishment of a coterie of loyal referees for journals and research projects. The paraphernalia of field formation is often hard-won, frequently involves excursions down blind alleys, and is a risk-taking business.[313]

An example in the field of education is the development and maintenance of its professional association, the British Educational Research Association (BERA) and its principal organ of dissemination, the *British Educational Research Journal (BERJ)*.[314] It understands its primary function as supporting a particular view of education and ultimately its practices, although these do not emanate in a straight-forward manner from the discursive construction. That is, it is possible to support all of the different epistemologies currently and in the future that swirl around in the allocated discursive space; that the issue of the differences between them can be resolved by focusing on perceived commonalities at the strategic and method levels, rather than at the levels of ontology and epistemology (the issue of truth is attended to, but only in a decontextualised and reductionist form; for example, cf. Moss, 2015); that it is possible to collect evidence that allows one to make unequivocal claims about how educational systems and people actually work and that these claims are in some sense transcendental; and that the collection of people who make up the particular community can come together and agree about educational judgements of institutions, texts and persons, and how they can be made. Indeed, the recent emphasis on awarding prizes for the best of this or that is evidence, first, of a particular approach to knowledge development and, second, of a commitment to current social practices rather than to critical evaluations of them.

But, more importantly, the field needs to establish three sets of criteria before it can be considered to be fully formed: first, it has to have created a set of criteria by which its knowledge can be evaluated; second, it needs to have formalised a set of definitional criteria that includes and excludes what is considered proper knowledge; and third, it needs to

---

[313] It is remarkable how many people in higher education have succumbed to the blandishments of such a discourse, even though they are also and at the same time committed to notions of social justice, equality and fairness.

[314] The bulk of these remarks were published as a BERA blog in 2018.

be able to offer a set of methodological criteria through which an initiate may operate – a set of procedures that delineates a practitioner from a non-practitioner. While some of these moves are more successful than others, they are always subject to decay, argument, dispute and change. The field itself always has to operate with and between other discursive fields, for example, the wider field of policy. Macro-political influences, therefore, have an influence on the way the field comes into being, and indeed practitioners (especially in the field of education) may deliberately shape their thinking to chime with policy moves, either actually in existence or projected.

These two discourses, and there are more, act as the background to what can be said about learning. More importantly perhaps, in most instances they take the place of criteria for determining truthful knowledge. Bearing this in mind, I now want to address the issue of knowledge and doubting.[315]

Knowledge and doubting

Here are some meta-level propositions that I have argued for in this book: i) we should read and try to understand the work of Ludwig Wittgenstein, a philosopher who died nearly 70 years ago; ii) there are five types of object in the world – discursive objects, material objects, relational objects, configurational objects and persons; iii) human beings have dispositional features; iv) learning and knowing are homologous concepts; v) there are four types of learning: cognitive, skill-based, dispositional and embodied; vi) doubting a proposition does not mean that one cannot know what it is about; vii) human beings can reflect on knowledge that they have already acquired; viii) a school effectiveness discourse is seriously deficient; ix) there are five conceptions of truth (there may be more, but they have not yet been invented, or codified): truth as correspondence, truth as coherence, truth as what works, truth as consensus and truth as warranted belief; and x) I am the author of this book. The question that should concern us, and does not concern enough people, is whether these are true propositions about the world. Wittgenstein's fundamental concern was to rework the notion of certainty, to include within it an idea of doubt, and to repudiate the full range of sceptical arguments.

---

[315] This was my initial starting point in this book.

Wittgenstein was interested in trying to answer the question of what it means to doubt something.[316] In *On Certainty* he suggested that ordinarily the sceptic doubts individual propositions and not meta-propositions, such as the enframings of individual propositions. In response to this, Wittgenstein (1969: §247) asked the question: 'What would it be like to doubt now whether I have two hands? Why can't I imagine it at all? What would I believe if I didn't believe that? So far I have no system at all within which this doubt might exist.' And further on in the book (1969: §274), he suggested that it is easy to doubt individual propositions in isolation, but much harder to do so if we place these propositions in a network of other propositions: '(e)xperience can be said to teach us these propositions. However, it does not teach us them in isolation; rather, it teaches us a host of interdependent propositions. If they were isolated I might perhaps doubt them, for I have no experience relating to them.' What this means is not that there are objects in the world that enter into relationships with other objects in the world, but that the meaning of these objects resides in the network of objects of which they are a part. Wittgenstein is here making a semantic point, and at the same time reaffirming the idea that doubting a proposition about a state of affairs in the world is not an invitation to adopt a sceptical position towards knowledge as such but an entirely legitimate part of knowing the world or acquiring knowledge of this world.

René Descartes (1988) developed the idea that radical doubt leads to foundational certainty. Wittgenstein was much more circumspect about the possibility of knowing something, even though he included as a prerequisite of this process of knowing that we should doubt the proposition if we are to know it (1969: §115): '(t)he game of doubting itself presupposes certainty'. However, Wittgenstein did not believe that every proposition is open to doubt or should be doubted as a necessary part of determining its truth-value, because some propositions are basic, and therefore we should call these propositions foundational or primitive (1969: §341): '(o)ur doubts depend on the fact that some propositions are exempt from doubt, are as it were like hinges on which those turn'.

---

[316] In *On Certainty* (1969), Wittgenstein addressed many more arguments against scepticism than I have referred to here. In line with the general argument of the book, I have sought to show that concepts should be understood as dispositional attributes of human beings, that they are acquired and that this renders much educational research redundant. One of these concepts is doubt or being doubtful. This is in line with the remarks made by Wittgenstein in *On Certainty*.

Furthermore, one can doubt something, that is, exercise a doubting disposition, only if the way of life that one has chosen to belong to has an attitude of trust and doubting already established within it.

For Wittgenstein, certainty rests on the possibility of doubt, despite his assertion that there are some primitive propositions that cannot be doubted. This last seems to me to be an unnecessary concession to those who argue that radically doubting everything can lead to foundational certainty. Doubt implies the possibility of epistemic, logical, rational and practically adequate corrections to any proposition that we might want to make, or that we are having to deal with, and, as Wittgenstein explained at some length, it is manifested in particular types of action. As with learning, doubting is an acquired disposition.

It is almost a truism to say that the self-aware sceptic is actually committed to what he denies, even if this is an exception to the general claim. In *On Certainty*, Wittgenstein repeatedly claimed that the sceptic does not understand the meaning of the words he is using (1969: §456): 'If, therefore, I doubt or am uncertain about this being my hand (in whatever sense), why not in that case about the meaning of these words as well?' *On Certainty* can be understood as a refutation of transcendental knowledge, or meta-knowledge as I described it in chapter 2, and this can be contrasted with an ordinary, everyday certainty of knowledge, to which he subscribed (1969: §7): 'Why do I not satisfy myself that I know or am certain that there is a chair over there, or a door, and so on. – I tell a friend, e.g. "Take that chair over there", "Shut the door", etc. etc.' It is also a continuation of the fundamental argument he proposed in the *Investigations*, that understanding the world is a semantic activity. Any investigation of the truth-value of propositional statements, then, such as those with which I began this section of the chapter, have to examine in the first instance the possibilities and, as importantly, limitations, of the words, word-sets or linguistically structured concepts that are being used with the purpose of determining meaning. The aim, first and foremost, is a semantic one.

This can hardly be called a completely satisfactory solution to the problems of knowledge and learning, although it might be a start. That these notions are complicated is a given, and that these solutions are incomplete is accepted; but what I hope the book does is provide some purchase on the most important issue of our times: the impoverishment of learning. It hardly needs saying, but I will say it anyway. This book has been a rejoinder to: empiricist and positivist conceptions of knowledge; detheorised and reductionist conceptualisations of learning; regressive and degenerative notions of curriculum; the propagation of simple messages about learning, knowledge, curriculum and assessment; the employment of punitive forms of power; the use of bureaucratic power mechanisms in new public management strategies; and the denial that values are central to understanding how we live and how we should live, with this valuing going all the way down, into our descriptions of the world, into those attempts we make at creating better futures and into our relations with other people. And then there is Brexit … The barbarians are at the gate.[317]

---

[317] This phrase is loosely transposed from the title of a book by J. M. Coetzee, *Waiting for the Barbarians* (1980).

References

Aggrawal, A. (2008) 'Appendix 1'. In A. Aggrawal, *Forensic and Medico-legal Aspects of Sexual Crimes and Unusual Sexual Practices*. Boca Raton, FL: CRC Press, 369–82.

Archer, M. (2002) 'Models of man: Transcendence and being-in-the-world'. In E. Cassidy (ed.), *Discerning Values and Beliefs*. Dublin: Veritas, 123–51.

Archer, M. (2007) *Making Our Way through the World*. Cambridge: Cambridge University Press.

Aristotle (1987) *De Anima (On the Soul)*. London: Penguin Classics.

Aristotle (2018a) *The Complete Aristotle, Part 2: Physics, or Natural Hearing*, trans. R. P. Hardie and R. K. Gaye. ShandonPress Kindle edition.

Aristotle (2018b) *The Complete Aristotle, Part 6: The Nicomachean Ethics*, trans. W. D. Ross. ShandonPress Kindle edition.

Augustine of Hippo (2003) *City of God*. Trans. Henry Bettenson. Harmondsworth: Penguin.

Augustine of Hippo (2017) *Confessions*. Trans. Henry Chadwick. Oxford: Oxford University Press.

Austin, J. L. (1962) *How to Do Things with Words: The William James Lectures*, ed. J. M. Urmson. Oxford: Clarendon Press.

Ayer, A. J. (1936) *Language, Truth and Logic*. London: Gollancz.

Bandura, A. (1977) *Social Learning Theory*. New York: General Learning Press.

Barthes, R. (1975) *S/Z*. London: Jonathan Cape.

Bergson, H. (1999) *Duration and Simultaneity*, ed. R. Durie. Manchester: Clinamen Press.

Bernstein, B. (2000) *Pedagogy, Symbolic Control and Identity: Theory, research, critique*. Rev. ed. Lanham, MD: Rowman and Littlefield.

Bernstein, B. (2002) 'From pedagogies to knowledges'. In A. Morais, I. Neves, B. Davies and H. Daniels (eds), *Towards a Sociology of Pedagogy: The contribution of Basil Bernstein to research*. New York: Peter Lang, 363–8.

Bertram, C. (2020) 'Jean-Jacques Rousseau'. In *Stanford Encyclopedia of Philosophy* (summer 2020 edition), ed. E. Zalta. Accessed 10 November 2020. https://plato.stanford.edu/entries/rousseau/.

Bhaskar, R. (2002) *Philosophy of Meta-Reality: Creativity, love and freedom*. London: Routledge.

Bhaskar, R. (2008a) *A Realist Theory of Science*. 2nd ed. London: Routledge.

Bhaskar, R. (2008b) *Dialectic: The pulse of freedom*. 2nd ed. London: Routledge.

Bhaskar, R. (2011) *Reclaiming Reality: A critical introduction to contemporary philosophy*. 2nd ed. London: Routledge.

Bhaskar, R., Frank, C., Hoyer, K.-G., Naess, P. and Parker, J. (eds) (2010) *Interdisciplinarity and Climate Change: Transforming knowledge and practice for our global future*. London: Routledge.

Blyth, A. (1981) 'From individuality to character: The Herbartian sociology applied to education'. *British Journal of Educational Studies*, 29 (1), 69–79.

Bollack, J. and Wismann, H. (1972) *Héraclite ou la separation*. Paris: Les Édition de Minuit.

Bourdieu, P. (1986) 'The forms of capital'. In J. G. Richardson (ed.), *Handbook of Theory and Research for the Sociology of Capital*. New York: Greenwood Press, 241–58.

Brandom, R. (1994) *Making It Explicit: Reasoning, representing, and discursive commitment*. Cambridge, MA: Harvard University Press.

Brandom, R. (2000) *Articulating Reasons: An introduction to inferentialism*. Cambridge, MA: Harvard University Press.

Brandom, R. (2004) 'The pragmatist enlightenment (and its problematic semantics)'. *European Journal of Philosophy*, 12 (1), 1–16.

Bredo, E. (1999) 'Reconstructing educational psychology'. In P. Murphy (ed.), *Learners, Learning and Assessment*. London: SAGE Publications, 23–45.

Bridges, D. (1999) 'Educational research: Pursuit of truth or flight into fancy?'. *British Educational Research Journal*, 25 (5), 597–616.

Bruner, J. (1996) *The Culture of Education*. Cambridge, MA: Harvard University Press.

Butler, D. L. (2015) 'Meta-cognition and self-regulation in learning'. In D. Scott and E. Hargreaves (eds), *The SAGE Handbook of Learning*. London: SAGE Publications, 291–310.

Callon, M. (1991) 'Techno-economic networks and irreversibility'. In J. Law (ed.), *A Sociology of Monsters: Essays on power, technology and domination*. London: Routledge, 132–61.

Cavell, S. (1979) *The Claim of Reason*. Oxford: Oxford University Press.

Chomsky, N. (1968) *Language and Mind*. New York: Harcourt Brace Jovanovich.

Coetzee, J. M. (1980) *Waiting for the Barbarians*. London: Penguin.

Collier, A. (2003) *In Defence of Objectivity*. London: Routledge.

Comenius, J. (2012 [1633–8]) *Didactica Magna*. London: Akal.

Comte, A. (2009 [1853]) *The Positive Philosophy of Auguste Comte*. 2 vols. Trans. Harriet Martineau. Cambridge: Cambridge University Press.

Condorcet, N. de (2012) *Condorcet: Political writings* (Cambridge Texts in the History of Political Thought), ed. S. Lukes and N. Urbinati. Cambridge: Cambridge University Press.

Daly, M. (1992) *Outercourse: The bedazzling voyage, containing recollections from my logbook of a radical feminist philosopher*. San Francisco: Harper.

Derrida, J. (1982) 'Différance'. In J. Derrida, *Margins of Philosophy*, trans. A. Bass. Chicago: University of Chicago Press, 1–28.

Derrida, J. (2016) *Heidegger: The question of being and history*. Chicago: Chicago University Press.

Descartes, R. (1988) *The Philosophical Writings of Descartes*, trans. John Cottingham, Robert Stoothoff and Dugald Murdoch. 3 vols. Cambridge: Cambridge University Press.

Dewey, J. (1938) *Experience and Education*. New York: Touchstone.

Diderot, D. (ed.) (1993 [1751–72]) *Encyclopédie, ou dictionnaire raisonné des sciences, des arts et des métiers*. Paris: Flammarion.

Donaldson, M. (1978) *Children's Minds*. London: Fontana.

Duminuco, V. (2000) *The Jesuit Ratio Studiorum of 1599: 400th Anniversary Perspectives*. New York: Fordham University Press.

Dunne, J. (1988) 'Teaching and limits of technique: An analysis of the behavioural objectives model'. *Irish Journal of Education*, 22 (2), 66–90.

Durkheim, E. (1939) *The Rules of Sociological Method*, ed. G. Catlin, trans. Sarah Solovay and John Mueller. 8th ed. Chicago: University of Chicago Press.

Durkheim, E. (1995) *The Elementary Forms of Religious Life*, trans. K. Field. New York: Free Press.

Eco, U. (1997) *The Search for the Perfect Language*. London: Fontana Press.

Edwards, R. (2015) 'The post-human and responsible experimentation in learning'. In D. Scott and E. Hargreaves (eds), *The SAGE Handbook of Learning*. London: SAGE Publications, 107–16.

Einstein, A. (1923 [1905]) 'On the electrodynamics of moving bodies. In A. Einstein, *The Principle of Relativity*. London: Methuen, 35–65.

Einstein, A. (2010 [1920]) *The Special and the General Theory*. Eastford, CT: Martino Fine Books.

Engeström, Y. (2001) 'Expansive learning at work: Toward an activity theoretical reconceptualization'. *Journal of Education and Work*, 14 (1), 133–56.

Fairclough, N. (2000) *New Labour, New Language*. London: Routledge.

Fenwick, T. and Edwards, R. (2010) *Actor-Network Theory in Education*. London: Routledge.

Fester, E. (2009) *Aquinas*. Oxford: Oneworld.

Flax, J. (1990) *Thinking in Fragments: Psychoanalysis, feminism and postmodernism in the contemporary West*. Berkeley: University of California Press.

Fodor, J. (1975) *The Language of Thought*. New York: Crowell.

Fodor, J. (1998) *Concepts: Where cognitive science went wrong*. New York: Oxford University Press.

Fodor, J. and Lepore, E. (2007) 'Brandom beleaguered'. *Philosophy and Phenomenological Research*, 74 (3), 677–91.

Foucault, M. (1961) *Folie et déraison: Histoire de la folie à l'âge classique*. Paris: Gallimard.

Foucault, M. (1963) *Naissance de la clinique: Une archéologie du regard médical*. Paris: Gallimard.

Foucault, M. (1969) *L'archéologie du savoir*. Paris: Gallimard.

Foucault, M. (1970) *The Order of Things: An archaeology of the human sciences*. New York: Pantheon.

Foucault, M. (1975) *Surveiller et punir: Naissance de la prison*. Paris: Gallimard.

Foucault, M. (1978a) 'La société disciplinaire en crise', interview-lecture delivered in Japan, in *Dits et écrits,* vol. 3: *1976–9,* 532–3.

Foucault, M. (1978b) *The History of Sexuality,* Vol. 1: *An Introduction.* Trans. Robert Hurley. New York: Pantheon.

Foucault, M. (1986) 'Of other spaces'. *Diacritics,* 16 (1), 22–7.

Foucault, M. (1997) 'Of other spaces: Utopias and heterotopias'. In Neil Leach (ed.), *Rethinking Architecture: A reader in cultural theory.* New York: Routledge, 330–6.

Foucault, M. (2010) *The Government of Self and Others: Lectures at the Collège de France, 1982–1983,* trans. Graham Burchell. New York: Palgrave Macmillan.

Frege, G. (1980 [1892]) 'Über Sinn und Bedeutung'. *Zeitschrift für Philosophie und philosophische Kritik,* 100, 25–50. Translated as 'On sense and reference' by M. Black in *Translations from the Philosophical Writings of Gottlob Frege,* ed. and trans. P. Geach and M. Black. Oxford: Blackwell.

Fukuyama, F. (1992) *The End of History and the Last Man.* New York: Free Press.

Furlong, J. and Oancea, A. (2005) *Assessing Quality in Applied and Practice-Based Research: A framework for discussion.* Oxford: Oxford University Department of Educational Studies.

Gadamer, H.-G. (1989) *Truth and Method,* trans. J. Weinsheimer and D. G. Marshall. 2nd ed. New York: Crossroad.

Gibbons, M., Limoges, C., Nowonty, H., Schwartzman, S., Scott, P. and Trow, M. (1994) *The New Production of Knowledge: The dynamics of science and research in contemporary societies.* London: SAGE Publications.

Giddens, A. (1986) *The Constitution of Society.* Cambridge: Polity Press.

Gilligan, C. (1990) *In a Different Voice: Psychological theory and women's development.* Cambridge, MA: Harvard University Press.

Gödel, K. (2003) *Collected Works, Volume II: Publications, 1938–1974.* Oxford: Oxford University Press.

Grace, G. (2013) 'Catholic social teaching should permeate the Catholic secondary school curriculum: An agenda for reform'. *International Studies in Catholic Education,* 5 (1), 99–109.

Greene, M. (2000) *Releasing the Imagination: Essays on education, the arts, and social change.* San Francisco: Jossey-Bass Education.

Griffin, S. (2000) *Woman and Nature: The roaring inside her.* Berkeley, CA: Counterpoint.

Haack, S. (1993) *Evidence and Inquiry: Towards reconstruction in epistemology.* Oxford: Blackwell.

Habermas, J. (1981) *The Theory of Communicative Action, Volume 1,* trans. T. McCarthy. Boston: Beacon Press.

Hacking, I. (1990) *The Taming of Chance.* Cambridge, MA: Harvard University Press.

Hall, S. (1980) 'Race, articulation and societies structured in dominance'. In UNESCO (ed.), *Sociological Theories: Race and colonialism.* Paris: UNESCO, 305–45.

Hammersley, M. (2002) 'Research as emancipatory: The case of Bhaskar's critical realism'. *Journal of Critical Realism,* 1 (1), 33–48.

Hand, M. (2006) *Is Religious Education Possible? A philosophical investigation.* London: Continuum.

Harré, R. (2011) *Theories and Things.* London: Sheed and Ward.

Hegel, G. (1977 [1921]) *Phenomenology of the Spirit,* trans. A. V. Miller. Oxford: Oxford University Press.

Heidegger, M. (1962 [1927]) *Being and Time,* trans. John Macquarrie and Edward Robinson. Oxford: Blackwell.

Heidegger, M. (1977) 'The question concerning technology'. In M. Heidegger, *The Question Concerning Technology and Other Essays,* trans. W. Lovitt. London: Harper and Row, 3–35.

Heidegger, M. (2012) *Bremen and Freiburg Lectures: Insight into that which is and basic principles of thinking* (Studies in Continental Thought), trans. A. Mitchell. Bloomington: Indiana University Press.

Hempel, C. (1965) *Aspects of Scientific Explanation and Other Essays in the Philosophy of Science.* New York: Free Press.

Hempel, C. and Oppenheim, P. (1948) 'Studies in the logic of explanation'. *Philosophy of Science,* 15, 135–75.

Hobsbawm, E. (1988) *The Age of Revolution: Europe, 1789–1848.* Ashton-on-Ribble: Abacus.

hooks, b. (1982) *Ain't I a Woman? Black women and feminism.* New York: Pluto Press.

Horsten, L. (2019) 'Philosophy of mathematics'. In *Stanford Encyclopedia of Philosophy* (spring 2019 edition), ed. Edward N. Zalta. Accessed 10 November 2020. https://plato.stanford.edu/archives/spr2019/entries/philosophy-mathematics/.

Howard, D. and Giovanelli, M. (2019) 'Einstein's philosophy of science'. In *Stanford Encyclopedia of Philosophy* (Fall 2019 edition), ed. Edward N. Zalta. Accessed 10 November 2020. https://plato.stanford.edu/archives/fall2019/entries/einstein-philscience/.

Hume, D. (2000 [1738]) *A Treatise of Human Nature*, ed. D. Norton and M. Norton. Oxford: Oxford University Press.

Husserl, E. (1913 [1900–1]) *Logical Investigations*, trans. J. N. Findlay. London: Routledge.

Husserl, E. (1973 [1939]) *Experience and Judgement*, trans. J. S. Churchill and K. Ameriks. London: Routledge.

Isaksen, R. (2017) 'Without foundation or neutral standpoint: Using immanent critique to guide a literature review'. *Journal of Critical Realism*, 17 (2), 97–117.

Israel, J. (2001) *Radical Enlightenment: Philosophy and the making of modernity, 1650–1750*. Oxford: Oxford University Press.

Jensen, O. and Richardson, T. (2004) *Making European Space: Mobility, power and territorial identity*. London: Routledge.

Kant, I. (1992) 'On pedagogy – über Pädagogik'. In *The Cambridge Edition of the Works of Immanuel Kant*, ed. P. Guyer and A. Wood. Cambridge: Cambridge University Press.

Kant, I. (2007 [1781]) *Critique of Pure Reason* (Penguin Modern Classics). London: Penguin.

Keynes, M. (1936) *The General Theory of Employment, Interest and Money*. London: Macmillan.

Kim, S. H. (2019) 'Max Weber'. In *Stanford Encyclopedia of Philosophy* (winter 2019 edition), ed. Edward Zalta. Accessed 10 November 2020. https://plato.stanford.edu/archives/win2019/entries/weber/.

Kohlberg, L. (1976) 'Moral stages and moralization: The cognitive-developmental approach'. In T. Lickona (ed.), *Moral Development and Behaviour*. London: Holt, Rinehart and Winston, 31–53.

Kolb, D. A. (1984) *Experiential Learning Experience as a Source of Learning and Development*. Englewood Cliffs, NJ: Prentice Hall.

Kress, G. and Bezemer, J. (2015) 'A social semiotic multimodal approach to learning'. In D. Scott and E. Hargreaves (eds), *SAGE Handbook of Learning*. London: SAGE Publications, 155–69.

Landow, G. (1992) *The Convergence of Contemporary Critical Theory and Technology*. Baltimore: Johns Hopkins University Press.

Latour, B. (1991) 'Technology is society made durable'. In J. Law (ed.), *A Sociology of Monsters: Essays on power, technology and domination*. London: Routledge, 103–31.

Law, J. and Hassard, J. (eds) (1999) *Actor Network Theory and After*. Oxford: Blackwell.

Leontiev, A. (1978) *Activity, Consciousness and Personality*. Englewood Cliffs, NJ: Prentice Hall.

Louth, A. (1996) *Maximus the Confessor*. London: Routledge.

Lowenfeld, V. (1949) *Creative and Mental Growth*. London: Lambert Brittain.

MacIntyre, A. (1981) *After Virtue*. Notre Dame, IN: University of Notre Dame Press.

Malesevic, S. (2004) *The Sociology of Ethnicity*. London: SAGE Publications.

Malotki, Ekkehart (1983) *Hopi Time: A linguistic analysis of the temporal concepts in the Hopi language*. Berlin: De Gruyter.

Marcuse, H. (1964) *One Dimensional Man*. London: Routledge.

Markosian, N. (2016) 'Time'. In *Stanford Encyclopedia of Philosophy* (Fall 2016 edition), ed. Edward N. Zalta. Accessed 10 November 2020. https://plato.stanford.edu/archives/fall2016/entries/time/.

Marx, K. (2009) *Capital*, vol. 1. Washington, DC: Regnery Publishing.

Maton, K. (2014) *Knowledge and Knowers: Towards a realist sociology of education*. London: Routledge.

Mazzucato, M. (2018) *The Value of Everything: Making and taking in the global economy*. London: Allen Lane.

McLeod, S. A. (2013) 'Kohlberg's stages of moral development'. *Simply Psychology*, 24 October. Accessed 10 November 2020. https://www.simplypsychology.org/kohlberg.html.

McLeod, S. A. (2018) 'Piaget's theory and stages of cognitive development'. *Simply Psychology*, 6 June. Accessed 10 November 2020. https://www.simplypsychology.org/piaget.html.

Merleau-Ponty, M. (1945) *Phénoménologie de la perception*. Paris: Gallimard.

Mill, J. S. (1963–91) *The Collected Works of John Stuart Mill*, ed. J. M. Robson. 33 vols. Toronto: University of Toronto Press.

Montesquieu (1892) 'Histoire véritable'. In *Mélanges inédits de Montesquieu*, vol. 2. Bordeaux: Gounouilhou and Paris: Rouam, 31–96.

Moss, G. (2015) 'Knowledge, education and research: Making common cause across communities of practice'. Keynote Lecture at the British Educational Research Association (BERA) Annual Conference, Queen's University Belfast, 15–17 September 2015.

Muijs, D. and Reynolds, D. (2011) *Effective Teaching: Evidence and practice.* Chichester: Wiley.

Mylonakou-Keke, I. (2015) 'The emergence of "syn-epistemic wholeness" from dialectic synergy of disciplines: A transdisciplinary social pedagogic model'. *Creative Education,* 6, 1890–907.

Nagel, T. (1974) 'What is it like to be a bat?'. *Philosophical Review,* 83 (4), 435–50.

Nagel, T. (2012) *Mind and Cosmos: Why the materialist neo-Darwinian conception of nature is almost certainly false.* Oxford: Oxford University Press.

Nicolescu, B. (2002) *Manifesto of Transdisciplinarity,* trans. K. C. Voss. Albany: State University of New York Press.

Nicolescu, B. (2014) *From Modernity to Cosmodernity: Science, culture and spirituality.* Albany: State University of New York Press.

Nietzsche, F. (1998 [1887]) *On the Genealogy of Morality,* trans. M. Clark and A. Swensen. Cambridge, MA: Hackett.

Noah, H. and Eckstein, M. (1969) *Toward a Science of Comparative Education.* New York: Macmillan.

O'Grady, P. (2002) *Relativism* (Central Problems in Philosophy). Durham: Acumen Publishing.

Online Etymology Dictionary. Accessed January 2019. https://www.etymonline.com.

Pedersen, S. (1993) *Family, Dependence, and the Origins of the Welfare State: Britain and France, 1914–1945.* Cambridge: Cambridge University Press.

Peirce, C. S. (1982) *The Essential Peirce,* ed. Nathan Houser, Christian Kloesel and the Peirce Edition Project. 2 vols. Bloomington: Indiana University Press.

Phillips, D. and Schweisfurth, M. (2008) *Comparative and International Education: An introduction to theory, method and practice.* London: Continuum International.

Piaget, J. (1962) *The Language and Thought of the Child.* London: Routledge and Kegan Paul.

Plato (1997) *Complete Works,* ed. J. Cooper and D. Hutchinson. Cambridge, MA: Hackett.

Popper, K. (2002) *Conjectures and Refutations: The growth of scientific knowledge.* London: Routledge.

Porro, P. (1990) *Enrico di Gand: La via delle proposizioni universali.* Bari: Levante.

Putnam, H. (1990) *Realism with a Human Face.* Cambridge, MA: Harvard University Press.

Quine, W. V. O. (1951) 'Two dogmas of empiricism'. *The Philosophical Review,* 60, 20–43.

Reich, R. (2015) *Saving Capitalism: For the many, not the few.* New York: Knopf.

Research Assessment Exercise (RAE) (2008) *Research Assessment Exercise.* London: Higher Education Funding Council for England.

Research Excellence Framework (REF) (2014) *Research Excellence Framework.* London: Higher Education Funding Council for England.

Rorty, R. (1979) *Philosophy and the Mirror of Nature.* Princeton: Princeton University Press.

Rorty, R. (1998) *Truth and Progress (Philosophical Papers 3).* Cambridge: Cambridge University Press.

Rousseau, J. J. (1979) *Émile, or Treatise on Education,* trans. Allan Bloom. New York: Basic Books.

Russell, B. with Whitehead, A. N. (1925–7 [1910–13]) *Principia Mathematica.* Cambridge: Cambridge University Press.

Sartre, J.-P. (2003) *Being and Nothingness.* London: Routledge.

Schleicher, A. (2015) 'Seven big myths about top-performing school systems'. *BBC News,* 4 February. Accessed 28 September 2017. www.bbc.co.uk/news/business-31087545.

Schon, D. (2005 [1959]) *The Reflective Practitioner: How professionals think in action.* San Francisco: Jossey-Bass.

Scott, D. (2017a) *Education Systems and Learners: Knowledge and knowing.* London: Palgrave Macmillan.

Scott, D. (2017b) 'The Parlous State of Educational Research'. BERA blog, 8 August. https://www.bera.ac.uk/blog/the-parlous-state-of-educational-research

Scott, D. (2019a) 'Virtues and dispositions as learning theory in universities'. In P. Gibbs, J. Jameson and A. Elwick (eds), *Values of the University in a Time of Uncertainty.* Cham: Springer, 31–44.

Scott, D. (2019b) 'Nationalisms, internationalisms and identities'. In D. Scott (ed.), *Manifestos, Policies and Practices: An equalities agenda.* London: UCL IOE Press, 155–69.

Scott, D. with Bhaskar, R. (2015) *Roy Bhaskar: A theory of education.* New York: Springer.

Scott, D., Posner, C. M., Martin, C. and Guzman, E. (2018) *The Education System in Mexico.* London: UCL Press.

Scott, D. and Scott, B. (2018) *Equalities and Inequalities in the English Education System.* London: UCL IOE Press.

Scott, D. and Usher, R. (2011) *Researching Education: Data, methods and theory in educational enquiry.* 2nd ed. London: Continuum.

Searle, J. (1984) *Minds, Brains and Science.* Cambridge, MA: Harvard University Press.

Searle, J. (1995) *The Construction of Social Reality*. New York: Free Press.

Searle, J. (2011) *Making the Social World*. Oxford: Oxford University Press.

Sellars, W. (1997) *Empiricism and the Philosophy of Mind*. Cambridge: Cambridge University Press.

Shilling, C. (2016) *The Body: A very short introduction*. Oxford: Oxford University Press.

Skidelsky, R. (2013) *John Maynard Keynes, 1883–1946: Economist, philosopher, statesman*. London: Penguin.

Skinner, B. F. (1953) *Science and Human Behavior*. London: Simon and Schuster.

Smith, M. (2009) *Rethinking Residential Child Care*. Bristol: Policy Press.

Spade, P. (1994) *Five Texts on the Mediaeval Problem of Universals*. Cambridge, MA: Hackett.

Spengler, O. (2013 [1934]) *The Hour of Decision*. London: Isha Books.

Standish, P. (2016) 'The disenchantment of education and the re-enchantment of the world'. *Journal of Philosophy of Education*, 50 (1), 98–116.

Strawson, P. (1959) *Individuals: An essay in descriptive metaphysics*. London: Methuen.

Taylor, C. (1985) 'What is human agency?' and 'Hegel's philosophy of mind'. In C. Taylor, *Human Agency and Language: Philosophical papers 1*. Cambridge: Cambridge University Press, 15–44, 77–96.

Taylor, C. (1998) *Sources of the Self: The making of the modern identity*. Cambridge, MA: Harvard University Press.

Taylor, C. (2011) *Dilemmas and Connections*. Cambridge, MA: Harvard University Press.

TLRP (Teaching and Learning Research Programme) (2010) 'TLRP's evidence-informed pedagogic principles'. London: Institute of Education. https://tinyurl.com/y685z7yn.

Tolman, E. C. (1932) *Purposive Behavior in Animals and Man*. New York: Century.

Topping, K. J. (2001a) *Peer Assisted Learning: A practical guide for teachers*. Cambridge, MA: Brookline Books.

Topping, K. J. (2001b) *Thinking, Reading, Writing: A practical guide to paired learning with peers, parents and volunteers*. New York: Continuum International.

Topping, K. J. (2003) 'Self and peer assessment in school and university: Reliability, validity and utility'. In M. S. R. Segers, F. J. R. C. Dochy and E. C. Cascallar (eds), *Optimizing New Modes of Assessment: In search of qualities and standards*. Dordrecht: Kluwer, 55–87.

Topping, K. J. and Ehly, S. (eds) (1998) *Peer-Assisted Learning*. Mahwah, NJ: Lawrence Erlbaum Associates.

Van der Meer, F., Battershaw, B. and Lamb, G. (1961) *Augustine the Bishop: The life and work of a Father of the Church*. London: Sheed and Ward.

Van Gulick, R. (2018) 'Consciousness'. In *Stanford Encyclopedia of Philosophy* (spring 2018 edition), ed. Edward N. Zalta. Accessed 10 November 2020. https://plato.stanford.edu/archives/spr2018/entries/consciousness/.

Vygotsky, L. (1978) *Mind in Society: The development of higher psychological processes*, ed. M. Cole, V. John-Steiner, S. Scribner and E. Souberman. Cambridge, MA: Harvard University Press.

Vygotsky, L. (1993) *The Collected Works of L. S. Vygotsky*. New York: Springer.

Watson, J. B. (1930) *Behaviorism*. New York: Norton.

Weber, M. (1964) *The Theory of Social and Economic Organisation*. London: Simon and Schuster.

Whitty, G. and Furlong, J. (eds) (2017) *Knowledge and the Study of Education: An international exploration* (Studies in Comparative Education). London: Symposium Books.

Whorf, B. L. (1956) *Language, Thought and Reality*, ed. J. B. Carroll. Cambridge, MA: MIT Press.

Williams, B. (1985) *Ethics and the Limits of Philosophy*. London: Fontana Press.

Wilson, E. O. (1998) *Consilience: The unity of knowledge*. New York: Knopf.

Winch, C. (2002) *The Philosophy of Human Learning*. London: Routledge.

Winch, C. (2017) *Teachers' Know-How*. Chichester: Wiley.

Wittgenstein, L. (1953) *Philosophical Investigations*, trans. G. E. M. Anscombe. Oxford: Blackwell.

Wittgenstein, L. (1958) *The Blue and Brown Books: Preliminary studies for the 'Philosophical Investigations'*. New York: Harper and Row.

Wittgenstein, L. (1961 [1921]) *Tractatus Logico-Philosophicus*, trans. D. F. Pears and B. F. McGuiness. New York: Humanities Press.

Wittgenstein, L. (1969) *On Certainty*. New York: Harper and Row.

Wrigley, T. (2018) 'The power of "evidence": Reliable science or a set of blunt tools?'. *British Educational Research Journal*, 44 (3), 359–76.

Young, M. (2005) *Bringing Knowledge Back In: From social constructivism to social realism in the sociology of education*. London: Routledge.

Young, M. and Muller, J. (2007) 'Truth and truthfulness in the sociology of educational knowledge'. *Theory and Research in Education*, 5 (3), 173–201.

Young, M. and Muller, J. (2010) 'Three educational scenarios for the future: Lessons from the sociology of knowledge'. *European Journal of Education*, 45 (1, part 1), 11–27.

Young, M. and Muller, J. (2015) *Curriculum and the Specialization of Knowledge: Studies in the sociology of education*. London: Routledge.

Zeleny, E. (2011) 'Galileo's Thought Experiment on Inertia'. Wolfram Demonstrations Project. Accessed 20 November 2020. https://demonstrations.wolfram.com/GalileosThought ExperimentOnInertia/.

Index

11+ test 211

acquisition 191–2, 196–7, 207–10, 213, 215, 247, 272
actor-network theory 26, 88, 127, 169, 171–2, 298
adult learning theory 160
affective learning 218
agency 63, 79, 92, 95, 128, 142–3, 161, 172, 234, 276–8, 280, 302
Aggrawal, A. 111
algo-heuristic theory 160
anchored instruction 160
andragogy 160
aptitude-treatment interaction theory 160
Archer, M. 231–2, 276, 282, 297
Aristotle vii, 46, 75, 76, 96–9, 238, 297
assessment ix, 16, 20, 56, 88–9, 131, 158, 164, 169, 179, 210, 221–3, 239–252, 262, 289, 296
attribution theory 160
Augustine of Hippo 108, 234, 265, 279, 297, 302
Austin, J. L. 14, 297
autonomy 129, 130, 132, 289
axiological theories 159
Ayer, F. 46, 61, 297

Bandura, A. 164, 173, 297
Barthes, R. 190, 297
Battershaw 302
behaviour 1, 6, 14, 20, 28, 34, 55, 58–9, 72, 76, 81, 85, 88, 102, 108, 111, 120, 124, 129, 133, 134, 138, 148, 151, 157, 159–66, 173, 176, 185, 191, 199, 203, 206, 215, 218, 220–1, 237–8, 251, 261, 263, 268–9, 275, 298
behaviourism 20, 25, 28, 34, 120, 157–62, 215, 302
Bergson, H. 270, 297
Bernstein, B. 47–9, 50, 66, 118, 119, 177, 227–8, 243, 266, 297
Bezemer, J. 12, 300
Bhaskar, R. vii, 10–11, 43–5, 53–4, 74, 91, 103, 113, 115, 128, 142, 150, 194, 197, 208–9, 213, 219, 226, 297, 299, 301
Blyth, A. 229, 297
Bollack, J. 195, 297
Bourdieu, P. 195, 297
bracketing 4, 40, 57, 163, 164
Brandom, R. vii, 26, 27–30, 52, 53, 297, 298

Bredo, E. 258, 298
Bridges, D. 8, 298
Bruner, J. 218, 258, 298
bureaucracy 259–62
Butler, D. L. 176, 232, 298

Callon, M. 171, 298
case 3, 4, 6, 8–9, 11, 16, 19, 22, 24, 27–8, 30, 32, 47, 54, 59, 64, 68, 73, 79–80, 94, 96–8, 107, 111–12, 114–16, 118, 128, 131, 133–4, 138, 142, 145, 148, 153, 156, 159, 164, 175, 190, 207–8, 222, 236, 249, 255, 270, 287
Cavell, S. 19, 235, 298
change vii, 4, 10, 13–14, 16–17, 25, 31, 32–4, 44, 48, 54, 58, 62, 67, 72–7, 80, 92, 94, 102–3, 108–10, 118–26, 131, 139, 142–3, 154–5, 159, 162, 164, 167, 169, 171, 174, 183, 185, 191, 195–6, 223, 227, 232, 236, 243–4, 264, 273, 277, 284, 291
chi-square tests 18, 77, 263
Chomsky, N. 23, 209–10, 213, 298
Christian godhead 40, 279
classic regression modelling 18, 77
classification 50, 140, 243, 272
coaching 34, 119, 156, 157, 173–4, 180, 203, 215, 249
Coetzee, J. M. 296, 298
cognition 20, 27, 34, 106, 118, 156–7, 173, 182, 203, 207, 214–15, 230, 232, 234, 238, 249, 259, 290
cognitive
   dissonance theory 160
   flexibility theory 160
   load theory 160
cognitivism 164–6
collaboration 40, 169
collectivism 95
Collier, A. 115–16, 298
Comenius, J. 229, 298
communication 40–2, 101, 124, 203, 251, 279, 289
community of practice 7, 25, 37, 42, 48, 60, 67, 84, 105, 107, 137, 174, 254, 284, 293
competence 12, 35, 41, 118, 124, 202–3, 250, 278
complexity theory 25, 40, 46, 169, 177, 217
component display theory 159
Comte, A. 50, 55, 298